Art and Aesthetics After Adorno

THE TOWNSEND PAPERS IN THE HUMANITIES *No. 3*

Art and Aesthetics After Adorno

J. M. Bernstein
Claudia Brodsky
Anthony J. Cascardi
Thierry de Duve
Aleš Erjavec
Robert Kaufman
Fred Rush

Published by
The Townsend Center for the Humanities
University of California | Berkeley

Distributed by
Fordham University Press
New York | 2010

Copyright ©2010 The Regents of the University of California

ISBN 978-0-9823294-2-9

Library of Congress Cataloging-in-Publication Data

Art and aesthetics after Adorno / J. M. Bernstein...[et al].
   p. cm. — (The Townsend papers in the humanities ; no. 3)
ISBN 978-0-9823294-2-9
1. Aesthetics, Modern—20th century 2. Aesthetics, Modern—21st century
3. Adorno, Theodor W., 1903–1969. Ästhetische Theorie. I. Bernstein, J. M.
  BH201.A78 2010
  111'.850904—dc22
                       2010018448

Inquiries concerning proposals for the Townsend Papers in the Humanities from Berkeley faculty and Townsend Center affiliates should be addressed to The Townsend Papers, 220 Stephens Hall, UC Berkeley, Berkeley, CA 94720-2340, or by email to townsend_papers@lists.berkeley.edu.

Design and typesetting: Kajun Graphics

Manufactured in the United States of America

Credits and acknowledgements for quoted material appear on page 180–81.

Table of Contents

Prolegomena to Any Future Aesthetics
Anthony J. Cascardi
7

Adorno After Adorno
Fred Rush
41

Framing the Sensuous: Objecthood and "Objectivity" in Art After Adorno
Claudia Brodsky
69

Poetry After "Poetry After Auschwitz"
Robert Kaufman
116

Aesthetics and the Aesthetic Today: After Adorno
Aleš Erjavec
182

"The Demand for Ugliness": Picasso's Bodies
J. M. Bernstein
210

Resisting Adorno, Revamping Kant
Thierry de Duve
249

Anthony J. Cascardi

Prolegomena to Any Future Aesthetics

Can truth do justice to beauty?
—Walter Benjamin[1]

Identity Crisis in Aesthetics

Published one year after his death, Theodor Adorno's *Aesthetic Theory* (1970) is without any doubt one of the most powerful and comprehensive critiques of art and of the discipline of aesthetics ever written. The work offers a deep and critical engagement with the history and philosophy of aesthetics and with the traditions of European art through the middle of the twentieth century. It is coupled, moreover, with ambitious claims about what aesthetic theory ought to be as a form of critique if it is to meet the demands made by artworks. As such, it opens the project of critical theory to the unique set of pressures created by the class of objects—meaningful, sensuous, and particular—that we have come to recognize as "works of art." But the forward-looking horizon of Adorno's *Aesthetic Theory* was the world of high modernism, where the existence of "art" had already come into question; its background was European art from roughly the time of Bach to the present. Much has happened since then both in practice and in theory, including revisions of aesthetic theory in light of a much broader view of the history of art.

Whether Adorno's ideas can be "followed" in the contemporary moment, and if so how, are not questions that admit of a simple answer. Indeed, there are questions to be raised about whether our present historical moment, in society as in art, is continuous with the world that Adorno knew. The collaborators in this volume take vastly different approaches to these issues, some by turning their attention to how Adorno helps us rethink the ways in which the art of the past must be reinterpreted in the light of subsequent history, others by reconsidering Adorno's project within the larger field of aesthetic theory, and still others by reasserting the transhistorical claims of art as a way of resisting the conceptual force-field that has made Adorno's work so influential. They hold in common a recognition of the power of Adorno's aesthetic critique, and they share a commitment to the place of aesthetic theory in response to historical developments that Adorno could not possibly have foreseen.

In spite of its detail and the density of its intellectual arguments, *Aesthetic Theory* can be read as presaging an aesthetics that Adorno did not live to write. The work was left unfinished, just as modernism itself. And yet what he did produce seems both to offer a trenchant critique of the field of aesthetics and to advance a set of ideas to which any future aesthetics would have to respond. These take as their point of orientation a set of remarks about the "difficulty" of art in the present time—its identity, its right to exist—coupled with a diagnosis of the perpetual instability of aesthetic theory. The "Draft Introduction" to the work cites a telling passage from the work of Moritz Geiger (1880–1937) that speaks to the ongoing identity crisis of aesthetics. Aesthetics, he says, is "blown about by every philosophical, cultural, and scientific gust; at one moment it is metaphysical and in the next empirical; now normative, then descriptive; now defined by artists, then by connoisseurs; one day art is supposedly the center of aesthetics and natural beauty merely preliminary, the next day art beauty is merely second-hand natural beauty."[2] While the history of aesthetics may be somewhat less random than this description suggests, aesthetics has nonetheless labored under ongoing uncertainties about itself. Hegel expressed the concern that art may not be a suitable subject for "systematic and scientific treatment" (hence for theory) at all. Before Hegel, in Kant, there are worries about whether aesthetic reflective judgments mark out a distinct "field." And, before Kant, Hume asked whether questions of taste would require something other than the resources of epistemology in order to be resolved. This is hardly all. In the course of attempts to grasp central questions about "beauty" and "art," aesthetic theory has often found itself in a centrifugal relation to its objects, attempting to transform itself into psychology, sociology, moral philosophy, and political analysis, among other things. Indeed, almost all the models on which modern aesthetic theory has been based have been drawn from extra-aesthetic domains. Aesthetic theory has attempted to imagine itself as a version of the theory of knowledge, as a philosophy of judgment, as a vehicle for morality, as a stand-in for political theory, and as substituting for a theory of community. It has looked to phenomenology, psychoanalysis, cognitive science, semiotics, ontology, pragmatics, communication theory, cultural studies, and ideology-critique for guidance. The peculiar lability of aesthetic theory has no doubt been a consequence of the fact that the social practice of "art" was itself in flux during the period when aesthetic theory began to take shape. Aesthetic theory developed in tandem with it. Such instability appears all the more striking now that the domain of art includes a much wider range of practices than ever before. If aesthetic theory is thought of as tied to the existence of "art" as a specific class of objects set apart from the rest of experience, then what becomes of aesthetics in an age when art seems intent on refusing that separation?

Adorno's writing suggests that these questions need to be addressed along two axes, one directed toward issues of history and practice, the other directed toward more conceptual concerns. As for history, aesthetics must reckon with shifts in the practice of art in relation to new technologies for communication and circulation. These, no doubt, are driven by the borderless extension of global capitalism even in the face of is various "crises" and collapses, by the inescapable allure of what Guy Debord presciently called the "society of the spectacle," and by a deep longing for meaningful social relations in a world of isolated individuals. For better or for worse, the practices of art have become entirely porous and open to new technologies of production and circulation, many of which represent themselves as *immaterial*, as happily divorced from the embodied world. Are these new practices continuous with modern modes of production as Adorno understands them, often implicitly, through Marx? Or are they something indeed radically different, representing a historical break that in turn obviates making distinctions between art and other kinds of material making? The more theoretical questions involve asking, first and foremost, whether thinking about art in relation to new modes of production within the framework of globalized capitalism remains a relevant concern and, concomitantly, whether attempts to align art with truth can help restore the value of art as a domain of meaningful sensuous particulars in a world that otherwise continues to believe that rationality is something radically other than, indeed higher than, whatever meaning is carried by art. Far from being outdated, the suggestion that art can stand as an example of what may be called "embodied meaning" seems all the more important in the world of global media capitalism.

Sense and Concept

In the "Draft Introduction" Adorno asked about the very possibility of constructing a theory of aesthetics in light of the fact that "theory" appears destined to let slip away the things that seem to matter most about art: that its meanings are borne by sensuous particulars, and that it makes sense while resisting full and complete rendering in any language that adheres to the sovereignty of abstract concepts. Artworks speak concretely, addressing themselves to the senses. They are meaningful but they are, in Hegel's terms, forms of *"embodied* meaning." The difficulty with aesthetic theory is that it has sought to assimilate the truth-content of art to the truth of concepts in their more or less conventional forms, which are disembodied and abstract. This would seem to suggest that aesthetic theory is bound to miss the very thing it hopes most to explain. Indeed, it could well seem that if art is forced to submit its truth-content to the demands of a discourse built around abstract concepts, the results might well resemble what Walter Benjamin described as "the burning up of the husk as it enters the realm of ideas" (*The Origin of German Tragic Drama*, p. 31). Benjamin's remark signaled two fears: first, that in discounting art's sensuous surface and grain, aesthetic theory would leave us with little more than a periphrastic reduction of the "thematic" content of the works in question; and second, that the transposition of art into the realm of ideas would blind us to the ways in which artworks help reveal what is incomplete in any form of knowledge that limits itself to concepts alone. Art is, or strives to be, a sensuous way of knowing that seems ever to be at odds with the theories designed to explain it. But in its wish to carry a form of knowledge that is concrete, art can nonetheless help articulate a critique of the ways in which the very notion of a "concept," hence of what counts as "rationality," has been split off from the world of sense.[3] And insofar as it is also conscious of the fact that the wish to reconcile sense and concept is bound to remain unfulfilled, art may be able to frame that critique in a way that is grounded in something other than the naive ideal of a return to a fullness of sense. Modern and contemporary art are as conscious of the illusions bound up in the notion of an "immediacy of sense" as they are resistant to the abstractions of pure concepts. What Adorno calls the "truth content" of art lies in the work "itself" but also in its historical formation, its cultural location, and in the sensory and affective responses it calls into being.

Of course, any encounter with art may well require some involvement with concepts in their more or less conventional forms: as sources of knowledge, or expressions of opinions, or statements of beliefs. One can hardly attempt to exclude from aesthetics the knowledge that a particular painting by Caravaggio is *of* the head of the Medusa; or the belief that Kenneth Branagh, the director of a film based on Shakespeare's *Hamlet*, is also, as an actor in the film, the prince of Denmark; or the informed opinion that the author of *Don Quixote* was in all likelihood born of *converso* ancestors. But such things are a matter of our cognition of these works, rather than of what they themselves "cognize" by virtue of their concrete existence *as* works of art.[4] To say that an artwork "cognizes" anything is of course a figure of speech, a catachresis whose purpose is to marshal an existing term to a meaning for which there is no adequate name. I place "cognize" in scare quotes because the kind of knowledge implicit in artworks does not resemble the knowledge we expect to have of objects as framed by propositional utterances. And yet this is the very thing that aesthetic theory has been at pains to explain: that while artworks are indeed objects, the truth-content of art is *of* the world while also offering critical reflections upon it. This truth-content is inseparable from the sensuous particularity of the works in question even while it remains irreducible to sheer sensuousness; it is a truth-content that is likewise inseparable from the fact that artworks are made. Indeed, Adorno located one of the great paradoxes of aesthetic theory in the fact that art offers us something that is at once made *and* true: "Today the metaphysics of art revolves around the question of how something spiritual that is made, in philosophical terms something 'merely posited' can be true. The issue is not the immediately existing artwork but its content [*Gehalt*]" (*AT*, p. 131).

Adorno's response to this puzzle, to which various contributors to this volume turn, revolves around one of the oldest issues in aesthetics, namely, the "semblance" character of art. What is made in art is semblance, and what must be rescued for truth is precisely the semblance-quality of art: "The question of the truth of something made is indeed none other than the question of semblance and the rescue of semblance as the semblance of the true.... Of all the paradoxes of art, no doubt the innermost one is that only through making, through the production of particular works specifically and completely formed in themselves, and never through any immediate vision, does art achieve what is not made, the truth" (*AT*, p. 131). Semblance must be "rescued" not only because it has been held suspect since at least the time of Plato but also because the commodity structure of capitalism has transformed most things into ghostlike appearances of themselves.

Beauty and Rationalization

In large part because artworks are in fact sensuous artifacts, they scarcely offer the kind of truth that can be formulated by conventional concepts, which must suppress those things that are particular and embodied about our engagement with the world. This is especially true of the ways in which art struggles against the concept in its dominant modern form, which has been complicit in creating the condition that Weber called "rationalization." While Weber argued that rationalization may be at work in all cultures, there is a historical component to the process of rationalization within the culture of modernity that seems to have ensured the disparity of sense and beauty. The specificity of rationalization in the West and increasingly around the globe, which Adorno located in the effects of social labor, goes unrecognized among adherents of the Romantic notion that art *must* establish itself as the antithesis of reason. Remnants of that stance can be seen even among critics who seem to argue against it. Witness Arnold Hauser's *Social History of Art*, which attempts to explain how art could leap toward a knowledge of things that lie beyond the bounds of science: "Art is a source of knowledge not only because it immediately continues the work of the sciences and completes their discoveries ... but also because it points out the limits of scientific competence and takes over at the point at which further knowledge can be acquired only along paths which cannot be trodden outside of art."[5] These arguments may be true, but they risk producing exaggerated versions of the very dichotomies they would hope to overcome.

The thesis according to which rationalization defines modernization means that certain norms of reason came to be regarded as if they were reason's *only* valid forms.[6] These forms were destined to exclude whatever is sensuous in the work of knowing. One critique of rationalization points out that all forms of reason are built upon some material ground; however, an aesthetic critique suggests that the sensuousness of art strives to assert what rationalized concepts have let slip away from the world. Thus, while the process of rationalization may well be pervasive in the West, and increasingly so globally, it remains nonetheless true that artworks can demonstrate its limitations within a particular historical framework. Herein lies the critical force that artworks carry in the context of their historical existence, but herein also lies a principal source of the frustrations, anxieties, and evasions of aesthetic theory over the long course of its history, beginning roughly in the seventeenth and eighteenth centuries and continuing, with but few exceptions, until the present day: how to theorize a field comprising works that are essentially sensuous and particular, historical and concrete. Aesthetic theory has been at pains to explain the fact that some essential component of truth seems to get lost in the course of any theoretical attempt to bring a work of art *itself* to cognition; there is just as little (or as much) shared between a theory of aesthetics and a work of art as there is between a theory of love and Botticelli's *Birth of Venus*. And yet the one can hardly exist without the other. The point is that while art makes claims as a form of knowing, it presents us with insights that are not reducible to their *conceptual* equivalents.

Artworks are sensuous, material, and particular; but they are not for that reason any less "true."

In attempting to locate whatever is distinctive about art, critics and theorists alike have sometimes called its noncognitive element "beauty" and have associated special qualities, pleasures, and emotions with it. Indeed, "beauty" is but one of the more familiar names for whatever it is that seems to elude the grasp of concepts in a work of art. But beauty is not all, and as Jay Bernstein has argued, modernism in particular has found it necessary to sacrifice whatever in "beauty" may oppose ugliness, require "harmony," or demand the felicitous integration of parts. (Bernstein's essay on Picasso in this volume speaks directly to this point.) Adorno offers one reason why this may be so: "[Modern art] has taken all the darkness and guilt of the world onto its shoulders. Its entire happiness consists in recognizing unhappiness; all its beauty consists in denying itself the semblance of beauty."[7]

And yet "beauty" has returned in the last several decades with a new critical edge, just as aesthetic pleasure has reasserted itself with a new political force in the work of photographers like Robert Mapplethorpe and Sebastião Salgado. "Beauty" has been the subject of a revival in recent writings on aesthetics, and this revival offers evidence of what the abstractions of theory had let slip away. A 1999 exhibit at the Hirshhorn Museum in Washington, D.C., under the title "Regarding Beauty" gives some indication of the desire to recapture the force of beauty for a field that seemed to have become increasingly fascinated by theories of history and politics, not to mention by the conceptual mystique of analytical philosophy. So too have a number of related writings, ranging from the anthology edited by Peg Brand, *Beauty Matters* (2000), to Dave Hickey's *The Invisible Dragon: Four Essays on Beauty* (1993); an earlier anthology, *Uncontrollable Beauty*, edited by Bill Beckley and David Shapiro (1988); Wendy Steiner's *The Scandal of Pleasure* (1995); and Arthur Danto's collection of essays *The Abuse of Beauty* (2003). These works speak, first, to the desire to recapture art's sensuous appeal from the theories designed to explain it and, second, to the desire to align the power of art's sensuousness with various moral and political projects (as in Elaine Scarry's *On Beauty and Being Just*, 1999). These, in turn, are indicative of a desire to claim, or to reclaim, the *importance* of art, a desire that appears ill at ease with the notion that art's importance ought to be self-evident. Standards of beauty may have changed since a century ago, when the character Adam Verver in Henry James's *The Golden Bowl* described art as providing human beings with a "release from the bonds of ugliness"; indeed, there is hardly a consensus about whether "beauty" and "ugliness" do, or should, stand opposed. Still, the appeal to beauty has put some pressure on theoretical debates, in part because it shows that there is more at stake in questions of aesthetics than matters of vogue or standards of taste. What is at issue is art's desire to serve as a form of sensuous cognition. This is something that aesthetic theory *ought* to be able to explain.

If aesthetic theory runs aground when asked to account for what is specifically "beautiful" about art, this is partly because the notion of beauty can seem frightfully thin when measured against the breadth and depth of what "art" can encompass, and even more so in view of the fact that "art" is a category whose boundaries seem to shift in relation to domains external to it (for example: nature, politics, society, religion, science). It is hardly clear whether, or how, the beauty of art differs from natural beauty, or how art is to be held apart from craft, if in fact it is. Indeed, "beauty" and "art" are both deceptively simple ideas that, in their simplicity, mask complex processes operating at both the historical and conceptual levels.[8] For instance, it remains unclear whether the concept of art can be applied to artifacts whose historical function was not so much "artistic" as religious (icon, chalice, temple, urn). But the additional problem, which surfaces at the theoretical level, is that notions like "art" and "beauty" seem not to work like other concepts, if indeed they work at all.

This question has been the subject of much debate since at least the aesthetics of Kant, and it is worth recalling.

In Kant's formulation, aesthetic judgments are unusual in being at once subjective and universal; they are rooted in particular feelings and yet they lay claim to universal validity. This is paradoxical, and while Kant attempts throughout the entire "Dialectic of Aesthetic Judgment" to resolve it, the results are unclear, even by his own standards.[9] And yet in spite of the failings of theory in this regard something seems to be right in Kant's idea that art is equally tied to the particularity of sensuous experience (and, moreover, tied to that particularity in its affective form) *and* grounded in the desire for claims that would have the same universality as other concepts. Kant's aesthetics is thus an expression of a desire that, however unfulfilled and in tension with itself, remains central to aesthetic theory: the desire to acknowledge claims that would make sensuous particulars the bearers of a kind of truth that is not beholden to preexisting categories and concepts. By appealing to the logic of what he calls "reflective" or "nonsubsumptive" judgments, Kant challenges us to find universal grounds of agreement on the basis of the particulars, rather than to presuppose that ground. And yet Kant leaves us with the question of whether the affects incited by representations of sensuous particulars can in fact resist judgment's normativizing force. This worry is heightened in Adorno's claim that the "bindingness" of every style may be a reflex of society's "repressive character" (*AT*, p. 207).

Seen in this light, it is hardly a surprise that aesthetic theory has so often been foiled in its attempts to provide any reliable calibration for terms like "beauty" and "art." But neither is it clear that the two—beauty and art—bear any essential relationship to one another. For one thing, the field of "art," toward which aesthetics has come to direct itself, is historical and so necessarily variable and unstable even in its distinction from "nature." Art beauty and natural beauty remain entwined. And yet it seems that the notion of "art" has also been variable at the level of what is expected of it normatively. "Art" has been taken as the designation of a particular class of works, as a name for things that are appreciated as more than "mere things," as a set of practices whose ends lie in something other than their usefulness, and as an honorific designation granted to artifacts that have achieved a significant degree of cultural distinction. Beginning with the avant-gardes (witness Duchamp's "readymades") it became clear that, while we do not call just *anything* a work of art, it is also true that just about anything *may* become a work of art.[10] The "nominalism" that Adorno associated with the work of Benedetto Croce may provide one response to this problem insofar as nominalism can proliferate concepts as the instances demand. But nominalism is a poor excuse for a theory, and rather indicates its frustrations. Indeed, the very idea of an aesthetic "theory" makes demands and introduces difficulties of quite a different order. As a "theory of art" aesthetics has wavered between a psychological empiricism, various forms of ontology (which have pursued questions about the essence of artworks), expressivism, functionalism (the uses of art), and the theory of values (in which the terms "art" and "beauty" are meant to impute judgments of quality and degree). As for its evaluative powers, aesthetic theory has been hard pressed to establish consistent or convincing links between "beauty" and the works to which this designation is intended to apply.

This embarrassment points up the more general problem of what may count as judgments of aesthetic value and taste, and of what may count as evidence for them. In response to aesthetic theory's ambitions in this regard, one might imagine the simple Wittgensteinian exercise of attempting to point to the beauty of a work of art, or to whatever particular element distinguishes it from a "mere thing." (Here, no doubt, is a place where Wittgenstein would say that language is "idling.") Adorno observes that the answer to the fundamental aesthetic question of why a work can be said to be beautiful amounts to the pursuit of casuistic reasoning rather than a priori logic. As judgments, aesthetic claims stand at odds with the determinability that attach between concepts and their "objects" in conventional terms. Adorno: "The empirical indeterminability of these reflections changes nothing in the objectivity of what they grasp.... That whereby it is possible to distinguish what is correct and what is false in an artwork according to its own measure is the elements in which universality imposes itself concretely in the monad" (*AT*, p. 189).

There is an important point to be gleaned from Adorno's insight that "universality" is evident in artworks and not simply in the judgments brought to them. This is that the "universality" of art is necessarily a concrete and particular universality, which is to say a form of universality that is fundamentally at odds with what we take to be the "concept" in its dominant form. This is true both at the level of individual works and as regards the more general notion of "art." The mounting evidence of decades of revisionism, a heightened self-consciousness about the contextuality of the languages of criticism, the reevaluation of art through various forms of ideology-critique, and, not least, an explosive heterogeneity among the practices that are taken to count as art, all suggest that any aesthetic theory with systematic and universalizing pretensions is bound to be defeated unless it can come to grips with the needs that drive theory to produce abstractions in the face of something as asystematic as the field of artworks. And unless aesthetics can somehow grapple with the fact of its own externality to art and proceed from that awareness to discover the deeper ways in which art still needs philosophy, one can be sure that notions like "beauty" and "art" will be *nothing more than* the reflections of isolated judgments or expressions of bare social interests and needs. To regard art, as Adorno does, as having a "need" for philosophy would be to pursue with an equally critical force the desires of art for a validity that might be recognizable in the culture of the "concept" *and* the unspoken needs of philosophy to anchor itself in the concrete. Regrettably, this project has scarcely begun. A few exceptions aside (among which may be counted the essays in the present volume), the result has been a series of merely partial encounters between aesthetics and art. But as the art of the late nineteenth and twentieth centuries began to put increasing pressure on some of the notions central to aesthetic theory—beauty, taste, the transparent immediacy of "experience" itself—it was hardly surprising to find that the philosophy of art soon reached the point where its only options seemed to be what Adorno characterized as a "dumb and trivial universality" on the one hand and "arbitrary judgments usually derived from conventional opinions" on the other (*AT,* p. 333). The bifurcation of the "sense" lodged in particulars and the universal demands of the rational "concept" are all too visible in this sorry choice.

Embodied Meanings

The questions of art's resistance to aesthetic theory and of the misrecognition of art by the theory designed to comprehend it are issues I take as central. How and why did this happen? At what cost did it occur? The general tenor of my response, for which I take Adorno's work in *Aesthetic Theory* as an instigation and as a provisional guide, has two prongs, one directed toward questions of history, the other directed toward more conceptual matters. One prong involves the development of aesthetic theory in relation to a desire for "embodied meaning" during the period in which one form of reason, the rationalized form, came to be institutionalized as normative.[11] To speak of "embodied meaning" is to register art's way of demonstrating the inadequacy of purely conceptual ways of knowing the world. It is at the same time a way of staking claims for the values that it makes in the world. To account for these facts we need to engage not only Adorno's negative-dialectical materialism but also Hegel's convictions about the role of art as a "sensuous manifestation of the idea," in spite of the fact that Hegel's claim was coupled with the belief that art could be surpassed by a form of spirit somehow more satisfactory than it—that is, by the Absolute. Art, he writes, "is not ... the highest way of apprehending the spiritually concrete. The higher way, in contrast to representation by means of the sensuously concrete, is thinking, which in a relative sense is indeed abstract, but it must be concrete, not one-sided, if it is to be true and rational."[12] For Adorno, by contrast, the possibilities of art are set by the untranscendable horizon of history. And from this historically bounded perspective it seems that the validity of "embodied meaning" was suppressed even in relation to some of the most compelling efforts to realize it, or that it was relegated to the status of *Wunschdenken*.

When seen from the perspective of conventional, "abstract" concepts, art may well appear inherently difficult and opaque; it seems resistant to paraphrase in part because the mode of paraphrase is reliant on propositional knowledge, on various forms of "knowing that." If art is opposed to any reductivism that would privilege its conceptual content, this is because there is something more than "conceptual content" in it. Its way of knowing the world, which is also a way of valuing it, is lost when only conceptual content is brought into view. As Robert Brandom explained, having conceptual content means playing a role in a form of reasoning whose goal is to make things explicit in terms of propositional utterances, that is, the sort of content typically expressed by declarative sentences: by "that" clauses, or by what Brandom describes as "content-specifying sentential complements of propositional attitude ascriptions. Because contents of this sort are the right shape to be sayable, thinkable, and believable, they can be understood as making something explicit. The claim is that to have or express a content of this kind is just to be able to play the role both of premise and of conclusion in *inferences*."[13] Moreover, the role of propositional utterances in making things explicit reinforces the sense that they serve as privileged means for disclosing the truth. By contrast, Adorno has much to say about the *opacity* of art (for example, "that artworks say something and in the same breath conceal it expresses this enigmaticalness from the perspective of language"; *AT*, p. 120). But *why* this opacity demands attention, and whether it can be grasped as the source of claims not to be dismissed for lack of clarity, requires a deeper understanding of the Weberian thesis about the role of rationalization in modern social life.

The notion of rationalization itself has antecedents in the philosophy of aesthetics, most notably in Schiller's *Letters on the Aesthetic Education of Man* and in Hegel's *Lectures on Aesthetics*. The critique of rationalization that reaches from Weber to Horkheimer and Adorno in fact begins as an aesthetic critique. For Hegel, this is a critique of a world of "reflection":

> The development of reflection in our life today has made it a need of ours, in relation both to our will and judgment, to cling to general considerations and to regulate the particular by them, with the result that universal forms, laws, duties, rights, maxims, prevail as determining reasons and are the chief regulator. But for artistic interest and production we demand in general rather a quality of life in which the universal is not present in the form of law and maxim, but which gives the impression of being one with the senses and the feelings, just as the universal and the rational is contained in the imagination by being brought into unity with a concrete sensuous appearance. Consequently the conditions of our present time are not favourable to art. (*LA*, p. 10)

The suppression of the immediacy of art and the emergence of a desire for the reconciliation of sense and concept emerge as part of a history in which the pervasive form of self-consciousness is "reflection"; reflection happens only with the loss of immediacy and carries with it what Hegel takes as the virtual guarantee that art will fail as the highest bearer of the truth (*LA*, pp. 10–11). Reflection stands at the root of the "abstraction" of the concept, of the loss of art's power to serve as the bearer of truth, and of the desire to surpass art in some higher manifestation of the embodied meaning. It is linked to Hegel's idealization of the "golden days" of classical antiquity and the Middle Ages, which serve as nostalgic points of reference for everything that art might achieve and as a basis for a mournful contrast with the present. If the prospects of an aesthetic critique in a rationalized society are truly limited, this is because art has in turn become constrained in its ability to disclose the truth. Art is a sensuous manifestation of the "Idea" but not in the highest possible way. Hegel's hope, which remained unachieved in the *Aesthetics*, was to make an opening for a more complex and adequate version of the "concept" than what art could provide. Indeed, Hegel's understanding of the history of art and of aesthetic forms (architecture, sculpture, painting, music, and poetry) is such that art itself makes "progress" by jettisoning that which is most central to it, namely, its sensuous form.

Some of the paradoxes of Hegel's aesthetics grow out of the tradition that he inherited. They begin with the "invention" of aesthetics as the theory of a new kind of "knowledge" by Alexander Baumgarten in his *Aesthetica* of 1750. Baumgarten's wish to make aesthetics a "science of sensation" was bound to be fraught with difficulty because it worked with accepted divisions of body and spirit. For Baumgarten, aesthetic cognition was double or, as he would say, "confused." Kant's response to Baumgarten was to say that aesthetics does not in fact give us knowledge in the form of knowledge of objects at all, not even, as Baumgarten thought, in a form that fuses together corporeal and mental elements.[14] The conditions underlying the misrecognition of art by aesthetic theory are the very same ones that allowed for the configuration of a relatively independent aesthetic sphere of culture, where art's irreducible materiality could be afforded a place under the pretense that art was also of benefit to those seeking knowledge, or aspiring to virtue, or interested in improving themselves or society. These things may well be true, and indeed are still heard among the "justifications" for art in contemporary pedagogical and political contexts. But the consolidation of a separate aesthetic domain was never and could never be complete. Art could neither be wholly divorced from the broader world of praxis, nor could reason in its purely rationalized forms suppress the validity of the claims that art makes sensuously. The two are linked by a structure of identity and difference.

This complex structure is often ignored by aesthetic theory. Indeed, the invention of modern aesthetics happens alongside the widespread acceptance of empirical and mechanistic views of the natural world, together with the institution of practices designed to support it; with the consolidation of nation-states; with the invention of liberal democracies; with the rise of commodity capitalism; with the establishment of bureaucratic institutions of the kind described especially well by Weber; and with changes in social practices related to the arts in a more direct and relevant way: the decline of patronage, the beginning of newspapers, the rise of café society, and the establishment of modern museums and concert halls as commercial institutions, first supported by paying subscribers and then by open ticket sales. By the time the field of literature had become what Pierre Bourdieu described as "a separate universe,"[15] there already existed a flourishing salon culture in which matters of taste could compete on equal footing with questions about politics or society. (Bourdieu writes: "The salons are also, through the exchanges that take place there, genuine articulations between the fields: those who hold political power aim to impose their vision on artists and to appropriate for themselves the power of consecration and legitimation which they hold, notably by means of what Sainte-Beuve calls 'literary press'; for their part, the writers and artists, acting as solicitors and intercessors, or even sometimes as true pressure groups, endeavor to assure for themselves a mediating control of the different material or symbolic rewards distributed by the state.")[16]

In identifying itself now with questions of taste of a more normative and "empirical" kind, now with "reflective" judgments that originate in subjective feelings of pleasure and pain, now with the aims of moral philosophy, now with politics, now with empirical approaches to "experience," now with the theory of material production, now with the dynamics of desire, now with the social organization of experience, and so on, aesthetic theory has consistently been pointing toward the very domains of praxis from which art has been set apart. Such separations may have been necessary in order for art to identify and validate itself as an integral and autonomous sphere of activity during a time when other such spheres were also consolidating themselves in independent ways.[17] But because these separations were not complete, that is, because art still retained recognizable traces of its relationship to what may more broadly be called the "praxis of life," the misrecognition of art by aesthetic theory can itself provide critical insights into the ways in which those extra-aesthetic domains were enmeshed in the conditions that rendered art unfamiliar. Indeed, the process of rationalization was not something that happened to any greater or lesser degree inside or outside of the aesthetic sphere but was completely woven into the fabric of Western modernity. In spite of its apparently autonomous existence, "art" was and has remained entwined with politics, history, morality, desire, and the materiality of production, even as these domains in modern life were themselves, in their own spheres, transformed by the suppression of the embodied concept. What art offers, which these domains may not, is a critical reflection upon these conditions. This is because art is semblance, hence not completely incorporated in the processes of rationalization.

As already hinted, the questions I am raising became especially sharp in the broad stretch of time that has come to be known as "modernity." This is the period when something like the "theory of art" began to fashion itself as coextensive with discourses concerned with truth and morality, politics and utility, and when the practice of "art" itself began to emerge as a domain of artifactual production no longer intelligible within the praxis of life. The result was the creation of a conceptual vocabulary for the theory of art that relied on the ancillary disciplines mentioned earlier, but that also came to invoke special, honorific terms like "beauty," "sublimity," and "disinterest" in order to describe the ways in which its objects and experiences did not conform to what those discourses counted as normative. Such considerations, and others like them, are crucial to an understanding of what became the field of "aesthetics" in the modern age. But it would be equally false to think that the underlying issues are in any sense unique to the culture of modernity. Recall that Horkheimer and Adorno never argued that rationalization, *qua* enlightenment, began with the displacement of myth. On their account, myth was already a form of enlightenment. Moreover, the question that Adorno identified as central to the metaphysics of art—how something made can also be true—is the recapitulation of an issue that is central to the Platonic critique of poetry. What the Platonic critique of poetry suggests, beyond what it says directly, is that art and the discourse of truth are joined by a structure of identity *and* difference; truth and beauty constitute an antinomy. On the one hand, each of them must exclude the other as part of its project of self-definition, and yet beauty presents itself as truth's forgotten face, just as truth strives to articulate what beauty is able to make manifest. If the historical component of any critical aesthetic theory involves showing how the antinomy of truth and beauty took the particular shape it did in the modern age, and if its critical task lies in an analysis of the misrecognition of art by conventional aesthetics, it does so in light of the distant ideal in which truth and beauty might each be able to say what the other holds dear. "The truth content of an artwork requires philosophy," writes Adorno (*AT*, p. 341). And yet, aesthetics has long failed to be the discourse of such recognition; indeed, the through-line of its development in Western modernity is the history of multiple evasions and displacements of this very fact. As a result, the truth of art has all too often been regarded as subordinate to some *other* truth, including the truth of the abstract concept; it has systematically been dislocated into art's cognate fields.

Alternatives

Adorno's "Draft Introduction" to the *Aesthetic Theory* points the way toward some alternatives. The importance of the "Draft Introduction" derives as much from the thoroughness of Adorno's critique of the discourses of aesthetics that precede him as from his commitment to the principle that art has always had the power to reveal things that theory seems to lack. Indeed, one goal of Adorno's *Aesthetic Theory* is to raise awareness of those things that aesthetic theory has allowed to be lost in our conception of art's engagement with the world. This restores art to the position of responding critically to the various theoretical approaches that have been devised to explain it, even while it participates in the same history that has conditioned aesthetics as a "theory of art." A sketch of Adorno's basic position, an outline of his critique of modern aesthetic theory, and some brief remarks regarding his own dialectical approach can serve as a further guide to these issues.

The "Draft Introduction" to the *Aesthetic Theory* begins with a powerful statement of the fact that aesthetic theory seems to be set systematically against what art reveals. The force of Adorno's point goes considerably beyond the truism that theory is concept-bound and so destined to ignore what sense seems directly to show. The ubiquitous and irreparable separation of any *concept* from any *thing* is not in and of itself the dilemma Adorno wishes to capture. As Terry Eagleton writes, "It is a pity that we lack a word to capture the unique aroma of coffee–that our speech is wizened and anemic, remote from the taste and feel of reality. But how could a word, as opposed to a pair of nostrils, capture the aroma of anything, and is it a matter of failure that it does not?"[18] There is indeed an answer to Eagleton's worry that in turn is the basis for Adorno's negative-dialectical approach: that "concept" and "thing" are in fact but two moments of the same world. As for aesthetic theory, the puzzle is that aesthetics seems to misrecognize art even while it seems committed to the idea that concept and sense *ought* to participate in one another; indeed, aesthetics seems to misrecognize the ways in which art is a form of cognition, albeit in the sensuous realm. As against the kind of theoretical work in which a conceptual apparatus is brought to bear on works of art from the outside or from "above," or in which the qualities of a particular work are used in order to generate normative principles or rules (for genre or style or periodization, or indeed for taste or "beauty" itself), Adorno acknowledges that art is a domain in which the expectations customarily placed on theory—for example, that it should have a certain level of generality, that it should provide a systematic and complete account of the cases it is meant to cover—may not hold. It is not enough for aesthetics to be inductive *or* for it to be deductive in its approach to art. This is because artworks refuse equally to grant access "from above" *and* "from below," "neither from concepts nor from a-conceptual experience" (*AT*, p. 343). But how, then, might one fashion a theory of art? The question begs response equally in the form of a vision of what the future of aesthetics might look like and in terms of a statement of the conditions that have informed it historically. What Adorno seeks is an account of something that idealism and materialism in aesthetics both ignore, namely, their undisclosed entanglements with one another. In Adorno's case the alternative lies in a realignment of aesthetic theory with the principles of negative-dialectical thinking: "The only possibility for aesthetics beyond this miserable alternative is the philosophical insight that fact and concept are not polar opposites but mediated reciprocally in one another" (*AT*, p. 343).

Adorno also means, of course, that aesthetic theory provides an index of the ways in which sense and concept are split from *and* implicated in one another. Since this process occurs historically, it would only make sense for aesthetics to be both historical and philosophical or, as Adorno, following Lukács, puts it, "historico-philosophical."[19] Rather than regard history as structured by underlying ideas seeking tangible expression in art—(much less by the "Absolute Spirit" of Hegelian dialectics)—Adorno takes art as a historically specific, material domain of culture composed of objects that cannot be reduced to mere matter. Artworks have a thingly character, but they are not "mere things." The "more than material quality" of artworks is given various names throughout the *Aesthetic Theory*, some more remarkable than others. In speaking of beauty, for example, Adorno refers to the quality of the "plus" or the "extra"; the same could be said of the unquantifiable extra measure that style "adds" to the ontology of a work of art. Often Adorno calls this element "spirit." Keeping track of "spirit" while dealing with artworks as artifacts means striving for the kind of account of art that modern aesthetics has by and large failed to produce because it has come to accept, or merely to lament, the vacuity of sense in comparison with the concept. Increasingly, the "philosophical" element in aesthetic theory has tended toward the overtheorization of artworks at the expense of what can best be called the force of their sensuous and material particularity. Along with this, the "historical" component of art has gone undertheorized, in spite of having been amply explored. During the period when art was theorized principally in terms of historical systems and subdivided by nation, century, and genre—as in the various taxonomies common in standard versions of the "history of literature," "history of art," "history of music," and so on—the various histories in question were derived largely from the categories established in Hegel's *Lectures on Aesthetics*, minus the speculative overlay and idealist underpinnings of the Hegelian system. Idealisim became orthodoxy.

By Adorno's account, the most prominent exceptions to the then-prevailing tendencies in aesthetic theory were to be found in the efforts of Walter Benjamin and Georg Lukács.[20] Consider, by contrast to their efforts, Adorno's critical assessments of the "mainstream" directions in modern aesthetics. In the course of the "Draft Introduction," Adorno passes under critical review a vast array of theoretically informed approaches to art: work-immanent studies, phenomenological aesthetics, a form of nominalism that he associates with Benedetto Croce, empiricist aesthetics, and hermeneutics, along with Kant's *Critique of Judgment* and Hegel's *Lectures on Aesthetics*. Given Adorno's critical assessment of this entire, heterogeneous tradition, his work might well be taken as constructing a space for the understanding of art by systematically excluding every conceivable approach to it: "art" would be defined as the structural remainder, as the thing that theory consistently fails to explain. But this is hardly the project that *Aesthetic Theory* sets for itself. Quite the contrary. Each of Adorno's negations is designed to disclose some element of aesthetic truth and each can in turn be incorporated into a dialectical understanding of the relationship between aesthetic theory and art. *Aesthetic Theory* aims to hold the "objective status" of art firmly in place rather than to locate it as a function of the affects or the judgments of the subject. (Adorno's critique of the association of art with subjective inwardness is evident in his early work on Kierkegaard.)[21] In his insistence upon art as an object-domain Adorno follows Hegel's response to Kant, who identified the task of aesthetics as universalizing the subjective judgment-power required for the mediation of the sensuous and supersensuous worlds. Adorno can hardly refuse Kant's idea that aesthetics must address itself to what the division of experience into the separate domain of cognition (sense) and morality (the supersensuous) fails to grasp. For Kant, this was "experience" as a whole. Adorno's aesthetics is Kantian in its commitment to the principle of art's incongruity with the realm of the cognitively true and the morally good. But it is resolutely un-Kantian in that it refuses to make art a function of subjectively grounded claims, even as universals. For Adorno, aesthetic theory is directed neither toward questions of taste and judgment nor toward questions of experience rooted in the subjective apprehension of forms. Rather, it offers a window onto a domain of works that are nonidentical with both the concepts we bring to them and to the materials of which they are composed. Artworks are things, and their "thingly" qualities ought to be respected; but artworks are not *mere* things. Insofar as they are woven into the fabric of social and historical relations, Adorno regards artworks as the "social antithesis of society."

Grounding this view is the claim that art plays a crucial role in preserving what I have been calling "embodied meaning." Terry Eagleton is no doubt right in pointing out that modern aesthetics began as a discourse about the body. This much was clear from the ways in which Burke and Hume engaged the question of sensation. In "The Standard of Taste," Hume, for instance, hoped to set judgments of taste on solid ground by identifying empirical grounds for agreement about aesthetic pleasure. But this also implies regarding artworks as bundles of stimuli. The result was something that Hume himself could hardly have imagined, namely, the obscuring of whatever was special about works of art. At the other end of the spectrum, the appeal to indeterminate and unknowable qualities as the key to the specifically "aesthetic" element in art (for example, the "je ne sais quoi"), or the linkage of art with the unfathomable creative powers of genius, yields a vision of aesthetics that is bound to seem remote from what artworks ask us to grasp as tangible, objective, and concrete. Aesthetic theory has a history of dividing art between one reductivism grounded in the empirical and another that gestures toward the ineffable. To this Adorno replies with a tersely articulated antinomy: "The beautiful is no more to be defined than its concept can be dispensed with" (*AT*, p. 51).

To be sure, one can replace an aesthetic theory *qua* theory of art with descriptions of aesthetic experience, as certain branches of phenomenology have sought to do. Insofar as phenomenology takes its bearings by lived experience, it might appear to be uniquely suited to the development of a philosophical aesthetics. The reasons are hardly obscure. Like art itself, phenomenology deals with the realm of embodied experience as complex, integrated, and irreducible. Its procedures defy any approach to the world that would begin from the "top down" or from the "bottom up." Phenomenology attempts to register the fact that any engagement with the world must commence "in the middle." It is equally discontent with the reduction of experience to its "conditions of possibility" and with mere descriptions of the content of experience. In the view of one of its most aesthetically minded practitioners, Maurice Merleau-Ponty, phenomenology is a philosophy that takes the facts of the subject's embodiment and of the materiality of the world as co-equal. Its philosophical task is to account for the engagement of the two in the production of meaning. Phenomenology is "a philosophy for which the world is always 'already there' before reflection begins ... and all its efforts are concentrated upon re-achieving a direct and primitive contact with the world, and endowing that contact with a philosophical status."[22] The point of departure for phenomenological reflection, the human body, occupies a position that is hardly "originary" but is itself remarkably in-between. "There is a human body when, between the seeing and the seen, between touching and the touched, between one eye and the other, between hand and hand, a blending of some sort takes place—when the spark is lit between sensing and sensible, lighting the fire that will not stop burning."[23]

Especially in the essays "Eye and Mind" and "Cézanne's Doubt" Merleau-Ponty gives an account of the ways in which art is an intelligent sensing of the world, offering an engagement with the world that gives evidence of the kind of knowledge that has been occluded by the dominance of "abstract concepts" in the preponderantly rationalized cultures of modernity. In Merleau-Ponty's view, the eye and the hand transmit the intelligence of the world. But, unlike "science," art (painting) is credited by Merleau-Ponty with an encounter with the brute meaning of the world. As such, it carries out the work of "thinking" in a manner that conceptual thought cannot accomplish. Moreover, art's intelligent sensing of the world is free from the desire to know things as true or false, and likewise free from the kinds of judgments about ends that are implicit in morality. The contrast between the certainties embodied in the visual domain of painting and the philosophies that ground certainty in the expurgation of doubt could hardly be greater: "A Cartesian can grant that the existing world is not visible.... A painter cannot grant that our openness to the world is illusory or indirect, that what we see is not the world itself, or that the mind has to do only with its thoughts or with another mind" ("Eye and Mind," pp. 186–87). Painting is thus as much a form of ontology as it is a mode of cognition: "Because depth, color, line, movement, contour, physiognomy are all branches of Being and because each one can sway all the rest, there are no separated, distinct 'problems' in painting, no really opposed paths, no partial 'solutions,' no cumulative progress, no irretrievable options" ("Eye and Mind," p. 188). Likewise, art is an engagement of the world that is itself a form of valuing, which is to say that it is a form of realizing and tracking value by means of material making and embodied perceiving. In it, values are not simply invoked or applied but enacted: as color, depth, line, volume, and so on. Painting thus becomes a mode of embodied meaning that returns us to those very things that have been alienated from the concept as a "simple abstraction": body, gesture, style, manner, tone, mood, and the like.

In Adorno's view, however, the phenomenology of art runs aground because it strives to be just as presuppositionless as the concept.[24] "It wants to say what art is. The essence it discerns is, for phenomenology, art's origin and at the same time the criterion of art's truth and falsehood" (*AT*, p. 351). Phenomenology understands that "essences" cannot be isolated from the continuum of existence. As Merleau-Ponty remarks at the very beginning of the

Phenomenology of Perception, phenomenology "puts essences back into existence, and does not expect to arrive at an understanding of man and the world from any starting point other than that of their 'facticity'" (p. vii). Artworks for their part call for reflection on experience by semblances of experience, in which we follow themes, reconstruct images, or relate empathically with what a given character may feel. Undialectical and nonreflective appeals to experience are bound to yield a revalidation of the subject when in fact the experience of art seems to require something closer to what Adorno calls a *"counter*movement to the subject" (my emphasis). As he put it, "[Aesthetic experience] demands something on the order of the self-denial of the observer, his capacity to address or recognize what aesthetic objects themselves enunciate and what they conceal" (*AT,* p. 346). The incomprehensibility to which we are given free and open access through appearances stands at the core of what Adorno calls the "enigma" of art. It is also art's best defense against the ravages of aesthetic theories that seem bent on schematizing it: "This incomprehensibility persists as the character of art, and it alone protects the philosophy of art from doing violence to art" (*AT,* p. 347). If aesthetic theory has an obligation, it is to bring the opacity of art to consciousness, to remain eloquent and articulate while resisting the temptation to regard the enigmas of art as puzzles to be solved: "The task of a philosophy of art is not so much to explain away the element of incomprehensibility, which speculative philosophy has almost invariably sought to do, but rather to understand the incomprehensibility itself" (*AT,* p. 347).

Merleau-Ponty's idea of essences put back into existence ranges well beyond mere facticity to a more complex form of experience. And yet Adorno's response to phenomenology may help clarify the fact that "embodied meaning" is not simply the result of concretizing an idea, much less of "subtracting" whatever in the concept is or was abstract so as to reach its material substratum.

It is rather an attempt to grasp the ways in which art, as a mode of material praxis, offers a sensuously intelligent way of grasping the world. If art is, in Hegel's famous phrase, the "sensuous manifestation of the Idea," then it is a manifestation in which the forces at work in bringing about the "manifestation of the Idea" are an integral part of the work itself. Art is the production of things that are not "mere things" in part because their material "madeness" brings forth a set of qualities that *mere* material things seem unable to disclose. Adorno offers this as his redescription of Benjamin's notion of the aura ("Aura is not only—as Benjamin claimed—the here and now of the artwork, it is whatever goes beyond its factual givenness"; *AT*, p. 45). These are not just sensuous qualities that *oppose* the concept, but a range of qualities, including affect and force, which go beyond the brute materials of any given work.

It seems only right, then, to consider philosophical appeals to the notion of "force"—as in Deleuze's appeal to the notion of *puissance* and to the "logic of sense"—in aesthetic theory. (Deleuze: "In art, and in painting as in music, it is not a matter of reproducing or inventing forms, but of capturing forces. For this reason no art is figurative.")[25] Can "force" and "sense" stand in some relation to the concept other than that of opposition or remainder? Phenomenology rests with the lived body, but it does not take power or forces into account. As Deleuze writes, "The lived body is a paltry thing in comparison with a more profound and almost unlivable Power."[26] If Deleuze's effort to develop a new aesthetics seems to be more radical than what phenomenology proposes it is largely because in place of "lived experience" Deleuze proposes an engagement with the forces that drive and organize it, including at the supra-individual level. In this he remains resolutely Nietzschean: forces present themselves as fundamentally aesthetic regardless of whether they are manifested in art or elsewhere. Whatever may provide the impetus for art cannot be limited to it; force is at work in every domain of human existence in spite of the fact that it has been so often masked by conventional understandings of the "concept" in its isolation from issues of power.

For Deleuze, the crucial relationships are between the concept, perception, and affects. These follow a combinatorial logic, in which no element is privileged over and above any of the others. It allows for what Fredric Jameson has called the Deleuzian "'flux' of perpetual change."[27] But Deleuze makes a lucid distinction among the elements that comprise this flux—among percept, affect, and concept. Rather than representing or imitating anything (least of all "ideas" in the conventional sense), or "realizing" the concept, as Hegel would have it, Deleuze regards art as a matter of recombining and objectivizing elements whose status remains co-equal. None of these is the ground for any of the others: there is no priority, implicit or otherwise, of concept over percept or affect, and so for all these terms. Drawing implicitly on the aesthetics of the baroque—to which Deleuze devoted an influential book where he explores the figures of the *pli* (fold) and the *bel composto* (artful arrangement)—art is the site where percept, concept, and affect combine like the threads of a fabric whose strands are completely interwoven with one another.[28] Or, evoking a different figure, it is a territory in which "every habitat, joins up not only its spatiotemporal but its qualitative planes or sections: a posture and a song, for example, a song and a color, percepts and affects. And every territory encompasses or cuts across the territories of other species, or intercepts the trajectories of animals without territories, forming interspecies junction points."[29]

Deleuze's insistence on combinations carries with it a resistance to the synthetic orientation of dialectical thought. Likewise, the Deleuzian alternative to the dialectical versions of aesthetics (including Adorno's "negative dialectics") strives to remain anchored in the flux of forces without falling into a materialist reductivism. True to his Nietzschean roots, and to a "transcendental empiricism" that is inspired by Hume,[30] Deleuze's philosophy regards itself as fundamentally aesthetic, not a theory of art. But it may miss the fact that concept and sense (including affects and percepts) always in fact mediate one another, with each one striving to complete what the other seems unable to do or say. And rather than think that an aesthetic philosophy can accomplish what art attempted to do in its role as a bearer of a truth denied by concepts, we might do better to ask how aesthetics came to misrecognize the very things it hoped to theorize. Given the changes in aesthetics and in art over the course of modernism and its aftermath, it might well seem that the task of aesthetic theory ought now to be an explanation of the conditions of the "impossibility" of art. But if this is so, then I would suggest that it is a task best begun by reflection on the history in which aesthetic theory was drawn to model itself along lines drawn from other disciplines, some quite inconsistent with the ambitions of art. Can the successor discourses to our many theories of art adequately respond to the ways in which beauty still stakes claims to truth? As the history of aesthetic theory makes abundantly clear, asking about the ways in which truth and beauty interanimate one another poses questions that the philosophy of art has only begun to take up.

Endnotes

1. Walter Benjamin, *The Origin of German Tragic Drama*, trans. John Osborne (New York, 1998), p. 31.

2. Adorno cites Geiger without specific reference in Theodor W. Adorno, *Aesthetic Theory*, trans. Robert Hullot-Kentor (Minneapolis, 1997), p. 332 (henceforth *AT*). See Moritz Geiger, *The Significance of Art: A Phenomenological Approach to Aesthetics* (Washington, D.C., 1986).

3. See Eckbert Faas, *The Genealogy of Aesthetics* (Cambridge, 2002), on the overemphasis on spirit rather than the body in most aesthetic theory.

4. Adorno writes, "Art itself thinks" (*AT*, p. 99).

5. Arnold Hauser, *Social History of Art* (London, 1951), p. 5.

6. See J. M. Bernstein, *Adorno: Disenchantment and Ethics* (Cambridge, 2001).

7. Theodor W. Adorno, *Philosophy of Modern Music*, trans. Anne G. Mitchell and Wesley V. Blomster (London, 1973), p. 126.

8. This is the formulation of Michael McKeon, *Origins of the English Novel, 1600–1740* (Baltimore, 1987), p. 20.

9. In the preface to the *Critique of Judgment*, Immanuel Kant writes of the deduction of the transcendental aesthetic that "the difficulty of unraveling a problem so involved in its nature may serve as an excuse for a certain amount of hardly avoidable obscurity in its solution"; trans. James Creed Meredith (Oxford, 1986), p. 7. Regarding the hope that aesthetic reflective judgment will span the gulf between the sensuous and supersensuous realms, Kant writes in the introduction that "it is not possible to throw a bridge from one realm to the other" (p. 37).

10. See Arthur Danto, *The Transfiguration of the Commonplace* (Cambridge, MA, 1981), and *Anything Goes* (Berkeley, 1998).

11. This is a major thrust of Bernstein's *Adorno: Disenchantment and Ethics*. But, whereas Bernstein speaks of the "complex concept," it seems to me that art's interest lies preponderantly with "embodied meaning." The differences lie especially in what the notion of "meaning" conveys, which "concept" (whether abstract, embodied, complex, or otherwise) does not.

12. G. W. F. Hegel, *Lectures on Aesthetics*, trans. T. M. Knox (Oxford, 1975), pp. 71–72 (henceforth *LA*).

13. Robert Brandom, *Articulating Reasons: An Introduction to Inferentialism* (Cambridge, MA, 2000), pp. 36–37. I am indebted here to Bernstein, who discusses Brandom's work in *Adorno: Disenchantment and Ethics*.

14. This is Kant's analysis in the *Critique of Judgment*, § 15, where Baumgarten and Wolf are referred to simply as "philosophers of reputation" (p. 69).

15 Pierre Bourdieu, *Distinction: A Social Critique of the Judgment of Taste*, trans. Richard Nice (Cambridge, MA, 1984), p. 6.

16 Pierre Bourdieu, *The Rules of Art*, trans. Susan Emanuel (Stanford, 1992), p. 51.

17 This is roughly the line that Jürgen Habermas takes, following Max Weber, in *The Philosophical Discourse of Modernity*, trans. Frederick Lawrence (Cambridge, MA, 1987).

18 Terry Eagleton, *The Ideology of the Aesthetic* (Oxford, 1990), pp. 342–43.

19 Cf. Georg Lukács, *The Theory of the Novel*, trans. Anna Bostock (Cambridge, MA, 1971), which bears the subtitle "A Historico-Philosophical Essay."

20 Adorno's many disagreements with Benjamin are well known. See the letters between them in Theodor W. Adorno, *Aesthetics and Politics* (London, 2007), pp. 110–41.

21 Theodor W. Adorno, *Kierkegaard: Construction of the Aesthetic*, trans. Robert Hullot-Kentor (Minneapolis, 1989).

22 Maurice Merleau-Ponty, *Phenomenology of Perception*, trans. Colin Smith (London, 2000), p. vii. Legitimate questions can be raised about the fact that Merleau-Ponty favors painting above all the other arts. One of the worries waiting to be expressed is that the fascination with painting may lead to a form of ocular-centrism that may in the end defeat the concreteness of its version of the concept and undermine the force with which it enacts its perspectives. In his defense is the argument that painting involves a kind of vision that is not the transformation of things into mental schemas but is, instead, a kind of corporeal thinking, one that deciphers and realizes signs that are given within the body. Painting may well be visual but it is not ocular-centric for Merleau-Ponty in the way that it is for someone like Descartes, who regards it as yet another mode for the conceptual possession of the world. See Maurice Merleau-Ponty, "Eye and Mind," in *The Primacy of Perception*, ed. James M. Edie (Evanston, 1964), p. 171. Moreover, Merleau-Ponty's approach to painting offers one possible response to an issue that has plagued aesthetic theory throughout its history: the antinomy of experience and judgment as a form of the strife between beauty and truth.

23 Merleau-Ponty, "Eye and Mind," p. 163.

24 Adorno does not say this without good reason. Merleau-Ponty writes that "Phenomenology is the study of essences; and according to it, all problems amount to finding definitions of essences: the essence of perception, or the essence of consciousness, for example"; *Phenomenology of Perception*, p. vii.

25 Gilles Deleuze, *Francis Bacon: The Logic of Sensation*, trans. Daniel W. Smith

(London, 2002), p. 56.

26. Gilles Deleuze, *Foucault*, trans. Seán Hand (Minneapolis, 1988), p. 39.
27. Fredric Jameson, *Late Marxism: Adorno, Or, the Persistence of the Dialectic* (London, 1990), p. 16.
28. Gilles Deleuze, *The Fold*, trans. Tom Conley (Minneapolis, 1993).
29. Gilles Deleuze and Félix Guattari, *What Is Philosophy?* trans. Hugh Tomlinson and Graham Burchell (New York, 1994), p. 185.
30. Gilles Deleuze, "Hume," in *Desert Islands and Other Texts: 1953–1974*, ed. David Lapoujade, trans. Michael Taormina (Los Angeles, 2004), pp. 162–69.

Fred Rush

Adorno After Adorno

CRITICAL THEORY IS A curious mixture of the utopian and the anti-utopian.[1] On the anti-utopian side, one of the primary impulses of early critical theory is to combat the "transfiguration of suffering" and its main apparatus, "idealism," by challenging the predilection of philosophy for ahistorical and systematic foundationalism, especially neo-Kantian and positivist developments in the foundations of the social sciences. So dedicated was Adorno to dialectically ferreting out remnants of "idealism" that he extended his critique of it to those who count as idealists only at a stretch, like Husserl and Heidegger. Nor were Adorno's own philosophical forebears exempt: he charged Lukács, Bloch, and, most tellingly, Benjamin at various times with utopianism stemming from etiolated idealism. Under every rock and upon every pedestal, it seems, was a Kantian of the wrong bent. Nor was Adorno of a particularly utopian disposition when he looked around him at what was, for him, contemporary culture. On the utopian side, Adorno's disparaging analysis of mass art and popular culture can seem to require a standard for "true art" no longer found in human experience, if it ever was to be found there in the first place. This approach to the value of contemporary culture on Adorno's part sometimes gives rise to charges that—if, indeed, his views are not just expressions of bitter antiquation—his dismissal of what many would be happy to allow as art is even *falsely* utopian.[2] The category of "false utopia" is distinctively Adorno's, so the criticism, when redirected at Adorno, has a special sting to it.[3]

The topic of this volume of essays, art and aesthetics after Adorno, assumes that Adorno's philosophy of art reorients the discipline of aesthetics as well as the objects over which aesthetic theories range. Only with this assumption in place would a treatment of art and aesthetics *after* Adorno be anything other than merely chronological and anodyne. Now, one might regard the importance of Adorno's aesthetics to be well settled; after all, isn't it obvious that Adorno has been quite influential both inside and outside the academy since the 1960s? But empirical questions concerning popularity are quite distinct from conceptual ones of leading significance. Moreover, what form the significance has taken—what *specifically* it is about the content of Adorno's aesthetics that makes it a bellwether—is a matter for interpretation, analysis, and disagreement.

Adorno's reconception of the very category of the "aesthetic" marks the significance and scope of his contribution to contemporary aesthetics and philosophy of art. But the force of this reorientation is often misunderstood. Correctly understanding the nature of aesthetics according to Adorno does not go far enough to settle the issue of his continued relevance for art or contemporary art theory. Conceiving of the activity of theoretical aesthetics as Adorno does calls into question the very possibility of the enterprise of contemporary aesthetics. If one grants the general thrust of his interpretation of what counts as properly aesthetic, it is quite possible that there are no contemporaneous objects that are aesthetic by the lights of that theory. Adorno holds that much of what many take to be the art most expressive of contemporary experience is not truly aesthetic. This claim has to do with the connection Adorno forges between the aesthetic vocation of art and the continuing struggle of subjectivity to keep its distance from modern forms of culture that threaten to engulf it. In other words, one might understand the issue framed by the phrase "art and aesthetics after Adorno" by placing emphasis on a sense of the word "after" that is somewhat antiquated in English but is still present in common usage of the German word "nach." This is the idea of practicing aesthetics as a follower of, or in accordance with, Adorno. Can one have an Adornian aesthetic any longer if Adorno's aesthetic claims are correct? Can there be an "Adorno after Adorno"? Adorno's anti-utopian and utopian tendencies intersect just here. On the one hand, Adorno's views on what can count as aesthetic experience might be thought to be overly ideal and demanding and, in this sense, utopian. If this is so, then his pessimism concerning contemporary art is (falsely) dystopian. On the other hand, if Adorno's claims concerning the nature of the truly aesthetic are more or less correct, his account may permit a much more realistic assessment of the potential of art for freedom. His views are then anti-utopian, revealing the false utopia of an ersatz aesthetic experience.

Art and Aesthetics in Adorno

False Reconciliation

Adorno's aesthetics is based on a Hegelian analysis of concepts. A concept is a process of self-differentiation that relates to other concepts in an overall dialectical logic, in which what are at lower levels of analysis separate concepts develop into their "opposites" (other concepts). This development takes place through a process of conceptual "negation" or "contradiction," in which apparently adequate and complete conceptions of the world turn out to be inadequate and incomplete when subjected to emerging requirements of developing rationality. The only truly determinate concept, Hegel holds, is the entire process of dialectically related concepts. Concepts are not representational items for Hegel, they are the basic ontological fabric of the world, and their development finally yields a single, entire system that is closed as to its logical features. Hegel's term for the relation of humanity to the world at this endpoint is "reconciliation" *(Versöhnung)*. Calling this endpoint a reconciliation registers that humans experience their relation to the world in an alienated form up to that point—the world is thought to consist in basic dualities, which cause one's experience of the world to be experience as of an "Other." This gradual elimination of alienated experience is fraught; each stage of thought is experienced initially as providing a firm footing only to be shown through failure to be insufficient in securing a stable view of the relation of humans to the world. The true end is experienced as a release from this development, as well as a return to what has been the hope from the beginning—a world in which humanity is "at home." Reconciliation marks the completion of the process of overcoming otherness and healing the divide between "spirit" and world.

Adorno demurs precisely at this point of Hegelian doctrine. He rejects the proposition that reason is driven to a final, most rational resting place. *Irreconcilability* is, then, a standing basic condition for Adorno—this is part of what he means when he reverses Hegel's formulation and asserts that "the whole is the false."[4] This denial of Hegelian teleology in Adorno is well known, but its import is often underappreciated. In particular, there is a tendency to overassimilate it to the German Romantic view that one finds in Fichte, Novalis, and Friedrich Schlegel that dialectic is infinite striving. Fichte and the Romantics hold that there is a stepwise, *progressive* dialectic, and that means they argue for at least a minimal positive relation of dialectic to what they call "the Absolute," the final cause for the activity. While there well may be remnants of this Romanticism in Adorno (of which more later) it is a mistake to think of Adorno's negative dialectic as a species of asymptotic approximation or a mere removal of the closure condition on Hegelian dialectic.[5] This can give the impression that any one stage of dialectic or dialectical transition would receive very much the same analysis as it would receive under the Hegelian understanding of dialectic, with the simple proviso that there would not be the underlying cumulative unfolding of the final end of dialectic at each and every stage. But the rejection of teleology governing the endpoint of the system (the system generally) requires reformulating the nature of *any one stage* of dialectic. Rejecting the overall ends-direction of dialectic leaves one, that is, with very potent skepticism at every dialectical stage, which skepticism must extend to the very issue of the possibility of dialectical transition and thus to any assurance of positive dialectical development. This is just to say that the stock Hegelian doctrine of *Aufhebung* itself must be radically reformulated.[6] Adorno never achieved a satisfactory reformulation of that doctrine, but for present purposes what is important to mark is that, for Adorno, dialectic can describe an "inward" spiraling-down as well as an "outward" stepping-up. "Progression" in this sort of dialectic consists in finer and finer negative assessments of purportedly stable categories. The cognitive superiority of one dialectical stage over another does not consist in resolving contradiction; it consists rather in driving the standing contradiction deeper into the given dialectical structure. From the canonical Hegelian perspective, this raises the concern that contingency infiltrates the deep structure of dialectic.[7]

In particular, Adorno's ethical outlook embraces contingency to an extent intolerable in idealism. Underlying his ethical views is a broad understanding of the significance for ethical understanding of what Weber called the "disenchantment" *(Entzauberung)* of nature.[8] Disenchanted nature gives rise to an awareness that one's ethical projects are, even with best intents, subject to circumstances beyond the control of even the most perceptive agents. This in turn is part of a more general recognition that human purposes have no guarantee that they will be answered by a purposeless world. All that one can hope for is coincidence of circumstance and intent. In the face of this realization, there are two basic positions open to one: naturalism and idealism. If one embraces naturalism, then classical understandings of normativity on the model of strict law seem problematic. If purposes are causal impulses on a par with the rest of the fabric of the universe, how can norms be any less contingent than any other part of the world? Idealism preserves the concept of strict ethical law in the teeth of purposeless nature, but only by positing that ultimate ontological structures are beyond the realm of empirical experience, governed as it is by natural law. The idealist accepts that the truth of ethical judgments and the realization of good will in the world are strictly indemonstrable. Kant's moral theory is a version of this option. Kant argues that what is ultimately valuable in ethics is good will, not its effects. Still, he realizes that finite discursive beings are also empirical beings and have interests in the worldly success of their ethical projects. Kant posits as rationally necessary a number of compensatory thoughts meant to secure a harmony between the empirically real and transcendentally ideal realms, thereby making it possible to persist in being ethical without being a defeatist. They are akin to what Kant calls "transcendental but merely regulative" principles. For Adorno, the Kantian doctrine of regulative reason and its sibling, the doctrine of reflective judgment, are of consequence.[9] This is not because Adorno wants to accommodate something like reflective judgment in his aesthetics or the Kantian idea of regulative posits in his ontology. The importance lies rather in what the doctrines display about idealism. They show idealism *in extremis*, that is, they reveal idealism's incapacity to face up to the residuum of theoretically salient contingency that it must admit. For Adorno, ethical judgment must fully acknowledge that even basic acts that we take to be constitutive of ethical agency may go astray. Nevertheless, many such acts do succeed if the conditions are right.[10] A philosophically respectable account of ethics would locate increased ethical success in the ontological conditions that make it the case that such action can in principle come off but, as a matter of empirical circumstance, can just as easily misfire.[11] Any other view is a version of reconciliation that requires positing a false utopia—in either a notional hereafter (Kant) or in the complete closure of a rational system (Hegel).

This detour through Adorno's ethical ontology is important because it is in his consideration of ethics that he develops most perspicaciously one of his main philosophical themes—one that is crucial for understanding his views on art. This is namely the issue of false reconciliation—"false" in the sense that *any* reconciliation, unless considered provisional, is de facto falsifying. Such falsification is a standing threat in culture and, in particular, in the making and understanding of art. Art is always under siege by the impulse to reconciliation, subject to various claimed reconciliations that would fix art's significance in terms of its representation or expression of the current state of culture in everyday understanding. Art is not truly art so long as it remains fixed in this way. Moreover, ethical goodness is dependent on retaining one's connection to an impulse that cannot be rationalized away. This impulse pertains to an inner nature of a "mimetic" (or close to mimetic) relation to things and others that is rational yet not controlling. This capacity is precisely what is under siege in modern life. Art is, in Adorno's estimation, a primary way to explore the relation of reason to impulse in a way that circumvents rationalization.[12]

Artists and Works

An artwork for Adorno is the historical outcome of an artist's innovative treatment of a given material. The phrase "given material" has to be immediately qualified. The material with which an artist works is precisely *not* a merely sensuous component such as sound, word, or paint. It is rather a historically developed set of practices and prior works that constitute the social world in which the artist finds himself. That this material is historical in turn conditions the sense in which it is "given." To an artist who is responsive to the historical nature of the material—one who sees art's materiality in terms of its historical development—the material is given as demanding change in order to maintain and advance its historical character.

Art for Adorno is a refuge from overadministered rationality and, as such, is a promising vehicle for developing a "less false" access to experience that can yield new understanding. Under conditions of modernity, where instrumental reasoning and discursive closure predominate, art's partly nondiscursive character is uniquely suited to both (a) introduce enough indeterminacy among standing concepts that one is able to begin to noninstrumentally imagine a next step in their development and (b) rescue the idea that nondiscursive elements of experience are inherently valuable. But art must also express the state of play between freedom and dominance present in the society at the time of its making. An analog of the divide in society between implicit demands of freedom and explicit lack of it is embedded in the work as a tension between two elements: (a') the superficial integration of the aesthetic components of the work, in many cases tending toward "totality," that is, near seamless synthesis, and (b') an undercurrent of disintegration, present in the work in the form of its "gaps" or, in the case of works that are self-conscious of this tension, "fragmentation."[13] An artwork is a dynamic entity whose unity is not a matter of integration at the expense of differentiation within the work but is rather the tension between integration and disintegration.

For Adorno art must be at the cutting edge of what counts as modern in order to fulfill this critical function. Its dialectical relationship to past art not only requires innovation on given material but also can be a response to the past that sees value in what has previously escaped, perhaps by mere accident, commodification. Largely following Benjamin, Adorno endorses the practice of artistically and critically investigating the marginalia of past and present cultures for materials that may be innovative just because of their lack of prior discursive importance. In fact, this lack of utility is but one component of the content of such ephemera; it is the conjunction of inutility with the property of being a *failed* commodity that is crucial. Such objects have a native dialectical structure—both part of and apart from capitalism—that is pregnant with artistic possibility. The importance of the materials of found, discarded culture is an aspect of Adorno's aesthetics that is often downplayed or missed; its demand for formal innovation in art does not entail that the material on which innovation operates comes from canonical high art and does not preclude the use of mass culture as its material. Nor is formal innovation limited to technical experimentation of the sort one finds in the Second Vienna School, in analytic cubism, or in Joyce and Beckett. Ironic juxtaposition, parataxis, and other rhetorical approaches to material can comprise critical art. Still, such art must oppose its own impulse to reconciliation in structural harmony; it must "will" its incomprehensibility.[14] For art to express such essential disunity and lack of freedom, it must undercut its own pretensions to authority and posit at the deepest point of its structure a skeptical impulse directed back on itself.

"The New"

The artist must struggle with the material against the material—he cannot so abstract himself from his given social environment that he doesn't feel its pull. Nevertheless, the artist can bring something new to the material that animates its latent tendencies, that is sensitive to elemental experience, and that is not exhausted by mass culture. Adorno at times characterizes what he takes to be wrong with mass culture in an extremely abstract way. His analysis has three levels. The first, and most abstract, is an attack on discursive experience generally. Generality of concepts—thinking of things as mattering in terms of their shared features—is the culprit. Any conceptual thought whatsoever threatens sensitive response. But this stringent and implausible form of noncognitivism does not sit well with Adorno's rejection of immediacy. One cannot think without generalizing, and art is after all a form of thought for Adorno. The second level of analysis is slightly less arcane. Concepts track given regularities and, therefore, by themselves are not spurs to think anew. Moreover, Adorno holds that the past experience that comprises concepts can rise to such a normative pitch that imagining other possible modes of experience is extremely difficult. Adorno holds that modern informational technology delivers fixity of concepts almost without a trace of their origins; it is part of the efficiency of late capitalism to do so. These first two points are formal; the third is not. Adorno is also concerned with the particular content of the concepts that are on hand for the artist. This is a more concrete dimension of Adorno's analysis that focuses on the power of certain kinds of generalized content, not just generic content but content-genera. It is the first two levels of analysis that are paramount to Adorno and the second one that, in his best moments, takes precedence. The problem is not generality; it is to generalize *in the right way*. The "right way" for Adorno involves vigilance concerning any putative resting place for artistic meaning. Criticism depletes the art object's reserve of stability that otherwise would cause it to relapse into the material status quo. Given the extreme efficiency of consumer culture in absorbing what were at one time expressions of artistic freedom and its capacity to craft new objects that limn aspects of what was once free art to create pseudofree "art," being an artist becomes increasingly difficult, and the shelf life—to take a term from 1950s consumer culture—of art is apt to be very short. Humans need pseudosubjectivity almost as much as they need the real thing, and they *think* they need the former more than the latter. A conductor like Arturo Toscanini is paradigmatic of Adorno's concern. The concatenation of Toscanini's music prodigy (which Adorno doesn't contest) and the Madison Avenue–style marketing of the excellence of the NBC Orchestra and of his own identity as "maestro" indicate a general and generic phenomenon, according to Adorno.[15] A work of true meaning is produced as a commodity, the nature of which is obscured by its association with the composer. Adorno considers the susceptibility—even the willed susceptibility—of high art to become pseudo-art to be inherent in European art music, a trend that starts quite early in the development of art-music, beginning with Beethoven and reaching something like an apogee with Wagner.[16] Even Mahler, a composer whom Adorno greatly esteemed, was only problematically able to balance composing with satisfying public expectations foisted upon him as the conductor of major orchestras.

Adorno After Adorno

Adorno Reception

Historically speaking, Adorno's philosophical views have had a rough reception within philosophical aesthetics, theoretically based art criticism, and what might be broadly called the sociology of art. There have been two basic lines of criticism, both of which complain that Adorno's theory places too much emphasis on subjectivity and thus compromises the responsiveness of criticism to contemporary art.[17] The two lines of complaint could not be more different, however, in their reasons for rejecting the focus on subjectivity. Poststructuralist criticisms of Adorno find the subjectivism at fault for what are, essentially, Heideggerian reasons, arguing that it must be replaced with a thoroughgoing aesthetic of "play" in which categories are subverting, not in virtue of an inner logic or dialectic, but rather because dialectic—even a "negative" one—is no longer relevant. For poststructuralists, Adorno's severe disappointment in mass culture and the mournfulness about art are just ossified remnants of a bygone, narrative self-understanding. The second line of negative reaction to Adorno emerges from the periphery of critical theory itself. The main representative of this line is Habermas, and the charge is that Adorno's account of subjectivity yields no viable position on the normativity of reasons. The problem here is not dialectic as such—appearances to the contrary, Habermas still avows some form of dialectical analysis—it is rather the negativity of the dialectic. For Habermas, Horkheimer and Adorno's *Dialectic of Enlightenment* (1944/47) is already a catastrophic misunderstanding of the potentialities of reason in modernity that is far too skeptical of Enlightenment as a source for free rationality. Habermas hammers home the allegedly pernicious continuity in Adorno of rational and aesthetic modes of awareness. Put in the terms of a category first crafted by Horkheimer, Habermas charges that Adorno falls into the dreaded camp of "irrationalism" *malgré lui*.[18] This is rhetorically astute on Habermas's part, whether or not the charge betrays misunderstandings of Adorno, irrationalism, or both. Because Habermas's criticisms have more to do with the pride of place Adorno assigns to aesthetic theory and experience than with the propriety of his aesthetics as such, I shall not explore them further here.

I wish to discuss two potential avenues along which Adorno's views might be extended, nevertheless, to achieve contemporary currency. The first involves an aspect of Adorno's work that is downplayed and might seem closest to poststructuralism. Although I believe that this is an aspect of Adorno that merits further discussion than it sometimes receives, it is likely that it will not be greeted as a very productive source for the work's contemporary salience, since it keeps in place Adorno's stringent formal progressivism. The second line of thought I shall sketch is much more recognizably Adorno's but, for that very reason, reintroduces a point that always looms in the background of Adorno-inspired contemporary criticism, that is, whether there is any application for Adorno's theory if the theory is correct about the structure of well-formed aesthetic objects.[19]

"Stabilized" Art

The Toscanini case shows that high art can be mass art—and a particularly pernicious form of mass art at that. Much of the phenomena covered by what Adorno meant by the term "mass art" is now called "media." It is safe to say that Adorno was hardly media-ready, even when judged against the standard of other upper-middle-class Weimar intellectuals. His own involvement with the popular art of his time was selective, prejudiced by prior theoretical commitment, and generally more a product of sociological study than of participation.[20] Still, it is a mistake to tax Adorno with the view that *all* popular art is regressive or that mere entertainment is odious. Although his writings on certain popular arts (jazz) can aggregate to give the opposite impression, Adorno was not dismissive of all popular art or even of all mass art.[21]

It is undeniable that Adorno tended to judge musical seriousness in terms of formal innovation. This alone might explain his distaste for jazz, which he alleges remains within the harmonic confines of Debussy and Ravel. The nerve of Adorno's account, however, is that jazz is a popular art that *pretends* to be serious: the subaltern of the Toscanini case. What concerns him is not so much the recycled harmonic Romanticism of the music but rather its pretense to be taken seriously as an expression of musical democracy—what would be for him a matter of false reconciliation. The musicological and sociological complaints are connected. Because the music is constrained by antiquated harmonic structure, its performance cannot qualify as an expression of collective freedom that measures up to today's requirements. Notwithstanding these biases, if they are such, popular art forms can be serious for Adorno if an artist deploys them in the context of autonomous art—here the examples are the use of folk music, jazz, and cabaret song, most notably in Mahler, Bartók, Berg, and Weill. Of course, such folk or mass art is no longer popular when it is given this different context, since the context calls for an ironic or satiric attitude toward the art so deployed absent from its truly popular experience.[22] In his music criticism from the 1920s and '30s, Adorno considers a type of composition he terms "stabilized" or "hybrid-negative" music, including among its practitioners Bartók, Janáček, Hindemith, Weill, and the Stravinsky of *L'histoire du soldat*.[23] This type of music integrates what would otherwise be regressive material with progressive elements. If the regressive material is subject to further critical assessment within the work, then it does not tell against the work's overall progressive nature—it is, in fact, what constitutes that nature. The case of Weill is illustrative. The regressive material would be cabaret-style swing jazz, which Weill handles with true critical acumen—Adorno cites the opera *Mahagonny* as exemplary.[24] Neoclassicism is the antipode.[25] Unlike hybrid negative or stabilized music, in which popular or historically remote musical forms coexist in a dialectical tension in a work, neoclassicism is insufficiently dialectical and, thus, purely regressive. The hope that the mere passage of time or their alleged folk nature alone can allow the forms to escape commodification is delusional. Inserting wholesale prior musical *Weltanschauungen* into the musical present fails to engage with the demands of modern times in its own terms. In truth, Adorno leaves imprecise the dialectical relation between the regressive and progressive elements in the music that allow for this critical status, and perhaps the imprecision is due to a lingering general formal bias against popular, folk, or mass music. He was never wholehearted about the ability of the composer to use dated material, distinguishing himself from other Marxist music critics of his time—for instance, his correspondent and friend Ernst Krenek. His main models for progressive art remain the Second Vienna School and, specifically, Schoenberg's atonalism.[26] (The analog in literature, Adorno's other main artistic concern, is Beckett.)

One might think that Adorno's allowance that art can be progressive by deploying diffuse cultural material offers a point of contact with poststructuralist criticism, which often seems to prize works of this sort. But this superficial similarity has to do more with the extensional overlap of the works counted as having potential aesthetic interest than with any theoretical détente. Inclusion of Adorno's theory in a world littered with pop culture deconstructions cannot have its basis simply in the category of stabilized art. Put another way, while Adorno allows that irony can be critical in artists like Weill, irony as it operates in much poststructural criticism is not critical by Adorno's lights. There are of course many varieties of irony abroad. One that has claimed a good deal of currency in poststructuralist circles was propounded, if not minted, in Jean-François Lyotard's monograph on the postmodern condition, which identifies irony with conceptual play.[27] Irony, on this understanding, is less concerned with the internal relation of the object of irony and the ironizing subject than it is with instituting a destabilizing movement from concept to concept. The poststructuralist understanding of the significance of irony, that is, depends on there being minimal conceptual barriers that would impede the sheer calisthenic movement of thought. For Adorno, irony would not be interesting unless it had a dialectical structure with requisite negativity. If one thinks of irony as having a dialectical structure, irony need not and indeed cannot involve diffidence about its object resulting from a scintillating play of concepts; rather, it consists in a dynamic tension *between concepts*—between the forces at work in innovation (distance) and the demands of history (commitment). Schoenberg is exemplary again; invention with dissonance is an achievement all the greater because of the deep appreciation of the historical undertow of harmony that informs it. Atonality has its dialectical bite in part because it is mindful of what it leaves behind.[28] This circumspection is what, to Adorno's mind, essentially marks Schoenberg as superior in musical comprehension to Boulez.

Aesthetic Experience

The point of departure for developing Adorno's aesthetic theory nowadays cannot, then, amount to a selective appeal to certain of the more mass-art friendly categories he deploys within the theory. It must come to grips with Adorno's reformulation of what counts as aesthetic experience. Modern aesthetics emerges in the eighteenth century in the empiricist theories of Addison, Hutcheson, and Burke and in the rationalist treatments of Wolff, Baumgarten, Winckelmann, and Lessing. There was a rich tradition in both camps with a good deal of variety on many issues. But there was general agreement that aesthetics is concerned with pleasure taken in sensuous experience. "Aesthetics," as Adorno uses the term, however, does *not* refer primarily to an account of art's significance in terms of either pleasure or sensuality. Adorno does discuss the sensuous aspects of art and considers them, at times, to be centrally involved in aesthetic experience proper. But sensuality is not a necessary condition on such experience, and it is usually not a sufficient one either. For Adorno what is "aesthetic" in the broadest terms about a work is a product of its negative dialectic, the aspects of the work that escape reduction to mass culture. The category of the aesthetic for him classifies *structural* features of the interaction of historical material and the innovation of the artist. Any aesthetics after Adorno that takes Adorno's analysis of the condition of subjectivity in late modernity seriously would have to be structural in this sense. It is in this structural or ontological register that there is a deep connection between aesthetics and ethics for Adorno. When he writes that "there is no good life in false life," he means not merely that there is no good life possible when many bad states of affairs obtain.[29] "Good life" and "false life" are for him ontological categories with discrete, integrated structures. False life is constituted by entirely general pathological structures that not only make good action highly problematic but also make it extraordinarily difficult to tell what would constitute a good action in the first place. The good often is misconceived under conditions of falsity, making it very unlikely that one could realize even part of a life that is good. Art that is properly aesthetic evades the "false life" of consumption; art's native ground is at the margins of society where consumption wins the day. These margins can dilate or contract in principle, of course. The point is not the protection of "successful" art; it is rather to protect the way in which true art fails. Art's success in evading consumption is dialectically tied to its potential failure, and not just possible failure. That is, to be art is to be a necessary failure, given time. Still, art can only succeed on its own terms if it can fail on its own terms. If its failure is dictated by the ever-shrinking margins of modernity—so Adorno—it is not its *own* failure. The falser the world becomes, the harder it is for art to evade the falsity "from without."[30] This compromises a main way humans can see over the horizon of falsity that continually presents itself as if it were a physical feature of the world.

Although it can seem as though Adorno sounds the death knell on art—and more than once—one never gets the sense that he gives up on art's alleged critical potential. But that is certainly a possibility. Like it or not, it may be that art can no longer deliver the philosophical punch that Adorno ascribes to it—a claim that is, in essence, a historically extended version of Hegel's "end of art" thesis. Adorno's aesthetic theory is, as usual, a bit ahead of the game, including within it an anticipatory form of mourning art's threatened demise and, therefore, intimations of the theory's own belatedness. In any case, it is far from clear that one can settle the case of "Adorno after Adorno" in Adorno's own terms. Adorno builds that very doubt into his theory.

Art and Aesthetics After Adorno

Given the self-imposed problems associated with a straightforward application of Adorno's aesthetics—the "Adorno after Adorno" problem—it is worthwhile to shift focus one more time and ask whether there are insights in Adorno's aesthetics that do not require adopting the full range of Adorno's views and yet remain suggestive of some basic strategies in the philosophy of art.

Formalism

One of Adorno's central insights is that general culture can and will subsume almost any art that is critical of it. This is not merely a matter of the sheer power of popular culture, or of the desire on the part of general culture to operate on the borrowed prestige of art. If it were just a matter of the former, there would be no rationality to the subsumption, and it is not a matter of the latter because most truly revolutionary art as such is not recognized as prestigious within general culture. General culture has an interest in assimilating the cutting edge simply on the grounds that what the edge cuts is society, as Adorno well knew. It is no good arguing that some art will never be domesticated in this way; the only argument is over how one is to think about the phenomenon. Some will not see it as fatal; like Benjamin, they may see it as a matter of art's evolution. Others, like Adorno, will see this as highly problematic. And, indeed, Adorno's favorites—Schoenberg and Beckett—*have* fallen prey to the phenomenon. Atonal music, sometimes of great sophistication, is a staple of horror films. And Beckett's oeuvre, except perhaps the most obscure later works, has been reabsorbed into the clowning from whence it came. It may be difficult to imagine how Pasolini's *Salò* might be made part of the next Volkswagen ad campaign, but that may say more about one's imagination than about possibility.

Of course artists and art theorists are aware that culture generally has a great deal of interest in domesticating art in ways that conceal the domestication. But it seems the main way in which artists and theorists attempt to forestall such domestication is to pack art with explicit countercultural content. Art is nowadays often message-centered, full of personal revelation, and trades directly in identity transmission. Whatever their other cultural pros and cons, these approaches would have been dismissed by Adorno as insufficiently formal. The grounds for the dismissal are, I think, worth serious consideration. Content-based art, even if the content is politically progressive, is much more apt to be incorporated into popular culture at large because content is inherently containable and submits to replication much more simply than does artistic form. Reacculturation of form can and does happen. But because formal experience of art is itself a difficult achievement even for the very practiced, requiring a good deal of knowledge and perceptual acuity, once one "gets it" one is less likely to view cultural expropriations as the real thing. Moreover, if Adorno is right, formal experience of art always involves a measure of self-skepticism concerning the sufficiency of one's responses. Of course stressing the formal experience of art hardly settles the problem of cultural subsumption. Difficulties shift to preserving responsive perspicuity over and against culture that aims at general responsiveness. Considering art from the perspective of performance may be key here. This is a recognizably Adornian idea, and there is a certain plausibility to the proposition that, say, someone who plays a musical instrument with seriousness is in a better position both to appreciate a musical work of art and to fend off pretenders than one who does not, although it is no guarantee, of course. Thinking of the significance of works from the point of view of performers has a degree of currency in the academy just now, but one has to stress that, no matter how desirable taking this point of view might be, actually taking it is very difficult for most of us, even those who practice criticism.[31]

There is a second point to Adorno's formalism worth considering. The formal experience of works impacts experience more deeply and from more angles than does the shallow stuff of message. One experiences formal qualities in art by means of formal (form*ing*) capacities. Such capacities not only have a hand in a wide range of human experience spanning the discursive and the nondiscursive; they also are centrally involved in the operation of imagination. Imagination is for Adorno a central political category and so, by implication, formal art has a better chance at base stimulation of a very important capacity for social and political change.[32]

Third, as I have noted, aesthetics in Adorno's sense has little to do with "feeling," at least as that concept is usually understood in modern philosophy and criticism. Adorno's aesthetics requires objective ascription of aesthetic properties and not the subjectivism usually associated with either the representational or expressivist branches of traditional aesthetic theory. Casual readers of Adorno sometimes miss this point because of Adorno's concentration on the issue of modern subjectivity. But Adorno does not have what one might call a subjectivist theory of subjectivism. What he is interested in is the plight and promise of subjective experience, where "being subjective" is precisely *not* a matter of boiling the invariant structures of the world down to the "possibility of experience," transcendental or otherwise. Reinterpreting aesthetic theory to deal with the residua of fixed categorical thought is crucial. Construing aesthetics to concern primarily feeling, pleasure, or beauty allows categorical thought too much leeway. It makes too many concessions to an instrumental specification of what can count as a fundamental object for aesthetic experience—otherwise meaningless affect. Adorno refuses this gambit. Whether one thinks that early critical theory overdraws the distinction between instrumental and noninstrumental reasoning (is mere predication *really* a prime instance of instrumental thought, as Adorno seems at times to think?), it is implausible to deny that some substantial overlap between the concepts of rationalization, reification, and instrumental thought charts the horse latitudes of theoretical aesthetics. Theoretical approaches to art must preserve the particularity native to art where the specific art in question requires this approach. Theories of art often dictate what count as proper modes of understanding or experience of art. In some cases, where the art itself calls for very theoretical engagement with it, theory itself needn't be problematic. But in cases where works are not quite so conceptual or where they are only partly so, theory must be on guard against itself.

Theory Theory

The late twentieth century was a period in which art criticism became more explicitly philosophical and, with that, more general and abstract. Literary theory was at the forefront of this development, but critical writing in the visual arts, in music, and in architecture soon followed. What Roland Barthes called "writerly" texts—by which he meant a select group of literary texts—was expanded to include all art.[33] Such art had meaning under, and only under, the critical microscope. More often than not, the microscopic inspection was followed by a critical dissection, meaning being a form of sacrifice on the part of the work. Adorno is representative of this priority of criticism or theory over art, even though he devotes much attention and effort to guarding against theoretical encroachment on the particularity of art.[34] Still, it is undeniable that when Adorno's aesthetic judgment deserts him, as it does in the case of all art music that falls outside the Austro-Germanic compositional line extending from Beethoven to Berg, it is because the theory distorts its relation to its object.

Anglo-American philosophical aesthetics blithely imports approaches to objects developed in metaphysics and epistemology into the aesthetic arena, and the potential for theory-object mismatch and theoretical predation is great. After all, metaphysical and epistemological theories in the United States, Britain, and Australia are themselves modeled to take account of allegedly foundational aspects of mathematics and the empirical sciences.

What is needed is a nonessentialist approach to art that is attentive to the conditions necessary for the theoretical reclamation of art's particularity. The particulars in question are hardly univocal of course; if they were, they wouldn't be particulars. Some art is perceptually demanding and qualitative acuity is demanded in its experience and criticism. Other art is explicitly historical, and understanding it involves attention to its expression of that feature. One could go on. No matter the attention to particularity called for, criticism must be sensitive to the fact that whatever descriptions, judgments, or interpretations are true or apt about the work, they are true or apt about *that* work. This is to say that criticism after Adorno will have to be multivalent. Art is not one thing. Not only are there the several arts—music, literature, painting, architecture, and dance—each of which diverges greatly from others, there are also within the several arts a great degree of plurality. The history of aesthetics is replete with attempts to analogize or reduce one art to another—architecture is "frozen music," *ut pictura poesis*, music is a language of its own, and so on. When one takes seriously the demand of particularity together with a caveat against hegemony across the arts, one comes up with what one might call "deep aesthetics."[35] The idea is basic: one deploys one's philosophical resources where and as needed. If understanding a particular work of architecture, say, requires an idea of embodied experience, then one will investigate the resources available in the phenomenological literature stemming from Merleau-Ponty and the emerging field of consciousness studies. Balzac's *Sarrasine* may indeed call for a writerly approach. The very concept of detail in painting, seemingly at home at the far end of the particularistic spectrum, may be properly subject to historical treatment.[36]

The quandary of "Adorno after Adorno" informs the question of art and aesthetics after Adorno, then, in two ways. First, it raises the possibility that aesthetics in the fashion of Adorno may cease to have a field over which to range. Of course, one can always play the game of arguing whether contemporary works of art *might* be cutting-edge for Adorno. But that is largely beside the point. The point is that there is no guarantee that the cutting-edge will be extant, and every reason to believe it will become even less so. Adorno's main claim is that greater sensitivity to particularity in art is in the service of exploring the mimetic impulse and its relation to noninstrumental rationality, which in turn informs the kind of resistance necessary to the ethical good. But one might demur from Adorno's account of the ethical good, from the impulse that he holds undergirds it, or from his position on the relations of aesthetics to both, and still think it a very bad thing for *aesthetics* to lose sight of its theoretical imitations. It is entirely open to one to challenge the idea that standard views on what theories are and what they are meant to accomplish are applicable in the context of art. Attention to Adorno's aesthetic theory can serve notice indirectly on aesthetic theory generally to pose the question of what might make such a theory adequate to its objects. In this way, Adorno's reorientation of aesthetics around what remains after culture has its say may inspire a move toward greater theoretical sensitivity to particularity and pluralism in aesthetics even if it is not able to go far enough down that road on its own.

Endnotes

Many thanks to Karl Ameriks, Lydia Goehr, Gregg Horowitz, and Christoph Menke for very helpful comments on a draft of this paper. Very different versions of it were presented at the Department of Philosophy at the University of Toronto in fall 2006, at the annual meeting of the American Society of Aesthetics held in Los Angeles in fall 2007, and at the Czech Institute of Arts and Sciences in Prague in spring 2008.

1. The English "utopia" has its proximate and controlling etymology in the Renaissance Latin of Thomas More's *Utopia* (1516), as do its many cognates in other European languages. More's term is an adaptation of the Greek οὐ τόπος, i.e., "no-place." More also plays upon the near-homophone Greek prefix εὐ (conveniently closer in sound in English than in Greek, as More notes in an appendix to the work), and connects the idea of no-place with that of a place of abundance or prosperity. Conceptually speaking, of course, there needn't be such a connection; i.e., there is no reason to assume that an imagined place that either doesn't or can't exist is a good place. But, historically speaking, there has always been a strong implication that a utopia is a good unreachable place, or even that it is unreachable *because* it is so good. English commentary on More sometimes deployed the word "eutopia" as a synonym. See, e.g., Sidney's *An Apology for Poetry* (1595).

2. Of course (1) "false" and (2) "negative" utopias (i.e., dystopias) are distinct categories. Conceptually speaking, one might have true utopias of either positive or negative character and false utopias of either kind as well. So, for instance, Adorno would likely hold the dystopia of Orwell's *1984* to be "false" because it projects a lack of human freedom predicated on something like capitalism to be the negative feature of that "utopia."

3. Many commentators on Adorno's aesthetics treat the phrases "popular culture" and "mass art" as if they were synonymous. They are not. "Mass art" is a term of art for Adorno that refers to art structured in terms of a Marxist understanding of the nature of commodity. There is a tendency to think that Adorno means the qualifier "mass" to signal the broad cultural instantiation or appeal of such art. While mass art often has that broad appeal—as one might think a commodified object would—it needn't in fact. The important point is that mass art is art that is intended for fungible distribution and delectation. "Popular art" is a sociological category that describes art of widespread influence and appeal. There is a great deal of overlap between the categories of mass art and popular culture under modern conditions, which are governed by a commodity concept of cultural significance. But there are times in the history of art when there is popular culture without mass art—i.e., when the concept of commodity either doesn't exist or has not sufficiently infiltrated art production. This is not to say, of course, that there might not be other features of the social significance of art that retard its progressive role. Adorno analyzes folk art in this way and rejects any analysis of such

art as a cure-all for overcommodification of contemporary art. Adorno's view is at heart Rousseauian. Art only emerges as a possible vehicle for fundamental human truths when it is commodified. It operates, as it were, under constant conditions of guerilla warfare.

4   Theodor W. Adorno, *Minima Moralia* § 29, in *Gesammelte Schriften* (hereafter *AGS*), ed. R. Tiedemann, 29 vols. (Frankfurt am Main, 1970–97), 4: p. 55 ("[d]as Ganze ist das Unwahre").

5   Kant has a view, articulated in the "Appendix to the Transcendental Dialectic" of the *Critique of Pure Reason* and again in the two introductions to the *Critique of Judgment*, that dialectical reason has positive asymptotic roles, but of course these are "merely regulative."

6   There is a dodge: one can attempt to recast Hegel as a transcendental philosopher. While that strategy might be plausible in limited contexts, it is decidedly less so as an overall account of dialectic in Hegel.

7   When one puts matters in this way, it becomes obvious why Kierkegaard held such interest for Adorno. Adorno's negative dialectic is very close to what Kierkegaard calls his "ironic inversion" of Hegel. Cf. Lydia Goehr's claim that Adorno's critique of Hegel utilizes a conception of the nonconceptual that is "borrowed from a domain or sphere external to philosophy" that she characterizes as "the musical or aesthetic domain"; Lydia Goehr, "*Doppelbewegung,*" in *Elective Affinities: Musical Essays on the History of Aesthetic Theory* (New York, 2008), p. 32.

8   See Max Weber, *Wissenschaft als Beruf*, ed. W. Mommsen and W. Schluchter (Tübingen, 1992).

9   See Fred Rush, "Dialectic, Value Objectivity, and the Unity of Reason," in *The Oxford Handbook of Continental Philosophy*, ed. B. Leiter and M. Rosen (Oxford, 2007), pp. 315–20.

10 Cf. Georg Wilhelm Friedrich Hegel, *Phänomenologie des Geistes*, in *Werke*, ed. E. Moldenhauer and K. M. Michel (Frankfurt am Main, 1970), 3: p. 447 ff. The outlook is broadly Aristotelian.

11 Much of the analysis here was developed in conversation with Christoph Menke, for which I am very grateful.

12 See pp. 55–57 for further discussion.

13 See *Ästhetische Theorie*, in *AGS* 7: p. 266 for a particularly clear statement of these ideas.

14 Incomprehensibility is not, for Adorno, primarily an epistemic matter—it is ontological. The structure of the art object is not comprehensive and, therefore, is not comprehensible.

15 See *Dialektik der Aufklärung*, in *AGS* 3: p. 182; *Minima Moralia* § 30, in *AGS* 4: p. 56; "Über den Fetischcharakter in der Musik und die Regression des Hörens," in *AGS* 14: p. 21; *Einleitung in die Muskisoziologie* VII, "Dirigent und Orchester," in *AGS* 14; 292–307; "Die Meisterschaft des Maestro,"

in *AGS* 16: pp. 52–67. Joseph Horowitz, *Understanding Toscanini: A Social History of American Concert Life* (1987; reprint, Berkeley, 1994), pp. 229–43, is an evenhanded treatment of Adorno on Toscanini.

16 See, e.g., "Resumé über Kulturindustrie," in *Ohne Leitbild / Parva Aesthetica*, in *AGS* 10.1: pp. 337–45; *Minima Moralia*, in *AGS* 4: p. 242 f. Sibelius is a particularly easy case according to Adorno, but to this group he would add all French music after Berlioz, not only the *chanson* tradition of Fauré, Chausson, and Poulenc, but also the much more controversial Debussy.

17 For the sake of exposition, I am not discussing the "social realist" criticism of Lukács.

18 Jürgen Habermas, *Der philosophische Diskurs der Moderne* (Frankfurt am Main, 1985), pp. 130–57. There is another less philosophical complaint that one hears now and then concerning Adorno's philosophy of art. It was once put to me, in a question and answer period following a paper I had read on the subject of Adorno's views on the political potential of artistic innovation, that the facts that the art world is no longer composed of artistic modernists, and that much of what used to count as the counterculture has been made into consumer products, amount to a "refutation" of Adorno. To be charitable, I supplied the required suppressed premise that Adorno's views were so formed by modernism that they were stalled within its bounds. This is a stock reaction to Adorno in some quarters. But Adorno's point is conceptual. One might attack the idea that marginalized subjectivity should be the primary content of art, but the mere fact that there is very little of this art around is neither here nor there. One may just as well interpret such nay-saying as the result of the problem, not its solution. That the counterculture has become a form of consumer culture—who could doubt that it has?—does not tell against counterculture *tout court*.

19 It is worth noting that Adorno's art theory is *precisely* unlike Danto's on a crucial point marking, as it were, a divergence between two Hegelian views on the role of theory in aesthetics. For Danto, the question of whether an art object counts as a "real" art object is otiose. The role of the philosophy of art is to take what the art world treats as art as data and answer the question of *how* that is so. Danto's is an entirely nonmetaphysical theory (in fact, it is antimetaphysical). For Adorno it always makes sense, and indeed is something on the order of an aesthetic duty, to ask whether a thing is *really* art or not. For a follower of Adorno, Danto's main work is question-begging. For a follower of Danto, Adorno has mistaken the proper nature of art theory.

20 Adorno's participation in the Paul Lazarsfeld–led Princeton Radio Research Project is sometimes put forward as a credential for Adorno's deep involvement in popular culture. Lazarsfeld found Adorno's work repugnant—empirically weak, obfuscating, and mandarin. But one

doesn't need to be the positivist Lazarsfeld to see in that work—much of it unpublished at the time—a disdain born of remoteness. Yes, Adorno could dance the foxtrot (apparently), but could he *foxtrot*?

[21] One might attempt to defend Adorno on jazz by arguing that he deploys the word "jazz" to refer only to mostly white, small combo, swing jazz as it would have existed in the 1930s—Paul Whiteman, for example. It is true that he uses the term in this way in one early essay, but in later writings—which would have had the benefit of the experience of more interesting forms of swing, bebop, hard bop, cool, modal post-bop, and even the stirrings of "experimental" jazz, had Adorno cared to educate himself about the history of that music—he does not back away from his rather broad claims. Of course, it is another question whether, if he had had sufficient knowledge of jazz, he would have affirmed his earlier views anyway. (I think he would have.) My point is simply that his lack of empirical knowledge leaves his philosophical claims about the music undermotivated.

[22] Adorno understands folk art to be expressive of collectivity and immediacy rather than the heightened isolation and subjectivity required of truly cutting-edge art.

[23] "Die stabilisierte Musik," in *AGS* 18: pp. 721–28 and "Zur gesellschaftlichen Lage der Musik," in *AGS* 18: pp. 729–77. Max Paddison, *Adorno's Aesthetics of Music* (Cambridge, 1993), pp. 44–47 provides an excellent discussion.

[24] By Weill's time the incorporation of jazz into art music was not uncommon by any means. Stravinsky's *Ragtime* (1918) is one of the first pieces in this mode, but there was an avalanche of such material in the 1920s: Poulenc, Milhaud, and Ravel were all experimenters. In Germany the appetite for jazz spilled out onto the stage in the form of "Zeitoper," most famously, Krenek's *Jonny spielt auf* (1925).

[25] Adorno's understanding of Stravinsky's neoclassicism is simplistic. His view that Stravinsky's earlier expressionistic works are proto-Fascist better stands up to scrutiny, as Richard Taruskin points out, now that we have Stravinsky's correspondence from that period in hand; *Defining Russia Musically* (Princeton, 1997), pp. 385–86. One might say as a shorthand: Adorno was able to take seriously the "Tristan chord" (difficult to characterize absolutely under either functional or nonfunctional analysis, but consisting of the following intervals: augmented fourth, augmented sixth, and augmented second above the root) but not the "Petrushka chord" (i.e., two major triads a tritone apart).

[26] This is the period dating roughly from 1908 (the fourth movement of the second string quartet, op. 10) to 1923 (when Schoenberg revealed to his circle of intimates his ideas for tone-row composition). The first through-composed twelve-tone piece is the *Suite for Piano*, op. 25 (1920–23).

[27] Jean-François Lyotard, *La condition post-moderne* (Paris, 1979).

[28] I recall my disappointment as a teenager when I obtained a copy of Schoenberg's *Harmonielehre* from the local public library. I was expecting an iconoclastic treatise whose subject matter would abandon all manner of tonality. Instead what I got was a book about tonal harmony, albeit at the far reaches of theory. One of the main points of the book was entirely lost on me then, i.e., that it is a valediction.

[29] *Minima Moralia* § 18, in *AGS* 4: p. 43 ("es gibt kein richtiges Leben im falschen").

[30] The novelist Paul Auster has written of Paul Celan's late poetry that it "set[s] the stakes so high that he must surpass himself in order to keep even ..., push[ing] his life into the void in order to cling to his identity; "The Poetry of Exile," in *Collected Prose* (New York, 2003), p. 359. Celan was a poet whom Adorno admired for just this reason.

[31] There are always counterexamples of course. Geoff Dyer specializes in writing about art with great understanding without even minimally practicing the art in question. See his *The Ongoing Moment* (New York, 2007) (photography) and *But Beautiful* (London, 1991) (jazz).

[32] Within the Frankfurt School the idea that imagination has political salience receives its most thorough treatment in the early work of Marcuse. Adorno's aesthetics, as well as his thought generally, has an attenuated relation to anything political. The degree of attenuation is a topic beyond the scope of this essay.

[33] Roland Barthes, *S/Z* (Paris, 1970), pp. 10–11; cf. "Qu'est-ce que l'écriture?" in *Le degré zéro de l'écriture* (Paris, 1972), pp. 11–17.

[34] Adorno is but one of several thinkers in the wake of German Romanticism who held that the structure of a theory should be as isomorphic as possible to the particularity of the experience it is to model. The tension in his thought between fidelity to the singularity of art and theory-driven analysis perhaps expresses a greater tension between neo-Romanticism and modernism in his thought generally.

[35] See Fred Rush, *On Architecture* (London, 2008).

[36] See Daniel Arasse, *Le détail* (Paris, 1996).

Claudia Brodsky

Framing the Sensuous: Objecthood and "Objectivity" in Art After Adorno

> No theory, not even that which is true, is safe from perversion into delusion when it abdicates a spontaneous relation to the object.
>
> The moment of the objectivity of truth, without which dialectics cannot be imagined ...
> —T. W. Adorno[1]

> [N]ow everyone wants to add something, to put something into the paint. If they don't, the work is called, a little pejoratively, "traditional." But painting doesn't back up. It spins its wheels a lot, yet somehow it tries to creep forward.
> —Frank Stella[2]

The Paradox of Affirming the "Impossibility" of Art

Unlike the schematic observations gathered in the posthumous *Ästhetische Theorie* (1970), whose definitive version, Adorno acknowledged shortly before his death, would "require" an "enormous effort" of "organization" to reach completion, the individual essays on artists and artistic media that Adorno wrote throughout his life—including, self-reflexively, an essay on the essay form itself—immerse the reader immediately in the special density of his dialectical thinking, a process of reflection at once opaque in origin and unremittingly rigorous in its development.[3] Just as these specifically focused essays often contain sharper theoretical insights than does Adorno's attempt to articulate an aesthetic theory in general, so the piecemeal quality of Adorno's final work-in-progress may have as much to do with enduring divisions within his view of what constitutes the aesthetic as with its own ultimately unfinished status, divisions that, as the present essay attempts to demonstrate, have lived on in the conception of art, in both the abstract and concrete senses, after him. In that they consider the aesthetic in each instance as the staging of something inassimilable, the essays allow Adorno to analyze the aesthetic in the course of sounding its fundamental resistance to analysis, an arresting sensuousness whose traditional conceptual qualification as "aesthetic" renders it no less impenetrable in its depths.

Among the most trenchant of the essays is Adorno's now canonical study of the peril of abdicating critical analysis of the aesthetic in the name of its appropriation and legitimation by "culture," that equivocal catchall, at once transparent and masking, for the objectification, social mediation, and commodification of art. An apparent attack on the self-importance of cultural criticism by the very theorist who made *Kulturkritik* central to *Ideologiekritik* in the last century, "Kulturkritik und Gesellschaft" ("Cultural Criticism and Society"), included in *Prismen*. *Kulturkritik und Gesellschaft* (1955), begins by skewering the inevitable narcissism of the culture of cultural criticism itself: "The cultural critic can hardly avoid the suggestion that he has the culture which culture lacks. His vanity comes to the aid of its own."[4] The progress of the essay defeats any such self-flattering "suggestion," even on the part of the critic who satirizes it. The development of its argument, at once dialectical and nonlinear, resembles less a work of discursive analysis than a discursive work of art. While avoiding the blinding power of dramatic theoretical gestures, its own predominant trope is *peripeteia*: a critique of cultural criticism proffered by one of its leading practitioners, the essay continually reverses the expectations it creates as well as those it rejects with regard to its subject.

That subject, so pervasive to everyday experience as to pass unperceived, is not the aesthetic nor any object of art *per se* but the mostly invisible web in which art is caught, the weave of interdependent relations, stemming from no single thread of causation, among culture, its socially approved arbiters or critics, and society. Working through a maze of critical prose rarely matched in complexity even by its author, the reader of Adorno's delineation of the intellectual—ideological as well as critical—interactions in which the aesthetic is embedded is granted no higher ground from which to order, let alone subordinate these. The relations that constitute Adorno's subject remain instead just that, relations; even though they refer to entities understood to be conceptual to begin with, the terms "culture," "cultural criticism," and "society" defy predictive definition in this essay with each new sentence predicate.

The one prediction and single phrase, however, for which the essay is most famous, is the peremptory definition of the act of "writing a poem after Auschwitz" as "barbaric" that occurs within the course of its lengthy penultimate sentence, one whose full, explicitly dialectical development will be more closely examined in what follows.[5] Made to serve as a touchstone of cultural criticism ever since, this widely cited statement would indeed be Adorno's most celebrated if, indeed, Adorno had ever made it *as* it has been universally cited, that is, as a definitive equation of the highest form of culture with the opposite of culture, barbarism. The logic of such a paradoxical equation would, in addition, effectively imitate that of its subject. For any statement declaring the fact of "Auschwitz" to have redefined the undertaking of all imaginative art *after* it would redefine art in much the same way that the camp concretely redefined the imagining of mass murder, determining it, precisely, in predominantly temporal rather than spatial terms. Like an act of annihilation aimed not at territorial expansion but at the erasure from all places on earth for all time of an inherently interterritorial, because already diasporic, people, art defined henceforth as barbarism would annihilate everywhere the possibility of art.

By exchanging rather than opposing acts of culture and barbarism in a single phrase, Adorno gives us an arresting glimpse of what it means for the concept of culture, or, for that matter, of a "culture industry," when the industry of murder includes culture in its mechanized routines. What, one may well ask, *is* music, for example, when its performance *in vivo* accompanies acts of extermination: is it still "music," a formal organization of sensory impressions abstractable from any performance or context, or is it barbarism brought to another, almost abstract level, barbarism that attacks the mind through the senses even in the act of destroying the body that houses those senses, that insists the mind know nothing is free of its power nor can be. And how can poetry still be "poetry" if the music that naturally inhabits it as meter, euphony, and beat is no longer simply "music," the purest, or least information-laden,[6] and thus most universal of the arts, but a means to destroy, along with the life of the body, the recollected and immediately receptive, aesthetic, and imaginative lives of barbarism's victims?

Negating the identity of art—affirming its undertaking to be "barbaric"— "*after* Auschwitz," Adorno's comment implies that history kills not only the victims of history but the survivors of history too.[7] Conveying the impossibility—*not of art but of that paradox*—is the challenge informing Adorno's thinking in general, and not only of a single phrase isolated and circulated like a Delphic oracle by the very culture it critiques. Any study of art *after Adorno*—the cultural critic culturally reputed to have proclaimed the impossibility of producing art once culture and barbarism have become indistinguishable—must first ask itself *what, for Adorno, objectively constitutes art to begin with*, or, if these are indeed the same, *what defines an art object* in Adorno's individual writings on art?

What Is an Art Object in Adorno?

> *I was not working towards harmony and I never think about harmony. I always think about whether something has resolution and an edge. In other words, an independence from me.... You know, closure leads to an endgame. I'm not in an endgame.*
> —Sean Scully[8]

> *Dialectics means intransigence toward all reification.*
> —T. W. Adorno[9]

If the difficulty in answering these apparently straightforward questions can be attributed to the particular intellectual demands of Adorno's writing, it also speaks, after Adorno, to another more general problem: the ongoing difficulty of defining the concrete reality of art today. To ask what an art object is in Adorno is both to pose a question that Adorno's writings on art bring forcefully to mind and to begin to rethink the aesthetic after Adorno by way of Adorno in ways that the theorist and cultural critic could not have foreseen. *Ars longa, vita brevis est* in deed, but no less in deed is life like art: uncertain of the identity of its object, the intellect hesitates, while the imagination goes to work, subjecting the mind to the challenge of understanding, among other objects, new forms of the production and conceptualization of art. Because dialectical thinking does not usurp but works with imagination against the rule of objectification, already in Adorno, and, through Adorno, after him, our understanding of the identity of the "object" of art becomes, no less than that of the subject who objectifies art, a problem.

Generically speaking, this should hardly be surprising. Perhaps the most important theorist of the aesthetic after Hegel, Adorno was, of course, a student and theorist of musical form to begin with, the same art form with which Hegel equated the passage of spirit out of aesthetic embodiment and into the conceptual prose of philosophy. Romantic music, in the *Lectures on Aesthetics*, dovetails with Romantic poetry to bring concrete objecthood itself to an end.[10] As Hegel describes it, the preponderance of "subjective" content in Romantic music overwhelms the perceptible contours of form, submerging the external markings of composition and structure in such an immeasurable outpouring of "interiority" as to render that content, now fully externalized, into its contrary: an uncontainable and thus subjectively uninterpretable exteriority. This is subjectivity so fully turned outside that it leaves nothing inside, subjectivity *as* mere sensuousness or, as Hegel remarkably calls it, "a mere sounding" (*ein blosses Tönen*).[11]

While the enormous power of Hegel's interpretation of Romantic music as the dissolution of meaningful artistic form may well meet its strongest counterweight in Adorno's analysis of modern music as, first and foremost, a formal art, it remains no less powerfully unclear what in Adorno's, as opposed to Hegel's, aesthetic theory defines an "object." This is not merely because music, of all the arts, may be the least likely exemplar of objecthood—transitory by nature, fixed only in its notation, inherently available to formal and performative variation—but because Adorno, writing on art in general, resists all exemplary definitions of what constitutes his theoretical object.

That resistance to defining and thus objectifying the object of one's contemplation is not adequately explained by the dialectic alone: with respect to *its* object, Hegel's dialectic of art appears unequivocal. The *Lectures on Aesthetics* divide neatly not only into three theoretically defined historical periods (Symbolic, Classical, Romantic) inhabited, in differing proportions, by three major genres (architecture; sculpture and painting; poetry and music) and a host of subgenres all defined by their expression or exclusion of mimetic content but also into objects defined dialectically in the first place by the very prevalence (or, in the Classical period, the purported equivalence) of subjecthood and objecthood they embody. In direct contrast with the objects of Hegel's dialectical aesthetics, Adorno's primary "object" of aesthetic analysis may hardly be one at all, but whether music, Adorno's initial and enduring practical preoccupation, is the origin or outcome of his conception of the aesthetic remains no less a real question.

For Adorno's aesthetic theory, like the intangible sensory nature of music, is, in its conceptual nature, inherently hard to grasp. Unlike Hegel's, his dialectical analysis does not understand itself as transitionally but rather as persistently "negative," and nowhere is that negativity and its ever-changing destruction of certainty in greater verbal evidence than in Adorno's differing articulations of what is, and is not, an art object. Still, and for the very same reason, it is within the difficulty of defining the art object negatively that Adorno's most illuminating contribution to the understanding of art in our time may lie.[12]

For, if "art" at present—or, at least, since Duchamp—appears to designate an infinite and fragmented field of particulars, none of which can be excluded *a priori* from, and few of which can rest secure *a posteriori* in, the name, the immediate difficulty in defining the object of art in Adorno is that "object" in Adorno goes by too many names. To some extent this owes to the history and lexicon of the German language itself. The indigenous, Old High German compound term "Gegenstand" (from *gagan* and *Stand*) is doubled in Grimm's *Wörterbuch* by the Latinate "Objekt," while the differently inflected German terms for "thing," "Sache" (descendent of the Old High German *sahha* and Old Saxon *saka*) and "Ding" (the preservation of *ding* in Old High German and twin of *Thing* in Old Saxon), also carry with them different senses of a kind of perceptual or conceptual "object" ("Sache" meaning both material thing and the matter under discussion; "Ding" meaning both material thing and the matter immediately—whether physically or conceptually—at hand). While "object" and "thing" in English obviously overlap with "Objekt" and "Ding," Adorno can and does employ the alternatives to these terms available only in German: "Gegenstand" as well as "Objekt," "Sache" as well as "Ding." Yet, just as these doubling words remain distinct from each other, not only historically but also semantically, so Adorno uses them *non*interchangeably. He sometimes employs "Sache" (but not "Ding") for example, when referring back to an "Objekt," but, even while employing them differently, he uses the alternate terms for "thing" both positively (as something real, or, that really matters) and negatively (as something solely construed as such by ideology). That the excellent translation of "Kulturkritik und Gesellschaft" by Samuel and Shierry Weber cannot incorporate these incongruences of synonymity and nonsynonymity into English is as unavoidable as the occasional substitution of "object" (in English) for "thing" (the German *Sache* or *Ding*) in their rendering. When, for example, Adorno writes a sentence employing three of the aforementioned German terms discretely, the English translation, in order to avoid an inevitable appearance of tautology or, at best, redundancy, is compelled to juggle the only two terms at its disposal as if two were three, making one ("object") appear where the other ("thing") had been:

> Gerade seine Souveränität, der Anspruch tieferen Wissens dem *Objekt* gegenüber, die Trennung des Begriffs von seiner *Sache* durch die Unabhängigkeit des Urteils, droht der *dinghaften* Gestalt der *Sache* zu verfallen.
>
> [Yet his very sovereignty, the claim to a more profound knowledge of the *object*, the separation of the idea from its *object* through the independence of the critical judgment threatens to succumb to the *thinglike* form of the *object*.][13]

That the meaning of Adorno's "dinghaft[e] Gestalt der Sache" might appear more obscured than clarified if translated instead in the only literal terms available in English as "thinglike form of the thing" does not alter the fact that the semantic distinctions between "object" and "thing" as between "thing" (*Sache*) and "thing" (*Ding*), and "object" (*Gegenstand*) and "object" (*Objekt*), are not immediately clear in Adorno either.[14] Their usage can be quantified, but understanding their status—as "object" and/or "thing"—remains as problematic as the relation between "Ding" (thing) and its substantivized verbal form, "Verdinglichung" (reification). Adorno uses the former for the most part in a neutral, even positive sense, to mean a "thing" *recalcitrant* to its own "reification,"[15] to being *conceptualized* as a thing, while he employs "Verdinglichung," the word for making something into a "Ding," uniformly negatively in the essay, to signify those irreversible acts of objectification that are the "death mask" of "life" itself.[16]

If "object" (*Gegenstand*) is the word Adorno uses instead of "thing" (*Ding*) to imply the product of an act of objectification that is at once an act of reification,[17] and if "object" (*Objekt*), used more frequently by Adorno, can convey, unlike "object" (*Gegenstand*) but like "thing" (*Ding*), either positive *or* negative connotations, the derivative terms, "objective" (*objektiv*) and "objectivity" (*Objektivität*), gradually shed any such semantic ambivalence in the essay.[18] First used in the wholly negative sense of the fictional impartiality claimed by culture critics on the basis of professional "information" and "privilege"—"Das Vorrecht von Information und Stellung erlaubt ihnen, ihre Ansicht zu sagen, als wäre sie die *Objektivität*. Aber es ist einzig die *Objektivität* des herrschenden Geistes [The privilege of information and position permit them to say their view as if it were *objectivity*. But it is solely the *objectivity* of the ruling mind]"[19]—the very notion of "objectivity," of an abstract capacity for being "objective" in general, for perceiving the reality of any "object" as such, undergoes, to use Adorno's terms, an evaluative "Umschlag" (reversal) within the course of a single sentence:

Kulturkritik teilt mit ihrem Objekt dessen Verblendung....
[Das volle Bewusstsein einer Gesellschaft von sich selbst]
zu hintertreiben, bedarf es nicht erst der subjektiven ideologischen Veranstaltung, obwohl diese in Zeiten des historischen Umschlags die *objektive* Verblendung zu verstärken pflegt.... [D]ass die Gesellschaft, so wie sie ist, trotz aller Absurdität doch ihr Leben unter den bestehenden Verhältnissen reproduziert, bringt *objektiv* den Schein ihrer Legitimation hervor.... Der Schein ist total geworden in einer Phase, in der Irrationalität und *objective* Falschheit hinter Rationalität und *objektiver* Notwendigkeit sich verstecken.

[Cultural criticism shares with its object the blindness of its object....To drive back {the full consciousness of a society of itself} does not require first a show of subjective ideology, although the latter serves to strengthen *objective* blindness in times of historical reversal.... {T}he fact that society as it is, in spite of all absurdity, does nonetheless reproduce its life under existing relations, *objectively* produces the appearance of its legitimacy.... The appearance has become total in a phase in which irrationality and *objective* falsity hide behind rationality and *objective* necessity.] [20]

Just as "objective" blindness is not the same "blindness" "cultural criticism shares" with "its object," but rather the real or "objective" condition of being blind; and just as a society that "objectively produces the appearance of its legitimacy" also lays the groundwork for the perception of that appearance as it really is, an appearance alone; and just as only "objective falsity" may be recognized for what it is, a real act of deception masked as "objective necessity," so the word "objective," used by Adorno to qualify the *nonobjective*, the blind and the untrue, negatively attains to the meaning of that which ideology can be seen to conceal and thus concretely reveals (through the "objective" fact of its concealment) to the world. An attention to *and* an abstraction from the concrete, perceptual "object," "objectivity" ultimately names the "power" of "the mind" to "fulfill" and so be unswayed by ideology, thereby changing the "theory" that is its articulation from speculation to action, to "real violence":

> Dass die Theorie zur realen Gewalt werde, wenn sie die Menschen ergreift, gründet in der *Objektivität* des Geistes selber, der kraft der Erfüllung seiner Ideologischen Funktion an der Ideologie irre werden muss.
>
> [That theory becomes real violence when it shakes and moves men is based in the *objectivity* of the mind itself, which is compelled by the fulfillment of its ideological function to stray from ideology.][21]

The "real violence" exercised by "theory" that "moves men" is "based" in "objectivity" that is not theoretically projected by but part of "the mind itself," an objectivity unconfined to objects and thus uncontrolled by ideology. In this startling observation Adorno defines theory as its opposite—a "violence" directly affecting men—and reveals the conventional sense of theory, that it must be abstracted from immediacy, to be part of the "ideological function" that "objectivity of mind" instead "fulfills" and goes beyond. Yet still more powerful than an object-free "objectivity of the mind" is an "objectivity" unconfined to the mind, one that Adorno attributes neither to objects, whether in themselves or as ideology presents and peddles them, nor to our enthrallment by or rejection of them, but to what he calls "truth."

The "truth" Adorno names—again, unlike Hegel's—is not the ultimate end or transcendence of the dialectical progress of the aesthetic in a synthesis of the mind with its object, the "objective" truth of a subjectivity rendered indistinguishable from the sensory, "a mere sounding." Nor does its "objectivity" rest upon the given reality of a perceptual object. Rather, "the objectivity of truth," according to Adorno, does not rest at all, but occurs at what he calls a "moment" defined only negatively by its passage: *"The moment of the objectivity of truth*, without which dialectic cannot be imagined (or conceived), is silently replaced by vulgar positivism and pragmatism—ultimately, bourgeois subjectivism."[22] The "moment" the object of art, embodying an objecthood unlike any other, brings to perception, succumbs to the inevitable process of its conceptualization by the "false" objectivities of "positivism and pragmatism." Yet, without that "moment" it would be impossible at any moment to conceive of the dialectic, to recognize the mind's real distinction from the object, and vice versa. Rapidly "replaced" in this sentence by its opposite—the incapacity, here called "bourgeois subjectivism," to perceive objects without falsely perceiving oneself in them—the "moment of objectivity" that Adorno ascribes not to man but to the most general of man-made abstractions, "truth," may in turn shed light on Adorno's concept of the most particular of man-made "things," the art object.

For, as opposed to a reified "culture-object" (*Kulturobjekt*), "death mask" not of "life" but of art, in whose contemplation "dialectic" risks "entrapment," the art object is composed, *like the dialectic*, of contradictory "moments."[23] Taking aim at "the contempt for 'objectivism'" that serves as "pretext for cynical terror" (whether in the "Soviet sphere" he criticizes or any other), Adorno describes an object-"immanent critique" that, "rather" than dwelling in "general knowledge of the servitude of the objective mind ... seeks to transform this knowledge into the power of the consideration of the thing itself" (*der Sache selbst*), one that,

> where it comes across something that does not suffice, does not rapidly ascribe it to the individual and his psychology, the mere cover for failure, but seeks to derive it from the irreconcilability of the *moments of the object*.[24]

That an art "object" can be made of, can contain, "moments," and that such "moments" rather than any specific content are what compose *its* "objectivity," like that of "truth," must render such an "object" nonobjectifiable in the very manner Hegel rejected as nonaesthetic, that of an "object" that is always changing, and thus not "properly" an art object at all.[25] Yet, an "object" made of "moments" may well be the only proper object of a subject that alternately perceives and fails to perceive it, "the mind" to whose own "immanent movement" Adorno had attributed the "overreaching claim" of "culture" to begin with: "the overreaching of the cultural claim, which is, however, immanent to the movement of the mind."[26] Occurring at the opening of the essay, between negative characterizations of culture, on the one hand, and its professional critics, on the other, the descriptive phrase "movement of the mind" is easy enough to overlook.[27] It is echoed and reflected, however, later in the essay, when Adorno defines the only objective basis of "immanent critique" to be an "object" in "movement" itself. Referring to what he calls the "self-movement of the object," Adorno describes the necessity of "freedom" to any "consciousness" that would "follow it," one that can oppose object-"immanent critique" to the all-engulfing "immanence of culture:" "Without such freedom, without the departure of consciousness from the immanence of culture, immanent criticism would itself not be thinkable: the self-movement of the object can only be followed by whomever does not already belong to it."[28]

For Adorno, the "object" of "immanent contemplation" is the opposite of an "object" in any traditional philosophical—whether ontological or dialectical—sense: it is not itself but, instead, at any "moment," "movement." Like, and along with, the "movement of the mind," the "self-movement of the object" makes "objectivity" possible, separating the object from the "immanence of culture" in which it is immersed, embodying and extending outward its "moments" of "truth." "Moments" of "objectivity" relate the "movement" of the "object" with that of the "mind," and the basis for that relation—for the perception that is never fixed long enough to merge with ideology, of an "object" that never "is" one in any static sense—is the form of immediacy without which there can be no art, let alone aesthetic theory, the experience by the subject of a "spontaneous relation to the object":

> No theory, not even that which is true, is secure from perversion into delusion when it has abdicated the spontaneous relationship to the object. Dialectic must protect itself therefrom no less than from entrapment in the cultural object.... The dialectical critic must and must not take part in culture. Only then does he do justice to the thing and himself.[29]

"The spontaneous relationship to the object" cuts through culture, its accretion of "information," its "reification" of objects. Such spontaneity, occurring and experienced involuntarily, inarticulately or, what we like to call "without thinking," is not conceptual but sensuous in nature, and its absolutely necessary involvement in the impact of the aesthetic of every genre and stripe has been confronted and acknowledged in theory of the aesthetic at least since Kant, who first transformed Plato's exclusion of the dangerous immediacy of the aesthetic from the day-to-day functioning of the rationally organized state into the no less dangerous premise that the immediate availability of aesthetic experience to any subject at any time is in fact necessary to the possibility of "free," that is, non-object-related and noncognitive, "moral" action.

Adorno's aesthetic theory, while related by the dialectic to objects, unlike Kant's, alters, no less than does Kant's critical analytic of aesthetic "judgment," how it is we conceive the aesthetic object we spontaneously perceive. For Adorno such an object is conceived "objectively," not as it is but in its "moments," moments perceptible only by a "mind" itself in "movement." Yet, for this to happen—for an object to be perceived as "moments" of the object—the immediate sensory reality of the aesthetic must be separated from its objectification: this, and not the destruction of the sensory, is the "real violence" of "theory." Finally, for perceived "moments" to be further perceived as the "movement" of the object rather than the mind alone, the sensory must be maintained while being perceived to change, given no objective identity but the identity of objecthood, of being and remaining some "thing" outside the subject. The sensory must be perceived "objectively," perceived at each "moment" as never before, for it to appear to move independently of the subject, to move as if "through" the mind on its own, and the basis for such a perception of the sensuous—not in itself, as if such perception were possible, or in its identity as an object (both equal grist for ideology)—is not sensuousness itself but abstraction.

Sensuousness and Abstraction in Schoenberg

> *In abolishing sensuous appearance, maturity and intellectualization of art virtually abolishes art itself.*
> —T. W. Adorno[30]

The "movement of the mind" and "self-movement of the object" occur in the interaction of sensuousness with abstraction. Nowhere is the negative dialectic between the two more evident than in Adorno's account of the artistic history of the artist he most admired, Arnold Schoenberg. While the thoroughly speculative "Cultural Criticism and Society," abruptly interrupted in closing by the naming of "Auschwitz," takes the equivocal relationships between culture and society, critic and culture, critic and society, and art and culture as its subject, the Schoenberg essay, arguably Adorno's greatest on a single artist, reveals, through the specific prism of the composer's technical development, a dialectical production of the "objectivity" of art closest to Adorno's understanding of the term. Combining analysis with commemoration, it regards Schoenberg's compositions both formally and historically from the individual angles defined by the intersecting dynamics of their internal structure, relation to tradition, and contemporary reception, drawing the sinuous abstractions of the cultural criticism essay into an individual narrative that, while concrete in each instance and particular, borders closely on the allegorical, the story of a single subject matter that is at once the story of art.

On Adorno's analysis, that subject matter first attains to objecthood by destroying the effortless identification of sensory—or *prima facie* "aesthetic"—experience with an object, "the customary crutches of a hearing that always already knows what is coming."³¹ In the place of these,

> [Schoenberg's music] demands, that the listener spontaneously compose its inner movement along with it, and exacts of him, as it were, praxis instead of contemplation. With this Schoenberg blasphemes against the expectation cultivated in contradiction of all idealist protestations that music present itself as a series of pleasant sensory stimulations to the comfortable listener.... With Schoenberg all comfortableness ceases.³²

Musical objects consist naturally of the tonal moments that constitute them, moments that, in music, compose "movement" by definition. Yet Schoenberg demands that the subject who perceives the musical object "compose its inner movement along with it." The argument for the composition in the subject of a movement *accompanying* (mit-*komponiert*) the internal movement of the object—for the perception of a made object as form of "praxis" rather than "contemplation"—is one that Schoenberg's music makes for Adorno, rather than the other way around. No dialectical critique is needed in the case of this musician for whom "the language of music was self-evident" and whose compositions, "instead of aiming at making abstractions"—a second-order language, or system of formal ideograms—out of musical sound, were thus able to "invest the concrete form of music with spirit."³³

It is rather Schoenberg's own "movement of mind" as artist—his "objectivization of the subjective impulse"—that proceeds dialectically in Adorno's analysis.³⁴ For in order to write music that moves in freedom from the culture of music, Schoenberg had to recompose the sensory material of music whose "language" he already intuited, endowing sound not with recognizable sonorous identity but with identifiable complexity. Music—Adorno's first theoretical and practical occupation—provides a name for such complexity: polyphony. Retrieving that technical term from the lexicon of Western musical history, Adorno "invests" it, objectively, "with spirit," stating, in the plainest descriptive terms, the formal content of its experience, what we actually hear when we perceive it: "the multiplicity of the simultaneous" (*die Vielheit des Simultanen*).[35] For Adorno no less than for Schoenberg, such a description describes musical and, moreover, aesthetic thinking. The separation of the sensuous from the contours of a single, identifiable object—the very division without which there would be neither theory nor art—requires that sensuousness and abstraction be brought together in "simultaneity," neither one definitively overshadowing, or overpowering, the other. And this remarkable combination of sonority *with* abstraction from sonorous familiarity, the ability to pull pure sound out of obscurity, was, Adorno argues, Schoenberg's greatest strength from the beginning. What its cultural reception dismisses under the "preferred reproach of intellectualism"—"reflection" that remains "external" rather than "immanent" "to the thing"—is an "intuitive" grasp of formal musical syntax that does not separate the intellectual from the aesthetic. And because neither structure nor sound is univocal in music, Schoenberg's refusal to subordinate one to the other produces a music of multiple simultaneities, of "identity in nonidentity," that appears doubly hard to hear.[36] The most common complaint against Schoenberg's music may thus be its "lack of melody"; yet it is not the absence of melody but the simultaneous presence of a multiplicity of melodies, of cotemporaneous musical "lines," that, rather than serving a single overarching theme, are and remain distinct, which makes the music of this composer—"a melodist to the core" for whom every part of music "sings"—appear antimelodic to the "formula"-bound listening habits it disorients and outstrips:

> The reproach of being an intellectual goes together with that of a lack of melody. But he was a melodist to the core. Instead of the accepted formula he produced new forms without cease. His melodic talent can hardly be contained within one sole melody; instead, all *simultaneous* musical events are profiled as melodies and the perception of them thus rendered more difficult. The original musical mode of reaction of Schoenberg is itself melodic: everything is actually "sung" in his music, even the instrumental lines. That lends his music its articulated nature, at once free in its movement and structured down to the last tone.[37]

Schoenberg's transformation of inherited melodic culture makes his music appear abstract. Yet, rather than reject melody in principle, he expands the melodic field, redefining even the conventional buttresses of "instrumental lines" as melody-bearing, and coordinating individual melodies as "simultaneous musical events." The disconcerting sound of melodies brought into structural instead of harmonious concert not only makes the immediate "perception of them ... more difficult"; it also conceals (even as it embodies), Adorno argues, its own profound rootedness in tradition. For Schoenberg's "multiplicity of the simultaneous" in music looks backward and forward at the same time; its dialectical organization is avant-garde in that it recalls a now distant musical (and social) past, the "objective" polyphonic structures, long buried under the ideology of aesthetic "subjectivity," of Bach. Redefining Schoenberg's vaunted "experimentalism" as the rigorous unearthing of a classical anachronism, the carrying of a now alien past into a future to which the limits of the present demonstrate it pertains, Adorno offers his most compelling analysis of art as indication of historical progress-in-regress, a dialectical model of modernity that, even as it lauds technical innovation as the concrete medium of aesthetic change, aligns rather than opposes *modernes* with *anciens*. I quote from this extraordinary interpretation of Schoenberg's "experimental" musical practice in relation to musical history at length, as it speaks directly to the question of the "objectivity" of the composition of art today:

> Schoenberg thinks the unfulfilled promise of Classicism through to its end and thereby breaks down the traditional façade. He took up again the challenge of Bach, from which Classicism, Beethoven included, withdrew, without however falling behind Classicism. Classicism had neglected Bach out of historical necessity. The autonomy of the musical subject outweighed every other interest and *critically excluded the historically transmitted form of objectivization*, preferring to make do with the appearance of objectivization, just as the unhindered interplay of subjects seemed to guarantee society. Only today, *now that subjectivity in its immediacy no longer reigns as the highest category*, but is perceived to be in need of complete social realization, can we recognize the insufficiency even of Beethoven's solution, *which extended the subject to the whole without reconciling the whole in itself*. Schoenberg's polyphony determines development ... *as the dialectical dissolution of the subjective melodic impulse in the objectively organized multiplicity of voices*.[38]

In the alternation of "objectivization" and "subjectivity" that Adorno outlines here, every step forward is, in hindsight, a step backward from a past moment whose "promise" remained "unfulfilled." This, and not the traditional Hegelian plotline of the development of art (itself belied by Hegel's own analysis of the production and interpretation of the aesthetic "symbol" as inherently "ambiguous" "sign"),[39] is what Adorno calls "historical necessity:" the necessity, "inhering in the movement of the mind," of negating the reification of the mind. Schoenberg is not Bach reborn; he is the anamnesis of Bach at a time when Bach cannot be recalled. His "experimental," twelve-tone technique presents the past of music as it now is, technically and thus historically estranged. Only insofar as he makes Classicism unrecognizable as "Classicism" by recalling a prior "objectivization" of musical form, does he carry Classicism *en avant*, to an "end" that makes its eclipse by subjective reification a part of history.

The avant-garde in Adorno's dialectical aesthetic history is thus not the *arrière-garde* but a kind of *arrière-arrière-garde*, avatars of forgotten forms whose "transmission" into the present of sensory experience makes them appear unintelligible, "abstract." As such, the "simultaneous multiplicity" of sound that characterizes the musical avant-garde also dramatizes the nonsimultaneity across time of senses and mind. Another word for such nonsimultaneity—the transmission of "classical" forms into present unrecognizability—is, Adorno suggests, "tradition":

> [T]he artistic extreme is responsible for obeying the logic of the thing [*Sache*], an objectivity no matter how hidden, or merely a private caprice, or abstract system. Its legitimacy however derives essentially from the tradition that it negates.... Not only the religious but also the aesthetic tradition is the remembering of something unconscious, repressed.... Tradition is present in works shunned as experimental and not in those whose own aim it is to be traditional.[40]

Tradition, in other words, must be lost in order to be found, and the founding of a "tradition" entails its certain loss. This was the fate of Schoenberg's "experimental" art, whose technique suffered its own stifling classicization by the "twelve-tone schools," "followers [who] succeeded only in displaying their own weakness, their impotent longing for security."[41] Such "hypostatization" of art in turn follows its own historical trajectory. Whenever "technical-aesthetic systems ... become models," retreating from "self-reflection," Adorno observes, "the system cripples the very impulse that had propelled it to begin"; as "fixed idea and universal recipe," it excludes whatever is "other" to its premises, all that stands outside its "analytic" scope.[42]

"Multiplicity in the simultaneous," a sensuousness always abstracted at any moment by an "other" sensuousness from itself, constitutes the "movement" and art of Schoenberg's music, and, inasmuch as that movement gives new "objective" life to Bach, its own life must be unsustainable, vulnerable to objectification, in the present. This fact of the irresolvable dialectic of art was lost least of all on Schoenberg, who, Adorno writes compellingly, himself "experienced" it as a subject: "The experience that no musical subject-object can constitute itself here and today was not wasted on him."[43] Indeed, rather than "waste" that "experience," ignoring, stylizing, or ironizing it, Schoenberg put it to good historic use: he betrayed it. In doing so, he made a "model" of musical innovation prove nothing less than the paradoxical impossibility of the end of art: that the "experience" of the impossibility of uniting subject and object in art "here and now" is equal to the impossibility of experiencing its opposite, the overcoming *or* annihilation of art by absolute abstraction.

For, beginning with his attempt to retreat from the rigors of twelve-tone technique, to dress it up externally in just those "traditional" "larger forms" its polyphonic structure rendered superfluous, Schoenberg belied his art by moving away from it, discarding its premise of "internal" forms turning "outward" in multiple melodic lines by exposing and then draping those lines in a sensuous skin of "manifest music" instead.[44] Schoenberg lived to make of his own music a kind of revenant "rattling mechanically," the skeleton of a previous incarnation revealed as such by an ill-fitting costume of traditional garb.[45] And because the fit of old music to new music is poor, and no composer, including Schoenberg, can alter this—can make a living body from a second skin of borrowed clothes—Schoenberg jettisons the life of music, tone. Viewing all sound as mere "façade," he strips it as he might strip history itself from the structure of music alone. The name for such sound as had once served not merely to adorn but to compose structure in Schoenberg is "color":

> Not the least of Schoenberg's acts integrating musical means was his definitive removal of color from the sphere of orna-

mentation and raising of it to a compositional element in its own right. It changes into a means for the elucidation of the contextual whole. Its being integrated into the composition, however, becomes its condemnation.... The more nakedly the construction represents itself, the less it requires coloristic assistance.... Mature music creates suspicion of all real sound as such.... The inclination to silence, which shapes the aura of every tone in Webern's lyric, is directly related to this tendency originating in Schönberg. *No less is its ultimate outcome, however, that, in abolishing sensuous appearance, maturity and intellectualization virtually abolishes art itself.*[46]

Whether, per Hegel, the aesthetic is the "sensory appearance" of the "idea," "sensory appearance" in Adorno is the experiential medium without which there can be no art. The desire to abolish all sensuousness may stem from the wish to preserve art from its own perversion, to abstract its "objectivity" from the always imperfect "here and now" of its reception and reification in history, yet such "intellectualization" of art, Adorno concludes, rather than saving art, "converges" with "barbaric" "enmity to art."[47] The penultimate sentence of the cultural criticism essay appears to state, of course, the exact opposite, to define instead a historic boundary beyond which the very composition of art and barbarism are one, and it is in the context of Adorno's historical account of Schoenberg's art that the full measure of his reflections on "writing a poem after Auschwitz" should be cited and read:

> Cultural criticism finds itself confronted by the last phase of the dialectic of culture and barbarism: to write a poem after Auschwitz is barbaric; *and this corrodes even the knowledge which articulates why it has become impossible to write poetry today.*[48]

The equation of art after Auschwitz with barbarism is, in the words of the Schoenberg essay, the reflection of a "tendency" toward "maturity and intellectualization" [that] "virtually abolish[es] art itself" (see note 46). As such it is in itself "anti-art," "barbaric," "corrod[ing]" our very ability to know and "articulate" exactly what is most worth knowing: *"why it has become impossible to write poetry today"* (emphasis added). By negating the independent objecthood of the sensuous appearance of art to come—by defining the future history of art as a history of barbarism in the making—such an abstraction from art does not render art itself but rather our ability to reflect upon it (in whatever form it appears to us) "impossible."

Easier to cite ad infinitum in part than to read once to its completion, Adorno's difficult, doubly negative observation here has proven positively apt: nothing has demonstrated the accuracy of its conclusion more effectively than the innumerable instances of its quotation that leave this conclusion out. Whether employed to introduce another plastic work of next-generation German or American art, or the—indeed unequalled—postwar achievements of the German-language poet, and survivor of a Romanian labor camp, Paul Celan (*né* Antschel), cultural critics have pointed to Adorno, or, rather, their monophrastic surrogate for him, in the conviction that they, with art on their side, have proven his prediction wrong.

The noncritical pieties that have invariably ensued—one part moral outrage to two parts praise for the ennobling virtues of art, as a rule—have instead served precisely to make Adorno's point. To consider art not only as fully available to but also as fully transcendent of human life is, in Adorno's aesthetic theory, to misunderstand both profoundly. Abstract and sensuous by nature, part of culture and free of culture, the objecthood of art is no substitute for the subjecthood of life and approaches barbarism when it pretends to be. Since art is instead already a part of life and of subjecthood, the medium of our abstraction from abstraction, of a sensuous immediacy not given but made, the abstract abolition of art, its "mature" prohibition, must also abolish history, the very possibility that every day is not "today," another anniversary of the act of total objectification, birthday of death by daily mass murder.

Schoenberg, Adorno notes, understood this perfectly, or at least as perfectly as the nonidentical lives of history and art would allow. Any art whose "promises" appeared capable of being "fulfilled in reality" is already an "emasculated" art; and anyone who, unlike Schoenberg, chooses "art" over "surviving" death by barbarism is, in a critical sense, already dead.[49] Rather than sacrifice sensuous life to art and the sensuousness of art to its totalizing abstraction, the late Schoenberg, Adorno concludes, produces art in the form of the "fragment," art that is itself a sensuous representation of the "impossibility" of art "here and now."[50] The brief "Jewish song" sung by the "Survivor from Warsaw" "represents the whole [of mankind]" not as its "model," or timeless "intellectualization," but as "victim," a body able to give voice to its own negation as voice and objectification as body, a subject that is *not* whole. Schoenberg's sensuous manifestation of knowledge of life annihilated, sung by one who knows himself alive only in part, is his refusal to "abdicate a spontaneous relation to the object," no matter how fragmentary, just as he refused to sacrifice life for art. For, in the absence of the "spontaneous relationship to the object" that allows us to experience what we do not know, life as well as "theory" undergo "perversion into delusion," the "barbarism" of an intellectualism *and* fascism according to which no object need be experienced since all objects outside the subject are superfluous. To return to the terms of the cultural criticism essay, Schoenberg's final fragments contain the "freedom" of "consciousness" to "go beyond" and so negate the identification of art with either pure sensuousness or intellectual objectification. In contemporary visual art in which the identity of the object of art is in question, we may call this negative freedom "framing."

The Sensuous Object: Color and Information

> *He makes you see and think of a great deal more than the objects before you.*
> —W. M. Thackeray on J. W. M. Turner[51]

If Clement Greenberg had not written, the artists he advocated might have had to invent him, but certainly modern art itself would never have gained the clear contours of a conceptual history. By defining the art object, specifically painting, as a made thing uniquely determined by its medium, Greenberg famously translated Kant's nonmimetic aesthetics and, in particular, his mathematical and dynamic sublime—exemplified in the Third Critique by infinite number and magnitude, the violent force of nature, and purely verbal reality of poetry—into the field of traditional aesthetic objects proper. Greenberg saw the sublime substantiated in the least Kantian of sublime perceptual objects, painting, and in so doing he not only severed modern art from the *trompe-l'oeil* presentation and reception of images but did so in a manner reminiscent of Hegel's theory of the origin of all art in the pyramids. The power of abstract expressionist painting for Greenberg, like that of Hegel's "properly" (*eigentliche*) "inscrutable" (*unentzifferbar*) "symbols" (*Symbolik*), was to render abstract the very notion of expression by expressing objective opacity, its own shaped reality, alone, remaining infinitely "enigmatic" (*rätselhaft*) in remaining material, nonrepresentational, to the core.[52]

Like Hegel and unlike Kant, Greenberg defined a particular moment in art containing within it the possibility of all art, a moment that Hegel, unlike Greenberg, circumscribed theoretically to be, "in its highest determination, a thing of the past" (*nach der Seite seiner höchsten Bestimmung für uns ein Vergangenes*).[53] That Hegel defined the "highest determination" of art as its specifically religious use and meaning, one that, paradoxically, already outstrips art itself, is a consideration as routinely deleted from the frequent citation of this first philosophical pronouncement of the "end of art" as is the dialectical negation with which Adorno immediately succeeds his own paradoxical equation of art after Auschwitz with barbarism. There is no doubt that, just as the pyramids, pummeled by natural and human history alike, still stand, and *art in its enigmatic determination as art* continues after Auschwitz to be made (including, not least of all, some of the greatest poetry ever to be written in German), the abstraction in art Greenberg championed as identical with art in its essence continues to be made with moving power or, in Adorno's words, with "the objectivity of truth," the "movement" of the object perceived rather than reified by that of the mind it brings about.

Yet, once we know that the art object is composed of moments in Adorno and recognize in Schoenberg's polyphony Adorno's fundamental theory of "multiplicity in simultaneity"—an aesthetic theory that makes movement rather than an identifiable object the defining quality of objecthood in art—we may begin to perceive the continuing schisms in contemporary visual art, both between nonfigural art and pervasive image reproduction and between the making of art objects and the making of art out of objects, as less definitive than they appear in their high-modern delineation by Greenberg or, for that matter, in the account of their origin in ancient Egypt given by Hegel.

As in Schoenberg, the sensory element of "color," here in a real rather than aesthetic-metaphoric sense, is central to the development of abstraction in modern painting, just as the crafted questioning of color in series of "black" or, alternatively, "white" paintings has composed a common step in the many diverse paths that have led painting away from the figure—paths forged in the work of Kazimir Malevich, Ad Reinhardt (whose comments on color's "uncontrollable" and thus "amoral" nature are well known), Clyfford Still, Frank Stella, Jackson Pollock, Mark Rothko, and Sean Scully among others.[54] Color being what it is, it has no proper ideological provenance or terrain, and the roster of "modern painters" who, since Ruskin, have made color—impossibly pure or composite color, thickly or thinly layered, materializing or dissolving before our eyes; color flattening the depth of objects or deepening the painted plane, presented in an indivisible spectrum or solid geometric shapes—into the "visceral" "things" and "building blocks" of modern art is similarly varied and long.[55] Including, of course, such twentieth-century masters as Henri Matisse and Piet Mondrian, bourgeois rebels *sui generis*, it extends back, with Ruskin, to the extraordinarily productive career, spanning over half a century, of the barber's son-cum-academician, Turner, whose aesthetically revolutionary *and* popularly appealing paintings remained as committed to the traditional mimetic genres of landscape, architectural, historical, and travel painting, as they were to the production on canvas of a central drama of color and light. To look at Turner's sunsets, daybreaks, and storm- and fire-filled skies, overpowering in their expanse the delicate structures and actions they touch, surrounding these mimetic objects in chasms of modulated color, whether in the form of mountains forever rising or in amorphous reflecting surfaces, is to wonder, first, in the age of Joshua Reynolds, how he got away with it, and second, if the dissolution of the object into an immediate vividness of color constitutive of the abstract art object hadn't reached its apex some two hundred years before "abstract expressionism" began.[56]

To this list of artists for whom color became the object of art, and depicted objects became in turn the body and occasion of color—no matter how exquisitely detailed or broadly brushed into being these objects may have been, in the manner of Turner or Matisse, respectively—we may, of course, add our own nominees. Scully includes Rembrandt, Masaccio, Vincent Van Gogh, and Giorgio Morandi in the tradition of painting color that is Rothko's and his own, and alongside these we may include several of Rothko's own near and exact contemporaries, each of whom presents the primacy of color to the shaping of perception, Wassily Kandinsky,

Morris Louis, Helen Frankenthaler, and Ellsworth Kelly, among others. Curt Barnes calls the effect the concentration upon "the painterly application of color" has had upon the history and definition of the art object "dialectical" and offers an excellent analysis of its recent evidence. First describing the attempt of Stella's shaped polyhedral and aluminum relief paintings to include three-dimensional space within painting without resorting to colorist methods—"never a colorist, Stella may not have understood the potential of color to create its own authoritative space, one that could rival and work in counterpoint to the physical"—Barnes highlights the role of color in deepening the "physical/pictorial," or spatial/planar, "dialectic" of modern painting:

> Sean Scully, James Biederman, Larry Brown, and others developed multiple-paneled pieces whose obtrusive physicalities depended primarily on the panel's varying thicknesses or distances from the wall plane. For all of these artists, the painterly application of color, the sensitive, complex, banal, historically charged practice of applying paint with a brush was key to the complex kinds of interaction they achieved with the painting support. Reframed in the physical/pictorial equation, paint could acquire new potentials for mystery and paradox, ambiguity and irony, and at the same time plant itself firmly in the physical continuum.... Paint application can parallel the shape of the support.... Color can move continuously across separate panels, or jump their boundaries.... The scale of painted form, as for example Scully's varying width of stripe, can contradict the topographic location—that is, the thickness—of the panels. And then there is the power of color itself to advance, recede, hover, pulsate, merge, expand, contract.[57]

A nonmimetic art object made of color applied to canvas, whether densely layered within irregular rectangles or poured into diaphanous curves it creates, is sensuousness abstracted from the objects of the world, a framing of sensuousness as such.[58] Sensuousness in itself—as present as it is unperceived in everyday objects—is made, through its framing, its separation from the subjective experiences of which it is a part, to embody the quality of objecthood even while resisting the blindnesses of conventional sight and conceptual reification. In the place of things known and ignored, sensuousness set apart from the things in which it takes part presents an unsettling "multiplicity of the simultaneous" in visual form: the sense of what is, as never before, and what is not available to the senses. Sensuousness framed creates an "object" of perception that, for no conceptual reason, commands rather than serves our attention, a thing whose experience has neither "timeframe" nor expiration date, that never appears one with any end it could serve. The framing of sensuousness in visual art after Adorno—the sensuousness without which Adorno declared there can be no art—allows us to see, or at least to approach the experience of seeing sensuous experience in itself, which is to say, it makes visible in at once immediate and modern allegorical form our own ability to abstract not (an abstract) meaning from (sensuous) pictures but the purely sensuous from the nonpictorial, the abstract. In the absence of mimetic mediation, in the identity of their appearance with their medium, sensuousness and abstraction contain each other in the manner of Hegel's permanently illegible "symbol." And for the same reason they are also free, in the manner of Kant's imagination and reason, to conflict violently, making of the mere act of sensuous perception a form of sublimity.

Such a description of sensuousness abstracted from objects appears at odds with that artistic tendency now long thought to have put abstraction to bed: the collection of circulated objects, images, and all species of information into an art object, often through flagrantly anti-aesthetic methods.[59] Mechanical acts of insertion and attachment by which an artificially composed three-dimensionality calls attention to itself, and technologies of reproduction that, lacking all real physical and conceptual boundaries, appear to emphasize the essential flatness of images, their kinship with information itself, rather than the three-dimensional subjects they represent, are sensuous only in the most explicitly arbitrary or implicitly secondary sense. These are art forms whose content Adorno condemned as "mere communication," whose "techniques" Scully identifies with "advertising," and that Barnes calls not art at all but "novel forms of 'documentation'" to which he opposes the physical/pictorial dialectic of painting as follows:

> Given an art world whose furnishings have to change like the frames in a music video to keep its public interested, it may now be time for us to move beyond the flattening accessibility of the literal to acknowledge the more persistent challenges of the visual.[60]

Habermas has referred in strikingly similar terms to the "flattening" of "the semantic threshold" that obtains whenever arbitrarily encountered objects are recontextualized as art: "Just as Joseph Cornell administers his found oddities to the imaginary place of a display cabinet, we can also see how the things one might encounter on a beach cross the semantic threshold, as soon as they are removed by the collector from the context of the place where they were originally discovered."[61] Yet perhaps the greatest and certainly most prolific of artists to have shuffled the decks of life and art together—to have made art out of the transposition, combination, and interchangeability of images and objects and treated the world as if it were a canvas, applying color equally to objects and images alike—espoused and practiced the view that such semantic distinctions are inimical to art, a deathly abstraction from an art object now defined as the original construction of a "context." Asked to comment on the "subjects of the photographs" employed in his series "Ground Rules" (1997), Robert Rauschenberg responds that the very question misses the point:

> That's one of the things that I feel is a distraction from the reality of a work. It pulls it out of context—makes it a foreign reference to something that has all been integrated into a new

life and relationship. Taking each image out of context is a question of manageability and encourages the separation that I think is false.[62]

The joys of juxtaposition—of transferring disparate unknown and familiar images together onto new, self-evidently extrinsic surfaces, coloring them and/or their support, mixing them with three-dimensional objects, found or fabricated or not—might seem in Adorno's view a fully negative version of aesthetic freedom, one that accepts ideological content as either unimportant or perversely integral to art. Of the method he employed in his unfruitful collaboration with Alain Robbe-Grillet—a case of two extremes that, *pace* Pascal, did not meet—Rauschenberg stated: "'I don't fiddle with the code of language, I accept it as a second nature which I don't put into question. The work that I do attack ... is the code of narrative.'"[63] One might say in response that, while leaving "the code of language" intact, Rauschenberg attacks narrative *tout court*: not the "code" or second-order system for combining different known grammatical and semantic identities, for sorting and joining the information that the messages of narrative transmit, but the structural possibility of achieving any form of meaningful sequencing that Hal Foster has called "narrative syntax," sequencing whose performance is consequential in effect.[64] Little distinguishes Rauschenberg's work more and distinguishes it from the separation of sensuousness and secondhand information called "abstract" art more thoroughly than such an "attack" on syntactic form: from Willem de Kooning, to Rothko, to Scully today, not to speak of their myriad contemporaries and predecessors, nothing could be more integral to nonfigural art than its syntax, the placement of each line, layer, and shape of pigment in relation to each other.[65] And perhaps nothing represented more dramatically the power Rauschenberg derived from defying or ignoring syntactic relations than his midcareer work *Hiccups* (1978), ninety-seven sheets of solvent-transfer images, as unrelated by any overarching formal structure as they are disconnected in content, whose aleatory extension, at nearly sixty-three feet, impeded its being seen in full even when fully exhibited.

Yet, confronted with compilations and translations of images by an artist who, as Faye Hirsch suggests, has "perhaps seen *too* much," a question regarding our own experience of his art arises: what do *we* see, who do not see with his eyes? Reviewing the *Ground Rules* series, Hirsch goes on to speculate:

> In a paradox that characterizes the series as a whole, the quality in the photographs of lost origins (of rarely knowing, for example, where they were shot) and their subject matter (the world's preoccupation with itself) seems even more hermetic when offered up in a package that so generously proffers the immediate, visually tangible pleasures of color. One almost expects to retrieve from them what can never be had.[66]

Adorno's dialectical theory of the "objectivity" of art indicates that "what can never be had" from "immediate" sensory "pleasures," whether of "visually tangible color" or familiar harmonic melody, is not merely information, the "lost origin" and "subject matter" of the particular art object, but the very freedom to appropriate all objects at which Rauschenberg aims. The negation of that freedom for Adorno, even as the "immediate" sensory "quality" of art—of "color" and "song"—remains in effect, makes "tangible" the decidedly mixed "pleasures" of art as "fragment." The intersection of exhaustion and exuberance that characterizes Rauschenberg's art objects—from the juxtaposition of the compositionally stunning *Combine* paintings with the surrealist association of objects in the freestanding *Combines*, to the unfinished *¼ Mile or 2 Furlong Piece*, which, started in 1981 and projected, at 189 contiguous panels, to be the longest art object in the world, has been exhibited only at stages of its development—expands Adorno's definition considerably: all art in Rauschenberg is merely a fragment of possible art, and all the world's information is art's "lost origin."

If Jasper Johns's very different handling of information seeks to depict the possibility that a "whole"—represented in the abstract ways in which alone we may perceive it, that is, as series, graphic symbol, or icon—"can be thrown," as Johns stated, "into a situation in which it is only a part"; and if Warhol's magnification of information into art instead elided the hierarchical opposition of part and whole, as of commercial object and art object, by negating, as Arthur Danto has observed, the "perceptual grounds" for "distinguishing art from reality" in the first place; then Rauschenberg, with an ever-expanding palette of reproductive processes and parts of the perceptual world at his disposal, submerges the cognitive opposition between sensuousness and information: between Hegel's hard, illegible symbols and his encyclopedic taxonomy of comparative art forms, between the pyramid at the origin of art and the "pyramid" of the postcard image. Rauschenberg suggests that pyramid and postcard pyramid, the origin and end of the production and experience of art, are one, and he does this in artworks that present recontextualizations of information to the senses.[67] Neither identical with nor possible without their particular sensory media, equally at odds with the "objective" "movement" of art and the objectification of art as kitsch, Rauschenberg's juxtapositional art resembles a "multiplicity of the simultaneous" effected in the absence of "polyphony," one piece of information and one sensuous medium no more necessarily conjoined to each other than to any other, one image as transferable at will as another. This is an "immediacy" that "flattens" not so much "semantic" thresholds as our very ability to perceive the difference between sensuous matter and abstraction.

It may be too neat, and certainly too glib, to say, even if only by way of illustration, that Rauschenberg's art represents in many ways the necessarily nonliteral translation of his literal dyslexia, the turning ever outward of his mind's internal eye toward an open lexicon of perceptual images embraced in all the seeming contingency of their actual appearance in the real world; and that the inexhaustible interrelatedness of Scully's compositions—of layer to layer of paint within each stripe, of stripe to stripe within and across blocks, and of each block of slightly different dimension and density to each other—is the anamnesis and animation, in an unfathomable interplay of geometry, color, and light, of a syntax already made clearly materially visible to and by him when he worked as a young typesetter, horizontally and vertically positioning blocks of different point sizes within fixed rectilinear spaces. For Scully's paintings allow us to guess at the depth behind the surface that the superficial imprint of typeface does not record, the weight and heft of the geometrical solid that sustains and holds it in place, here simulated not by an object attached combine-like to the canvas but by surfaces betraying other surfaces of paint and, emerging from between their uneven delineation, the present view and future prospect of the contradiction of solidity, light.[68]

In taking and assembling information out of context, Rauschenberg, by contrast, renders information sensuous. By substituting no formal aesthetic syntax for the "lost" syntax of history, he lends the images he places on surfaces the self-contradictory immediacy of wistfulness. Abstracted from the "origins" of their individual significance and circulation by culture, Rauschenberg's are images and objects applied to the pursuit of something other than happiness. The shadow of their own uselessness that they cast upon the viewer projects not the continuing conceptual reification of the object but the space and occasion for a disorienting perception of depth. Shorn like orphaned words and letters of syntactic relation and construction, it remains entirely unclear, however, what this unfamiliar depth portends.

If the paradox of the impossibility of art after Adorno was that the survivors of barbarism have not survived barbarism, just as fragments can no longer be fragments, parts that remain of what was never whole, then the paradox of the possibility of art after Adorno is that the object of art itself is split. Yet this, we may now also say, is the difficult guarantee of its "objectivity." The critical "movement" the viewer must make between abstract forms rendered sensuous, thick, and uneven with history, in an irreversible sedimentation of pigment, and images and objects whose abstraction from history casts all historical experience in an eerie light, maintains a "spontaneous relation to the object" while perceiving in it "the multiplicity of the simultaneous." In abstracting information, and in making color informative in its own right, these art objects are certainly antithetical to each other, yet no more so than is the undertaking of "cultural criticism" itself, whose "flagrant contradiction," Adorno reminds us, is first made known to us by way of the senses themselves:

> Whoever is used to *thinking with his ears*, must be annoyed by the sound of the word culture-critique not only because, like "automobile," it is pieced together of Latin and Greek. It recalls a flagrant contradiction. Culture does not suit the culture-critic.[69]

Adorno describes Schoenberg's compositions in the same heterogeneous terms used here, as "music of the intellectual ear."[70] Unlike the trajectory toward the overcoming of art recursively traced by Hegel, the objecthood of art after Adorno persists in "pieced together" antithetical relations perceived whenever, thinking with our eyes or ears, we abstract the object from its reification. Just as the art object embodying a "movement" of "moments," of "multiplicity in simultaneity" is any "thing" but an "object" in Adorno, so this act of abstraction—"spontaneous" in its "relation to the object," historical in its transmission or "tradition"—is temporal, experiential, and not abstract. It "objectively" perceives the apparently impossible object, whole "fragment," and "flagrant contradiction" that art frames as sensuousness for the mind.

Endnotes

[1] T. W. Adorno, "Kulturkritik und Gesellschaft," in *Prismen. Kulturkritik und Gesellschaft* (Frankfurt, 1955), pp. 29, 22: "Keine Theorie, und auch die wahre nicht, ist vor der Perversion in den Wahn sicher, wenn sie einmal der spontanen Beziehung auf das Objekt sich entäussert hat"; "Das Moment der Objektivität der Wahrheit, ohne das Dialektik nicht vorgestellt werden kann." All subsequent citations from "Kulturkritik und Gesellschaft" are from this edition. (All translations from the German, unless otherwise indicated, are my own.)

[2] Frank Stella quoted in Felicity Barringer, "Matisse: He's Kind of Cast a Spell on Me," *Artnews* 92 (April 1993): p. 150.

[3] T. W. Adorno, *Ästhetische Theorie*, ed. Gretel Adorno and Rolf Tiedemann (Frankfurt, 1970), "Editorisches Nachwort," p. 537. Adorno and Tiedemann state of the unfinished volume: "Ihr Bruchstzuckhaftes ist der Eingriff des Todes in ein Werk, bevor es das Gesetz seiner Form ganz verwirklicht hatte" ([The] fragmentary nature [of *Aesthetic Theory*] is the intervention of death in a work before it has realized the law of its form; p. 538). The self-critical essay, "Der Essay als Form," in which many of Adorno's reflections on cultural criticism are mirrored, first appeared in Theodor W. Adorno, *Noten zur Literatur,* vol. 1 (Frankfurt, 1958).

[4] "Der Kulturkritiker kann kaum die Unterstellung vermeiden, er hätte die Kultur, welche dieser abgeht. Seine Eitelkeit kommt der ihren zu Hilfe"; Adorno, "Kulturkritik," 7.

[5] Ibid., p. 31: "[N]ach Auschwitz ein Gedicht zu schreiben, ist barbarisch." The three-part sentence in which these words appear is cited in full and further analyzed later in this essay.

[6] It is exactly this already abstract quality of music, as pure medium of sensation, that has made it a model for modern abstract art. Cf. Clement Greenberg, "Towards a Newer Laocoon," in *Clement Greenberg: The Collected Essays and Criticism,* vol. 1, *Perceptions and Judgments, 1939–1944,* ed. John O'Brian (Chicago, 1986), pp. 23–37 (31): "Aside from what was going on inside music, music as an art in itself began [after Romanticism] to occupy a very important position in relation to the other arts. Because of its 'absolute' nature, its remoteness from imitation, its almost complete absorption in the very physical quality of its medium ..., music had come to replace poetry as the paragon art. It was the art which the other avant-garde arts envied most, and whose effects they tried hardest to imitate.... [T]he advantage of music lay chiefly in the fact that it was an 'abstract' art, an art of 'pure form'... incapable, objectively, of communicating anything else than a sensation, and because sensation could not be conceived in any other terms than those of the sense through which it entered the consciousness."

[7] The most thorough consideration not only of Adorno's statement and

the ongoing critical reaction to it but also, perhaps most importantly, of Adorno's own dialectical response to the controversy his comment ignited, is Robert Kaufman's "Poetry's Ethics? Theodor W. Adorno and Robert Duncan on Aesthetic Illusion and Sociopolitical Delusion," *New German Critique* 97 (Winter 2006): pp. 73–118. See esp. pp. 98–104 for Adorno's reflections on his earlier statement in the 1965 lectures on metaphysics subsequently incorporated into *Negative Dialectics* (1966) and the centrality of aesthetic "semblance" to the conception of "negative dialectics" itself. See also pp. 113–14 for Kaufman's fine reading of the relation Adorno draws between the "seeming impossibility" of "poetry" after Auschwitz and that of "life," and his interpretation of Adorno's insight that "the apparent *unavailability* of [the] semblance-character" of art is itself a "negative knowledge that can be gained only through the attempt at semblance-character" (114).

8 Sean Scully, quoted in R. Eric Davis, "Sean Scully's Preoccupations: An Interview," *On Paper* (July–Aug. 1998): pp. 24–29 (29).

9 Adorno, "Kulturkritik," p. 25: "Dialektik heisst Intransigenz gegenüber jeglicher Verdinglichung."

10 Perhaps it should be underscored at this point that the use of the term "objecthood" in the present analysis of the art object after Adorno relates, first, to the Hegelian subject-object dialectic, including the abstraction—or, in the case of the aesthetic object, the nominalization—of the "object" Hegel predicts; and, second, to Adorno's development of the notion of an object-immanent "objectivity" to counter the underlying subjective bias of "objective" reasoning in Hegel. The significance attributed to "objecthood" here should not be confused with the meaning given it by Michael Fried, who, employing the term to reference the rejection of "pictoral illusion" and "anthropomorphism" in favor of the creation of "Specific Objects" advocated by Donald Judd, viewed its achievement as the goal of a specific movement in modern art—minimalist, or as Fried calls it, "literalist," "non-art"—that, in his view, seeks to replace art, defined as "object" and "painting," by "singleness of ... shape." See Michael Fried, "Art and Objecthood," *Artforum* 5 (June 1967): pp. 12–23, later incorporated in *Art and Objecthood: Essays and Reviews* (Chicago, 1998), see pp. 148–53 esp. As the attempt is made here to demonstrate, "objecthood," understood dialectically instead of derivatively, i.e., as deriving from the givenness of objects, suggests nearly the opposite of Fried's description of the anti-art view of art as "nothing more than objects." Rather, it refers to our dynamic experience of a "thing" made to remain outside us, to resist reification in Adorno's sense, an object that, *in that it originates in relation to a subject* (no matter how contingent or determined that relation may be), must contradict the subject's view of it as "nothing more than" an object, whether that "nothing" equates to mere externality, instrument, or even mirror of the self. In the pages that follow, objecthood, then, names the inassimilable, because sensuous and

abstract, quality of the art object, the quality that compels the subject who perceives it to follow out its "movement" mentally, an "objectivity" composed of sensuousness framed or sensuousness made by framing. Finally, while Fried understandably employs "objecthood" historically to distinguish divergent paths through the conflictual landscape of visual art in the second half of the last century, this analysis understands under "objecthood" the quality, difficult (as Hegel already demonstrated) for any path of aesthetic development to maintain over time, in which distinct kinds of art objects—abstract and figurative; painterly, sculptural, and photographic; combined, copied, and found—converge in the challenge each poses to the mind through the senses and, through the mind, to the future history of art.

A similar view to Fried's early critique of Judd's rejection of the painted illusion of space for real space, and of the "'relational'" rendering of "'space in and around marks and colours'" for "specific," three-dimensional "objects," is developed by Donald Kuspit; see "Nuance and Intensity in Sean Scully: Humanism in Abstract Disguise," in *Sean Scully: Body of Light* (Melbourne, 2004), pp. 45–51 (48, 50).

[11] See G. W. F. Hegel, *Vorlesungen über die Ästhetik*, vol. 13–15 of *Theorie Werkausgabe*, ed. E. Moldenhauer and K. M. Michel, 20 vols. (Frankfurt, 1977), 14: pp. 140ff. On the further equation of "sound" with "sign" in Hegel, and consequent circularity of the notion of the "end of the aesthetic" his dialectical history of art forms proposes, see my "From the Pyramids to Romantic Poetry: Housing the Spirit in Hegel," in *Rereading Romanticism*, ed. Martha Helfer (Amsterdam, 2000), pp. 327–66.

[12] Cf. Adorno, "Kulturkritik," p. 15: "Versperrt ist dem Kulturkritiker die Einsicht, dass die Verdinglichung des Lebens selbst nicht auf einem Zuviel, sondern einen Zuwenig an Aufklärung beruhe und dass die Verstümmelungen, welche der Menschheit von der gegenwärtigen partikularistischen Rationalität angetan werden, Schandmale der totalen Irrationalität sind" (The cultural critic is blocked from the insight that the reification of life rests not on too much but on too little enlightenment, and that the mutilations that present, particularistic rationality inflicts upon man are the stigmata of total irrationality).

[13] T. W. Adorno, "Cultural Criticism and Society," in *Prisms*, trans. Samuel and Shierry Weber (Cambridge, 1981), pp. 17–34 (23; emphases added for clarity). On at least one important occasion, when redundancy in English is not at issue, the Webers similarly translate *Sache* as "object," perhaps so as to underscore preceding uses of the latter term: "No theory, not even that which is true, is safe from perversion into delusion once it has renounced a spontaneous relation to the *object* [*Objekt*]. Dialectics must guard against this no less than against enthrallment in the cultural *object* [*Kulturobjekt*]. It can subscribe neither to the cult of the mind nor to hatred of it. The dialectical critic of culture must both participate in culture and not participate. Only then does he do justice to his *object*

[*Sache*] and to himself" (p. 33). We will return to this passage.

14 Throughout *Ästhetische Theorie*, for example, "Objekt" is used whenever Hegel's "subject-object dialectic" is directly under discussion (see pp. 244–62 esp.), but that is where Adorno's specification of "object" as word or meaning more or less ends. While "Gegenstand" and "Sache" are sometimes distinguished from "Objekt" in their connotation of concrete things, that distinction, untenable in its English translation, often does not hold up well in Adorno's own phrasing, "Gegenstand" sometimes taking on a connotation of mimetic content along with its literal meaning of "object," and "Sache" conveying at least the following disparate senses: that of an intellectual issue or question; of a literal "thing"; or of a dialectically required apposite term to "Objekt": "Die Subject-*Objekt*-Dialektik trägt bei Hegel in der *Sache* sich zu. Zu denken ist auch ans Verhältnis von Subjekt und *Objekt* im Kunstwerk, soweit es mit *Gegenständen* zu tun hat. Es ändert sich geschichtlich, lebt jedoch nach auch in den un*gegenständlichen* Gebilden, die zum *Gegenstand* Stellung beziehen, indem sie ihn tabuieren (p. 244–45); "Im Gebilde ist Subjekt weder der Betrachter noch der Schöpfer noch absoluter Geist, vielmehr der an die *Sache* gebundene, von ihr präformiert, seinerseits durchs *Objekt* vermittelt" (p. 248; emphases added for clarity). The Lenhardt translation, T. W. Adorno, *Aesthetic Theory*, trans. C. Lenhardt (London, 1984), of the passages that follow renders "Sache" alternately as "the thing under discussion" and "object," and redefines "Gegenstände" as "concrete tangible things" (rather than maintaining its literal meaning, "objects"), but translates "ungegenständlichen" as "non-representational," and finally "Gegenstand" as "object," these last three semantic versions of a single word all occurring in the course of two consecutive sentences: "In Hegel the subject-object dialectic occurs in the *thing under investigation (in der Sache* [sic]). Another problem might be that of how subject and object are related when art deals with *concrete tangible things* [Gegenständen]. This relation has changed historically, and yet it lives on even in the *non-representational* [ungegenständlichen] works of today, for they too take a position on the *object* [Gegenstand], if only tacitly: they taboo it....The subject in a work of art is neither the viewer nor the creative artist nor some absolute spirit. It is spirit, to the extent to which it is embedded in, and mediated and performed by, the *object* [Objekt]" (pp. 234, 238; emphases added for clarity).

Such a lexical analysis of the Lenhardt and Weber translations is aimed not at critiquing their individual versions of Adorno's texts, but rather at indicating the real uncertainty of how we are to view and name the "object" variously designated in those original texts themselves, an uncertainty that the problem of the translation of "object" makes evident, but only insofar as it is already part and parcel of the full thrust of Adorno's theory of art.

15 The sense of "Ding" as a "thing" resistant to ideological "reification" or

"Verdinglichung" already appeared in the past participle form of a related verb, of which "Ding" is the root, in the epigrammatic definition of the artwork in *Minima moralia* (1951; reprint, Frankfurt, 1993), p. 142: "Jedes Kunstwerk ist eine *abgedungene* Untat" (Every artwork is a crime that has been paid for [or paid off; from *dingen*: to pay someone to commit a crime]; emphasis added).

16 "Leben verwandelt sich in die Ideologie der Verdinglichung, eigentlich die Maske des Toten" (Life transforms itself into the ideology of reification, properly the mask of the dead); Adorno, "Kulturkritik," p. 24. The impenetrable "Ding" and its derivatives appear in the following instances in the essay: "unabdingbares Element" (ineluctable, or, literally, un-unthingable element; p. 11); "dinghafte Gestalt der Sache" (thingly form of the thing; p. 13); "Verdinglichung des Lebens" (reification of life) and "[L]ieber soll das Ende aller Dinge kommen, als dass die Menschheit der Verdinglichung ein Ende macht" ([O]ne would rather the end of all things come than mankind put an end to reification; p. 15); "als Mass aller Dinge" (as the measure of all things; p. 17); "wie gelungene Verdinglichung, also Trennung" (as successful reification, that is, separation; p. 25); "der Gegensatz der von aussen und von innen eindringenden Erkenntnis selber als Symptom jener Verdinglichung" (the opposition of knowledge imposing itself from inside and from outside as itself symptom of that reification; p. 28); "[D]ie Methode [macht] ... eben jene Verdinglichung sich zu eigen, die sie zum kritischen Thema hat" ([M]ethod makes ... the very reification that is its critical theme its own; p. 29); "Begriffe verdinglichten Wesens benutzt, wie die Gesellschaft selber vedinglicht ist" ([It] uses concepts of reified essence or being insofar as society itself is reified; p. 29); "Je totaler die Gesellschaft, um so verdinglichter auch der Geist, und um so paradoxer sein Beginnen, der Verdinglichung aus eigenem sich zu entwinden" (The more total the society, the more reified the spirit, and the more paradoxical its beginning to disentangle itself from reification on its own; p. 30); "[D]er absoluten Verdinglichung ... ist der kritische Geist nicht gewachsen, solange er bei sich bleibt in selbstgenügsamer Kontemplation" ([C]ritical spirit is no match for absolute reification as long as it remains in self-sufficient contemplation with itself; p. 31). In contrast to "Ding," "Sache" is used, often idiomatically, to convey both material and conceptual connotations of "thing;" see pp. 13, 23, 27, 28, 29.

17 Cf. "Indem [der Kulturkritiker] Kultur zu seinem Gegenstand macht, vergegenständlicht er sie nochmals. Ihr eigener Sinn aber ist die Suspension von Vergegenständlichung" (In that the cultural critic makes culture into his object, he objectifies it again. Its own meaning, however, is the suspension of objectification); Adorno, "Kulturkritik," p. 12.

18 See ibid., pp. 12, 28, 29, 30, for uses of "Gegenstand"; pp. 13, 19, 22, 27, 28, 29, for positive and negative uses of "Objekt."

[19] Ibid., p. 9 (emphases added for clarity).

[20] Ibid., pp. 19–20 (emphases added for clarity).

[21] Ibid., p. 20 (emphases added for clarity). See also: "Kultur ist ideologisch geworden nicht nur als Inbegriff der subjektiv ausgeheckten Manifestationen *des objektiven Geistes*" (Culture has become ideological not only as the very essence of subjectively fashioned manifestation of *the objective mind;* p. 24, emphasis added for clarity).

[22] Ibid., p. 22: "*Das Moment der Objektivität von Wahrheit*, ohne das Dialektik nicht vorgestellet werden kann, wird stillschweigend durch vulgären Positivismus und Pragmatismus—in letzter Instanz: bürgerlichen Subjetivismus—ersetzt" (emphasis added).

[23] Ibid., p. 29.

[24] Ibid., p. 27: "Solche Kritik bescheidet sich nicht bei dem allgemeinen Wissen von der Knechtschaft des objektiven Geistes, sondern sucht dies Wissen in die Kraft der Betrachtung der Sache selbst umzusetzen.... Wo sie aufs Unzulängliche stösst, schreibt sie es nicht eilfertig dem Individuum und seiner Psychologie, dem blossen Deckbild des Misslingens zu, sondern sucht es aus der Unversönlichkeit *der Momente des Objekts* abzuleiten" (emphasis added).

[25] It is for their own objective permanence and inscrutability, as well as the embalmed bodies they remove in perpetuity from the world, that Hegel identified the Egyptian pyramids as the "symbolic proper" (eigentliche Symbolik) or true origin of art, in direct contrast to the ongoing metamorphosis of organic bodies celebrated by the Hindus. See Hegel, *Vorlesungen über die Ästhetik,* 13: pp. 290–94, 393, 452–65, in particular, and Brodsky, "From the Pyramids to Romantic Poetry," pp. 351–62.

[26] Adorno, "Kulturkritik," p. 8: "Die Überspannung des kulturellen Anspruchs, die doch wieder der Bewegung des Geistes immanent ist."

[27] Ibid.: "Solche Vornehmheit macht der Kulturkritiker zu seinem Privileg und verwirkt seine Legitimation, indem er als bezahlter und geehrter Plagegeist der Kultur an dieser mitwirkt" (The cultural critic makes the distinction [of culture] into his own privilege and gives up his legitimation in collaborating with culture as its paid and honored pest).

[28] Ibid., p. 22: "Ohne solche Freiheit, ohne Hinausgehen des Bewusstseins über die Immanenz der Kultur wäre immanente Kritik selber nicht denkbar: der Selbstbewegung des Objekts vermag nur zu folgen, wer dieser nicht durchaus angehört."

[29] Ibid., p. 29: "Keine Theorie, und auch die wahre nicht, ist vor der Perversion in den Wahn sicher, wenn sie einmal der spontanen Beziehung auf das Objekt sich entäussert hat. Davor muss Dialektik nicht weniger sich hüten als vor der Befangenheit im Kulturobjekt.... Der dialektische Kritiker an der Kultur muss an dieser teilhaben und nicht

teilhaben. Nur dann lässt er der Sache und sich selber Gerechtigkeit widerfahren."

30 T. W. Adorno, "Arnold Schönberg, 1874–1951," in Adorno, *Prismen*, p. 211: "Mündigkeit und Vergeisterung der Kunst mit dem sinnlichen Schein virtuell die Kunst selber tilgen." All following citations from this essay will be from this edition.

31 "[D]ie üblichen Krücken eines Hörens, das immer schon weiss, was kommt," from Adorno, "Arnold Schönberg, 1874–1951," p. 181.

32 Ibid.: "[Schönbergs Musik] verlangt, dass der Hörer ihre innere Bewegung spontan mitkomponiert, und mutet ihm anstelle blosser Kontemplation gleichsam Praxis zu. Damit aber frevelt Schönberg gegen die im Widerpruch zu allen idealistischen Beteuerungen gehegte Erwartung, dass Musik al eine Folge gefälliger sinnlicher Reize dem bequemen Hören sich präsentiere.... Bei Schönberg hört die Gemütlichkeit auf."

33 Ibid., p. 182.

34 "Bei Schönberg wird die Objektivierung des subjektiven Impulses zum Ernstfall" (With Schoenberg the objectivization of the subjective impulse becomes a serious matter); ibid., p. 191.

35 Ibid., p. 181.

36 "Dem [des Blauen Reiters Programm des 'Geistigen in der Kunst'] hielt Schönberg die Treue, nich indem er auf Abstraktion ausging, sondern indem er die konkrete Gestalt der Musik selber vergeistigte. Daraus wird ihm der beliebste Vorwurf gemacht, der des Intellektualismus. Die immanente Kraft der Vergeisterung wird entweder verwechselt mit einer der Sache äusserlichen Reflexion, oder es wird dogmatisch Musik von jener Forderung der Vergeisterung ausgenommen, die als Korrektiv der Verwandlung von Kultur in Kulturgut für alle ästhetischen Medien unabsweisbar ward" (Schoenberg remained true to the Blue Rider program of "the spirit of the mind in art," not in proceeding from abstraction, but in endowing the concrete form of music itself with intellectual spirit. This is the basis of the preferred reproach against him, that of intellectualism. The immanent power of fusing art with intellect is either confused with a form of reflection that is external to the thing, or music is dogmatically exempted from the demand of such intellectual effort, that which became the necessary corrective to the transformation of culture in cultural good for all aesthetic media), ibid., p. 182. "[Schönbergs] ist eine Musik der Identität in Nichtidentität" ([Schoenberg's] is a music of identity in nonidentity), ibid., p. 188.

37 Ibid., p. 184: "Der Vorwurf des Intellektuellen geht mit dem des Mangels an Melodie zusammen. Aber er war der Melodiker schlechthin. Anstelle der eingeschliffenen Formel hat er unablässig neue Gestalten produziert. Kaum je kann seine melodische Eingebung mit einer einzelnen Melodie

hinaushalten, sondern alle *gleichzeitigen* musikalischen Ereignisse warden als Melodien profiliert und damit gerade die Auffassung erschwert. Die ursprüngliche musikalische Reaktionsweise Schönbergs selbst ist melodisch: alles bei ihm eigentlich 'gesungen,' auch die instrumentalen Linien. Das verleiht seiner Musik das Artikulierte, zugleich frei Schwingende und bis zum letzten Ton Gegliederte" (emphasis added).

[38] Ibid., p. 192: "Schönberg denkt zu Ende, was der Klassizismus versprach und nicht hielt, und darüber zerbricht die traditionelle Fassade. Er hat die Bachische Forderung wieder aufgenommen, der der Klassizismus, Beethoven einbegriffen, sich entzog, ohne dass Schönberg doch hinter den Klassizismus zurückgefallen ware. Dieser hatte Bach aus geschichtlicher Notwendigkeit vernachlässigt. Die Autonomie des musikalischen Subjekts überwog jedes andere Interesse und *schloss kritisch die überkommene Gestalt der Objektivierung aus*, während man mit dem Schein der Objektivierung vorlieb nehmen konnte, so wie das ungehemmte Zusammenspiel der Subjekte die Gesellschaft zu garantieren schien. *Heute erst, da die Subjektivität in ihrer Unmittelbarkeit nicht länger als höchste Kategorie waltet,* sondern als der gesamtgesellschaftlichen Verwirklichung bedürftig durchschaut ist, wird die Insuffizienz selbst der Beethovenschen Lösung, *die das Subjekt zum Ganzen ausbreitet, ohne das Ganze in sich zu versöhnen,* erkennbar. Schönbergs Polyphonie bestimmt die Durchführung ... *als dialektische Auseinanderlegung des subjektiven Melodischen Impulses in der objektiv organisierten Mehrstimmigkeit*" (emphasis added).

[39] Cf. my "Szondi and Hegel: 'The Troubled Relationship of Literary Criticism to Philosophy,'" *Telos* 140 (Fall 2007): 45–63, for an extended discussion of Hegel's analysis, in *Lectures on Aesthetics*, of the inherent semantic and historic "ambiguity" stemming from the identity of the "symbol," "in the first [and last] place," as "sign."

[40] Adorno, "Schönberg," p. 189: "[D]as künstlerische Extrem zu verwantworten, ob es der Logik der Sache, einer wie sehr auch verborgene Objektivität, oder bloss der privaten Willkür oder abstrakten System. Seine Legitimität aber zieht es wesentlich aus der Tradition, die es negiert ... Nicht nur die religiöse, auch die ästhetische Tradition ist Erinnerung an ein Unbewusstes, ja Verdränglichtes.... Tradition ist gegenwärtig in den als experimentell gescholtenen Werken und nicht in den der eigenen Absicht nach traditionalistischen."

[41] Ibid., pp. 206, 208.

[42] Ibid., p. 206.

[43] Ibid., p. 211: "Die Erfahrung, das kein musikalisches Subject-Objekt heut und hier sich konstituieren kann, war an ihm nicht verschwendet."

[44] Ibid., pp. 207, 187.

[45] Ibid.

⁴⁶ Ibid., p. 210: "Unter Schönbergs Akten der Integration musikalischer Mittel war nicht der letzte, dass er endgültig die Farbe der Sphäre des Schmückenden Entriss und zum Kompositionselement eigenen Rechtes erhob. Sie verwandelt sich in ein Mittel der Verdeutlichung des Zusammenhangs. Solche Einbeziehung in die Komposition aber wird ihr zum Verhängnis.... Je nackter die Konstruktion sich darstellt, um so weniger bedarf sie der koloristischenHilfe ... Mündige Musik schöpft Verdacht gegen das real Erklingende schlechthin ... Die Neigung zum Verstummen, wie sie in Weberns Lyrik die Aura jeden Tones bildet, ist dieser von Schönberg ausgehenden Tendenz verschwistert. *Sie läuft aber auch nicht weniger hinaus, als dass Mündigkeit und Vergeisterung der Kunst mit dem sinnlichen Schein virtuell die Kunst selber tilgen*" (emphasis added).

⁴⁷ "Emphatisch arbeitet in Schönbergs Spätwerk die Vergeisterung der Kunst an deren Auflösung und findet sich so mit dem kunstfeindlichen und barbarischen Element abgründig zusammen " (The intellectualization of art in Schoenberg's late work works emphatically toward the dissolution of art and so converges abysmally with the anti-artistic and barbaric element), ibid.

⁴⁸ Ibid., p. 31: "Kulturkritik findet sich der letzten Stufe der Dialektik von Kultur und Barberei gegenüber: nach Auschwitz ein Gedicht zu schrieben, ist barbarisch; *und das frisst auch die Erkenntnis an, die ausspricht, warum es unmöglich ward, heute Gedichte zu schreiben*" (emphasis added).

⁴⁹ Ibid., p.213.

⁵⁰ Ibid., p. 214.

⁵¹ Cited in Oliver Meslay, *Turner: Life and Landscape* (New York, 2005), p. 102.

⁵² Greenberg states of abstract artists what could well be stated of him: "Purists make extravagant claims for art, because usually they value it much more than any one else does"; Greenberg, "Towards a Newer Laocoon," p. 23. He famously defines the "purity" arising from a knowing separation of the arts, and of "painting" from the representation of things and communication of messages proper to "literature" (thereby inverting Lessing's own epoch-making argument regarding the descriptive properties of spatial-pictoral, rather than temporal-verbal, media) as follows: "Purity in art consists in the acceptance, willing acceptance, of the limitations of the medium of the specific art"; "The history of avant-garde painting is that of a progressive surrender to the resistance of its medium (32, 34).

⁵³ Hegel, *Vorlesungen über die Ästhetik*, 13: pp. 25.

⁵⁴ Reinhardt's provocative pronouncement—"There is something wrong, irresponsible, mindless about color, something impossible to control. Control and rationality are part of any morality'"—is cited as part of an argument on behalf of color in Glen Dixon, "Sean Scully," *Artforum* 34 (Oct. 1994): 97.

In his Norton lectures, *Working Space* (Cambridge, MA, 1986), Stella contributes to the debate surrounding the divide between abstractly sensuous color and representational shape by attributing the "lack of a convincing projective illusionism,... of a self-contained [pictorial] space" in painting since Pollock and Morris Louis to "a misguided search for color," linking, by contrast, his own early black paintings with Caravaggio's "ability to create the sensation of real space" (11–12).

55 See Dixon, "Sean Scully," p. 97, on the felt "sensuality" of color in Rothko and Scully; see Reinhard Ermen, reviews of Rothko and Scully exhibits, Basel and Düsseldorf 2001, in *Kunstforum International* 155 (June/July 2001): 425–28, esp. 427, on Scully: "[E]r hat seine Streifen zu einer Art Baukasten weitergedacht ... konkrete Körper, die die Farben vor oder zurücksetzen und den Betrachter ... in den Bildraum einlassen" ([H]e has thought his stripes out into a kind of building block ... concrete bodies that set the colors forward or backward and let the viewer ... into the picture space).

Reminiscent of Adorno's analysis of the peculiar objecthood of the art object, Jonathan Lasher has written persuasively of the ability of Mondrian's paintings to "present the visual in purely objective terms" while "taking on a resonance that is not 'objectively' there" when they are "completed in the mind of the viewer"; see Lasher, "New Math," *Artforum* 34 (Oct. 1995): 83. In his eloquent essay on Rothko's development and achievement, "Bodies of Light," *Art in America* (July 1999): pp. 60–70, 107, Scully states the decisive effect of Matisse's new, non-"descripti[ve]" use of color (in *The Red Studio*) on Rothko: "It was Rothko's exposure to Matisse's painting *The Red Studio* (1911), when it came to New York in 1949, that opened a huge door to his own future. *The Red Studio*, as radical as Picasso's *Les Demoisiselles d'Avignon* (1907), was painted with a flat red colour that completely covered—and thus simplified and unified—the entire surface of the painting. This work profoundly affected Rothko and made it possible for him thereafter to put down color without bothering to model it for the sake of description."

56 Rothko himself had evidently come to the same conclusion, if slightly differently conceived, suggesting, according to Tate curator Norman Reed, that "Turner had learned a great deal from him"; interview with Sir Norman Reed, "Rothko's Rooms," dir. Keith Alexander, 2000. Extending beyond this happy admission that the history of abstract color painting had proceeded backwards, Rothko's acceptance of Reed's proposal that the Tate house his Seagram paintings rested in no small measure, Reed reports, on the proximity of the room to be devoted to them to the Tate's gallery of Turners.

57 Curt Barnes, "Travels Along the Dialectic: Hit-and-Run Observations on Interdimensoinality," *Art Journal* 30 (1991): pp. 26–32 (28).

58 Kuspit, citing Scully's use of the term in discussing Van Gogh, explains

the particular sense of "Suchness" created by Scully's own abstract sensuousness as follows: "In the altered state of consciousness, which is Scully's abstract painting, geometry becomes intense and colour becomes profound. Their Suchness becomes self-evident. The doors of perception are flung wide open.... The sublime Suchness of relational patterns and of moving light becomes evident"; "Nuance and Intensity," p. 50.

[59] Historically astute and experientially accurate accounts of the enduring participation of abstraction in art are offered, by contrast, by Kuspit, especially in his writing on Scully. See, in particular, his "Sean Scully," *Artforum International* 38 (Sept. 1999): p. 168; "Nuance and Intensity," pp. 45–51, and "Sacred Sadness," in *Sean Scully: A Retrospective* (London, 2007), pp. 14–18. For Kuspit, Scully's paintings do more than merely prove "that abstraction is not dead;" rather, they "epitomize the essentials of abstraction and give them what one might call, literally and figuratively, new depth"; "Sean Scully," p. 168.

[60] Adorno, "Kulturkritik," p. 17; Davis, "Sean Scully's Preoccupations," 29; Barnes, "Travels Along the Dialectic," p. 32. In distinction from, but no less opposition to, Warhol's objectivization and weirdly transcendent historicization of the imagery and methods of commercial art, Scully views art made with the circulatory aims and "techniques" of advertising as "a pure and unbridled form of capitalism," i.e., a form exercised in necessary disregard for the "consequentiality" of art; see "Interview with Eric Davis," in Sean Scully, *Resistance and Persistance: Selected Writings* (London, 2006), p. 135.

[61] Jürgen Habermas, "A Modernism that Turned into a Tradition: Glosses and Associations," in *Sean Scully: Body of Light*, pp. 39–42 (40–41). Habermas continues: "Sean Scully objects to the flattening of this threshold" (41).

[62] Faye Hirsch, "Weatherman: Robert Rauschenberg's *Ground Rules* Series," *Art on Paper* 2 (Nov.–Dec. 1997): pp. 10–15 (14).

[63] Hal Foster, review, *Artforum* (Sept. 1979): pp. 72–74 (74).

[64] Ibid.

[65] While Rothko's creation of overlapping shapes and borders of color that we experience not as affixed to canvas but afloat has often led to especially mystical ruminations on the content of his work, an excellent account of the visual syntax that, relating "the surface figures" of his paintings, composes at the same time their extraordinary, apparently untethered spatial effect, is offered in Sheldon Nodelman's "Rediscovering Rothko," *Art in America* (July 1999): pp. 58–65, 106 (62). Of Rothko's now "classic works from 1949 onward," Nodelman writes: "Rothko's great discovery, and the key to the unprecedented achievement of these paintings, was his exploitation (for the first time systematically and at large scale) of a fundamental perceptual mechanism, relational

contrast, as a means for creating apparent spatiality" (pp. 61–62).

66 Hirsch, "Weatherman," p. 13.

67 See Majorie Welish, interview with Jasper Johns (Feb. 22, 1990), in "When Is a Door Not a Door?" *Art Journal* 50 (Sep. 1991): pp. 48–51 (50); see Arthur C. Danto, *Philosophizing Art: Selected Essays* (Berkeley, 1999), p. 65.

68 See Davis, "Sean Scully's Preoccupations, " p. 2; cf. Kuspit, "Sacred Sadness," p. 17: "[The] structured plane [of Scully's paintings] is suspended over and generally blocks out an amorphous plane of implied depth…. Whatever the mood suggested, this double layer effect confirms that the paintings are formal masterpieces. They acknowledge the physical surface of the canvas while subverting (transcending?) it, by creating the illusion of 'behind' the surface … as though Scully was an archaeologist digging up the darkness, with its rotting colours, in search of a living memory of light."

69 Adorno, "Kulturkritik," p. 7: "Wer gewohnt ist, *mit den Ohren zu denken*, der muss am Klang des Wortes Kulturkritik sich ärgern nicht darum bloss, weil es, wie das Automobil, aus Latein und Griechisch zusammengestückt ist. Es erinnert an einen flagranten Widerspruch. Dem Kulturkritiker passt die Kultur nicht" (emphasis added).

70 Adorno, "Schönberg," p. 193.

Robert Kaufman

Poetry After "Poetry After Auschwitz"

NOTHING IN THEODOR W. ADORNO'S controversial oeuvre knows so charged an afterlife as that notorious 1949 aphorism: "[A]fter Auschwitz, to write a poem is barbaric" (*nach Auschwitz ein Gedicht zu schreiben, ist barbarisch*). Ubiquitous as those words become in a reception history extending impressively far and wide and continuing still, their epigrammatic sting has more often than not been radically detached and misleadingly abstracted: detached from the contexts and multiply oriented directions of the 1949 essay titled "Cultural Criticism and Society" that had housed them; detached from that essay's explicit analysis of what it might mean for art and culture's emancipatory engagements to be rethought in relation to a contemporary capitalist-administrative society putting the world's confrontation with the National Socialist genocide behind it and extraordinarily interested in integrating and neutralizing art and culture's tendencies toward protest and critique; detached also from the essay's knowing, unsparingly self-critical analysis precisely of aesthetic and cultural criticism's "critical" awareness and oppositional impulse to deny the force of the aforementioned sociocultural and socioeconomic dynamics of assimilation and co-optation; and detached, finally, from that aphorism's construction of a simultaneously essay-ending and discourse-generating gesture, which—far from any banning, enjoining, stigmatizing, or the like—rather presents lyric poetry as objectivating the strongest version of a postwar dilemma certainly shared, on lower frequencies, by much philosophy and criticism (and as being in accord with Adorno's, Benjamin's, and other Frankfurt School figures' and kindred artists' lifelong views that lyric carried unique critical powers). Not to mention that Adorno had composed his refractory thought so that the infamous words were embedded within a long, complexly frictive German sentence subsequently parceled, in the best-known English translation, into three separate sentences whose effect might seem strikingly different from that comprehended in the original.[1]

Adorno had actually, if naively, imagined that his barbed, tensile aphorism, provocation though it surely was, would nonetheless straightforwardly join other immediate postwar efforts to make thought and writing grapple with and palpably enact a questioning of the meanings of humanity's "after-living"— its *sur-vival*—of the 1933–1945 Third Reich, of what Paul Celan's poetry would soon begin to call *that which happened (das, was geschah)*, that which happened not only to the immediate victims of the genocide but also to the world itself and to the ongoing aftermath of human experience.[2] In this essay I pursue poetry's immanent explorations and contributions, not only to the initial "poetry after Auschwitz" question but also to what comes historically after that initial question.

It turns out that one of later-modernist, later twentieth-century poetry's most consequential responses to the "what follows 'poetry after Auschwitz'?" query will be, in significant part: "poetry after 'poetry after Auschwitz.'" It will be among this essay's abiding concerns—as it was among the abiding concerns of the poetry itself—to show how and why this "following" involves more than mere statement of obvious, inevitable, next-step outcomes, more than mere play on the words "follow" and "after," more even than the combination of conceptually determined logic itself plus linguistic-temporal sequencing or succession; instead of all these, what's operative in poetry after "poetry after Auschwitz" proves to be extraordinarily hard-won recognition of actual, specific historical developments and conditions of possibility that would go largely, if not completely, unapprehended but for artistic-aesthetic—in this case, poetic—agency, effort, and achievement. For not least interesting are the profoundly historical character and meanings *of* poetry after poetry after Auschwitz. This poetry after poetry after Auschwitz will compel, via its particular aesthetic illuminations, the re-opening of several other crucial historical questions that had only appeared to be—or had appeared to be *only*—literary, cultural, or aesthetic and that had at any rate seemed settled, or destined to remain mysterious, but now urge their renewed necessity and contemporaneity and, in a certain sense, their ability to shuttle us to certain extrapoetic and extra-aesthetic matters. What *really* finally happened to modernism, from within and without, to cause its demise; *did* modernism actually die? Why does a reinvention of lyric-Romantic critical agency with a difference—or rather, a rediscovery *and* reinvention of the lyric-Romantic strains secretly animating so much modernist poetry and art—loom so large in these investigations of modernism's life and afterlives? How do both these historical investigation-engagements (of lyric-Romantic critical agency; of what finally happened to modernism) constellate themselves together with developments in today's poetry, poetics and aesthetics, criticism?

In Celan himself, the Romantic strains at least would not seem newsworthy. A deep, rich, and explicit relationship to Hölderlin and other German Romantics suffuses Celan's poetry and the critical literature. Less obvious is that Hölderlin's curious status—that of a radically experimental Romantic lyric poet whose revivification early in the twentieth century gave him new life as a guiding spirit of modernism, a lyric constructivist par excellence who'd grasped that paratactical construction, far from refusing mimesis' semblance-expression, actually constructs new mimetic-expressive, and thus new experiential, capacity (a description that, re-placed into the direst and most desperate of contexts, likewise describes Celan's art)—already stands as one of the foundation stones of modernism's own self-conception as a radical reinvention or continuation of Romanticism. One thereby eventually arrives—or should—at the curious and curiously undiscussed question of whether Celan's poetry is itself still modernist.

We'll return to this consideration, but suffice it to say here that with a crucial and by no means determinist or simply oppositional twist, Celan devastatingly reimagines rather than eschews the richest of Romantic-modernist meditations on and enactments of how lyric poetry, and aesthetic experience more generally, spark a sensing of *life*; of generative, living form; of the critical sensing of an expressivist-constructivist agency synonymous with dynamic artistic-aesthetic form, synonymous with imaginative, forming activity. Such meditations will hold even, and especially, for the incomparably grim limit-cases of life, of nonlife as life, that Celan's poetry engages. Celan's work suggests, moreover, how poetic form's abilities to configure or constellate an in-motion structure or force-field composed from the very materials of our understanding-experience of life, reality, recent sociopolitical catastrophes, and what's taken place in their various aftermaths, and of lyric modality, can allow us to tell the time—or tell some missing times—of the histories demanding our attention.

For reasons that will emerge more fully in what follows, postwar American poetry's remove from this drama's ostensible main (German, European) stage will carry its own special charge. For the moment it's enough to observe that American poetry's role will prove less a parallel with, than another chapter in and extension of, Celanian literary history, even as American poetry likewise finds itself becoming a crucial testing ground for the reception and activation of Frankfurt School aesthetics and critical theory (for situational reasons that Adorno and his colleagues had imagined might well obtain). Like some of its European and Latin American contemporaries, American poetry after 1945 often seeks to hold on to modernist achievements while reaching back to various Romantic practices and theories. From at least Ginsberg and other Beat poets onward, it cannot be gainsaid how crucial the Romantic currents within but unacknowledged by modernism become to American poetry's fraught attempts to come to artistic terms with the Holocaust. (The generally unremarked double strangeness of William Carlos Williams's famous introduction to *Howl* bears noting as an example of how perplexed even the best-intentioned or most astute figures in American poetry could be when confronted with this unprecedented donnée: Williams's introduction offers not a word about poetic form, be it line, meter, image, diction, or anything else; but Williams does see fit, in focusing on the poet's personal experience, amazingly if not bizarrely to equate Ginsberg's experiences with the experience of those who'd just survived Hitler's concentration camps.)[3] Indeed, a more general effort freshly to see and hear the Romantic poetics and the Romanticism-conceived notion of reflective critical agency (itself perhaps just another way of saying life, organic form, or expressivist-constructivist form) inside what was formally revolutionary in Poundian modernism (despite Pound's, Eliot's, and others' denials of the Romantic sources) is central to those tendencies within the postwar poetry and criticism seeking to retain yet reorient attractive legacies of modernist experimentalism.

But of course this experimental art and criticism proceeds with an especially acute awareness of why the defeat of Nazi Germany should occasion an ever more urgent reconsideration of aspects of modernism—aspects at one with modernism's anti-Romantic, antidemocratic strains—that had once seemed to make critical agency, if not reflection itself, beside the point. (We need only remember Eliot's and related salvos against the Hamletian sublime, their dire warnings about the sociopolitical dangers of aesthetically sparked interpretation altogether.)[4] Postwar experimental poetry thus consciously involves itself in a terrible, unavoidable irony: The reconsideration of and recommitment to critical aesthetic reflection—to mimesis's or semblance's enactment of living form—is brought to bear on an unprecedented mass destruction in and of real life, brought to bear on the calculated, systematized elimination of millions of *lives*. Though certainly cognizant of the special—and here specially charged—resources that German poetry, poetics, and aesthetics (from *Naturphilosophie* onward) hold for thinking about this compound question of life and critical reflection, American later-modernist poets quite understandably tend, after World War II, rather to emphasize their recourse to and rethinking of the English-language poetry whose literary and social histories lie sedimented within the formal donées of the very art these postwar Americans are in the process of making. In this light, but with an intentionally internationalist twist, they return especially to Whitman's extensions of Emersonian transcendentalism and to the British Romanticism informing Emersonianism. The result appears as a collectively composed, militant though extraordinarily pained tone poem configured to stretch at least from Percy Shelley's 1821 protest against early industrialism's suppression of "the poetry of life" to Muriel Rukeyser's revivifying intent to underscore, if not transpose, that poetry's music, ethics, and politics when she answers an incomparably blood-soaked era's death message with *The Life of Poetry* (1949).[5]

Near the far end, if not already the afterlife, of this history come Celan's poetry and Adorno's critical meditations. I try in what follows to do justice to the particularity of each, to their work in their lifetime and after, by undertaking sustained engagement with some other very well-known particulars whose poetry and criticism exist in urgent dialogue with Celan, Adorno, and their cohort, focusing above all on the American postwar poet notorious for "saving" experimental modernist poetry exactly by means of an unabashed yet rigorous tracing, and a subtle rewriting and refunctioning, of the Romantic roots of modernist poetic, and especially lyric, practice in an effort to have life make real contact with especially recalcitrant aspects of the historical, to make otherwise missing histories live after, or at least live in and as, their apparent disappearance.

It's not unheard of, but neither is it exactly common for a challenging, much-recited, and often orally discussed poem by a significant and influential poet to have received virtually no published commentary, particularly when many of that poet's works have been treated in articles and books, and where there are abundant testimonies concerning the poem's influence on poets and critics alike. Because the very title of the 1976 or 1977 Robert Duncan poem in question signals a concern with some of the great sociopolitical and ethical—and, finally, historical—questions engaged by later twentieth-century American poetry and culture, it might be tempting to explain the absence of published commentary via some version of a repressed or semi-subterranean political unconscious. But that would probably mislead us, for among the intriguing features of this poem's circulation and reception histories appears to be—including most recently, in the months just after September 11, 2001, and then again at the beginning of and throughout the Iraq War—a rather widespread awareness of the stakes and issues the poem calls forth; and this may in turn suggest that the poem's lately renewed reception, by poets and by some critics, hints at relations rather different from those most frequently articulated, in these last few decades, among aesthetic form or Romantic and modernist formalism and the generally competing counternotions of politico-ethical *engagement*, or of the political unconscious itself. In short, we may here be encountering an object lesson in how hastily applied notions of a political unconscious actually intensifies formal-historical suppression and forgetting. At any rate, what perhaps instead underlies the three-decades' absence of published commentary is a daunting sense that so *much* is involved in this poem that its political-ethical enunciations or mappings might take forever; that there might also be sidestories and backstories whose narrative events are perhaps not well enough known or even available for reconstruction; and finally, the overwhelming sense that, formally and stylistically, this poem's resolute, almost unleavened abstraction can feel strange, off-putting, so that the poem can be and often is mentioned as a rigorous though unsatisfying experiment. (It's apparently been deemed unsatisfying because its level of abstraction and emphatic recourse to philosophical diction far surpass even that of the Duncan poems where formalist aesthetic abstraction, while a crucial element, nonetheless tends to be constructed, apparently unlike the poem at hand, in tension with concrete imagery and at least semigraspable allusiveness, as well as with familiar or semifamiliar historical and mythological materials—the sort of *constellating* that Duncan felt he'd learned from Ezra Pound and, with far more openness to modernism's Romantic legacies, from Charles Olson and, especially, H.D. [Hilda Doolittle]).[6]

Here's the poem, which Duncan wrote sometime in '76 or '77, possibly in his San Francisco home but probably in Paris during an extended working visit; the poem subsequently appeared in his book *Ground Work: Before the War*, published four years before his 1988 death.

A SONG FROM THE STRUCTURES OF RIME RINGING
AS THE POET PAUL CELAN SINGS :

Something has wreckt the world I am in

I think   I have wreckt
    the world I am in.
It is beautiful.   From my wreckage
this world   returns
to restore me,   overcomes its identity in me.

> Nothing has wreckt the world I am in.
>   It is nothing
> in the world that has
>   workt   this
> wreckage of me   or my "world" I mean
>
> the possibility of no thing so
>   being there.
>
> It is totally untranslatable.
>
> Something is there that is it.   Must
>   be   nothing ultimately   no
> thing.   In the formula derived
>   as I go
> the something is   Nothing   I know
> obscured in the proposition of No-thingness.
>
>   It is Nothing that has
> wreckt the world I am in so that it is
>   beautiful,   Nothing in me
>
>   being
> beyond the world I am in
>   something
> in the world longs for
>
>   nothing there.[7]

Without the words "Paul Celan" in its title, this would be a very different poem: an arresting or—depending on one's judgment—not so arresting attempt to enact once more, on the far side of late modernism, a Romanticism-derived interweaving of familiar dramatic, generative, destructive, and reconstructive encounters among world, self or subject, thingness or objectness. It would appear to be an exploration of the alternately animating and abjecting experience of consciousness; a meditation on the potentially transformative character of the aesthetic or the beautiful; and, ultimately, a whole lot of nothing—no *thing, nothingness,* the blank or nothing status of so-called nonobjective, nonconceptual thought, and so forth (with these blanks threatening, at moments in the poem, to seem as if they'd been written on flowing banners of ribbon meant to be manipulated elegantly though parodically by fugitive stagehands from either the Reduced Hegel Company or its crosstown rival, the High Diggers).

Yet the ear, eye, and rest of the body register genuine poetic technique, feeling, and structure, starting with the poem's circular, seemingly unending lyric movement of undoing, negating, redoing. One hears the allusions to, the resonances and rewritings of, poetry's own history, working backward from the final line's play on the final line of Wallace Stevens's "The Snowman" (with its "Nothing that is not there and the nothing that is"), tracing back further still toward the negatively capable Nobodies and Nothings in Dickinson, Keats, Shakespeare, and too many more to count. Those nothings and zeros or cipher-spaces or estranged numberings start to bring other registers of poetic structure and experience into focus. There's a hint of Duncan's trying out the sort of metrical and rhythmic play with number and form more typical of his friend the Objectivist poet Louis Zukofsky, for Duncan has given this poem twenty-eight lines and, as often for him, an almost but not quite identifiable pattern of rhythm and rhyme, where the point is rather to invoke teasingly and then let dissolve the suggestions of established metrics, sound likenesses, forms, and genres—here with suggestions of a fugitive rhyme scheme, of a double sonnet, of there possibly being two octets, two sestets, two *volta*s (though just where, or just before, a doubled *volta* might be marked, we encounter the at once decisive and ambiguous line "It is totally untranslatable"). As it happens, sound affinity, word and phrase repetition with more and less difference, and bare-bones homonymic rhyme ("*n-o*" and "*k-n-o-w*," for instance) do much of the poem's texture work.

But these formal features fall quite literally under the sign of the Romanian-born Celan, whose German-language poetry, inextricable from the experience of the Holocaust and its aftermaths, Duncan had been reading for some time. (And "Celan" in the poem's title begins, on reflection, to amplify linked sound allusions the reader might have dimly begun to sense on first encounter, linkages the poem itself appears to hear as being conjoined with the other internalized poetic histories of nothing: namely, the nobodies and no ones and nothings in Celan's own poetry; in, for instance, the well-known "Psalm.")[8] Like other veterans of the Black Mountain College experimental arts scene and kindred communities, Duncan had known the 1950s and 1960s translations of Celan by poet-translators Cid Corman and Jerome Rothenberg, the signal events being, for Duncan, the 1959 publication of Rothenberg's Celan translations in Rothenberg's journal *Poems from the Floating World* and in the Rothenberg-edited City Lights Pocket Poets anthology *New Young German Poets*.[9] But it seems to have been a sustained reading and rereading in the early-mid 1970s of Celan both in German and in translation—especially in Michael Hamburger's 1972 facing-page German and English *Selected Poems of Paul Celan* (and possibly also in Joachim Neugroschel's 1971 likewise facing-page *Speech-Grille, and Selected Poems*)—that simply knocked Duncan out.[10] Amid all that reading, Duncan accepted the 1977 invitation from a group of French poets to come to Paris. A number of these French poets had known, worked with, and in some cases translated Celan (and had been translated by him) during the postwar decades that he lived and worked in Paris (until his 1970 suicide), and they had long been avid readers of Duncan as well. It appears that this living with Celan's poetry, combined with the anticipation or experience of being around a number of Celan's French colleagues (including the poets Jacques Roubaud, Jean Daive, Claude Royet-Journoud,

Anne-Marie Albiach, Emmanuel Hocquard, and Raquel Levy) provided the stimulus for Duncan to compose the poem.

Duncan's Celan poem was first published in Paris in 1977 by Hocquard and Levy's Orange Export Ltd. in an English-language edition of, per Duncan's request, nine rectangular palm-sized copies, for which Duncan had also requested, without further explanation, that these minipamphlets or chapbooks of the single poem be no fewer than three and no more than five pages in length, and that no page have fewer than two, nor more than eight lines.[11] Seven years later the poem appeared in a more standard manner—that is, across a single page—in *Ground Work: Before the War*. Duncan begins *Ground Work* with an important preface on prosody, "Some Notes on Notation." Carrying evident significance for Duncan's thinking about Celan in relation to how poetry jointly composes soundings and mutenesses, and how such composing works finally to create the poem's experience of time (and thus, formally, a key aspect of poetry's relation to historical experience), the preface emphasizes that the volume's poems all work with various silences, with "[s]ignificant pauses for the syncopation of suspense or arrest," including "caesuras as definite parts of the articulation of the line, with turnings at the end of the verse, with intervals of silence in the measures between stanzas," so that caesura-spaces make "[s]ilences themselves [into] phrases, units in the measure, charged with meaning." The poem threads these charged, silence-filled measures into "[t]he cadence of the verse" in relation to "the dance of [the] physical body." These various pauses, suspensions, arrests—these caesurae—will have everything to do with the effort to convey history's arrests, pause-interruptions, its own caesuras. And, simultaneously, they will signal the effort to pry open a place in time—the stop-time space of the poem—in which the materials of what did happen, or what could have happened differently, can be replayed, reanimated, reconfigured.

Duncan's emphasis on prosodic measure and poetic form more generally thus begins to ask that we grasp these as at every point constituting a structure and phenomenology of historical silences and of what was silenced in them: "The caesura space becomes not just an articulation of phrasings but a phrase itself of silence. Space between stanzas becomes a stanza-verse of silence: in which the beat continues"; "silence itself is sounded, a significant or meaningful absence, its semiotic value contributing to and derived from our apprehension of the field of the poem it belongs to." In some poems, specific, even visually identifiable techniques derived from other poets participate in this silence-construction: "The space-period-space [" . "] taken over from the later poetry of William Carlos Williams, at first undefined, now means ... a sounded silence, followed by the period in which the beat stops, and out of that cessation the beginning of the beat again." Finally, while initially for the reader the "literal time of the poem is experienced as given, even as the literal size of a painter's canvas is given," among the poem's effects is the reader's awareness of the construction of temporality itself—and of what would fill any particular historical temporality—for ultimately, "[w]hat is advanced in the process of the poem is the configuration of ... given time."[12]

Duncan proceeds to say a good deal more about prosody; the meditations reflect decades of work toward a music able to do justice to the social history and ethical commitments inside of, summoned, or kindled by his poetry. Of particular importance to Duncan are what his letters and essays identify as Wordsworthian and Emersonian notions about the philosophical and aesthetic courting of experience and, indeed, an especially Emersonian admission of or even insistence upon the grounding of open, process-focused experience in the encounter with grief. To that sort of overarching philosophical sense (which he often traces through not only Wordsworth and Emerson but also William James, John Dewey, Alfred North Whitehead, and beyond), Duncan brings specific lessons in poetic form and style, based partly in Dickinson's genius for compression and Whitman's opposite impulse of expansion.[13]

All this side and background information is important not so much for sourcing as for an understanding that Duncan himself appears to have regarded such context, in the act of writing "A Song from the Structures of Rime Ringing As the Poet Paul Celan Sings," as preparatory for what poets like Michael Palmer have called one of Duncan's "masterpiece[s] of elegy and negative lyricism," though who and what are being elegized is no small question.[14] Suffice it to say for the moment that, rather than stepping into the place of Celan, or of others who directly experienced the National Socialist genocide, Duncan's poem works toward discovering what it means for American poetry and culture, in their remove but also their connectedness, to participate in attempts to generate reflective experience of, and in, the Holocaust's aftermath. The poem's title already starts to tell as much; this "Song from the Structures of Rime" (bringing within the poem's title the larger *Structures of Rime* sequence) is "ringing"—chiming—rather than equally "singing" "As the Poet Paul Celan Sings." *As* vibrates with multiple meanings that seem to fuse: *like* the poet Paul Celan; but also, *while* the poet Paul Celan sings, so that in Duncan's poem the fundamental gestural-dynamic of the aesthetic's necessarily metaphorical *as if* transforms itself into what is, in line with the givens of the poem's presumptive true fictions, a literalization accomplished when *as* transforms itself into temporality. The poem is now felt to intervene in and reopen time, and therefore history's medium, in the very act of echoing, citing, and alluding to Celan's song. We'll return to this point later, but it's worth pausing here to remark Duncan's suggestion that not only social but likewise artistic-aesthetic history is being reanimated, an action that renews with an at-first barely noticeable sting the question of there having been an unacknowledged—in direct proportion to its having been an inconceivably murderous—caesura in modernism, and whether the very ability to ask or raise the question is itself somehow modernist.

The *Structures of Rime* was one of several open-ended sequences or series—including the *Passages*—that Duncan began in the 1950s as part of what he conceived, in dialogue with Charles Olson, Robert Creeley, Denise Levertov, and others as an open-form and composition-by-field poetics. These sequences worked their way through various of Duncan's books across three decades, ceasing only with the poet's 1988 death. Duncan spelled "rime" archaically, and throughout the *Structures of Rime* he appears to have Coleridge and other eighteenth- and nineteenth-century poets in mind for their play on the poetic and scientific meanings of the word. We're evidently meant to encounter rhyme poetically as sound-likeness and as synonym for the poem or for poetic form per se, but also to engage "r-i-m-e" scientifically yet still also obviously poetically, as another term for hoarfrost or for condensation as it approaches the condition *of* frost. Hence, the temporary solidity assumed by water eventually dissolves back into fluid, literally to become physically ungraspable substance-as-movement-or-process, but whose movement continues to carry with it charged notions of poetic and aesthetic structure, concretization, dissolution and condensation, and sequence. The activity of apprehending these metaphorics—of grasping that the figures when artfully and convincingly constellated get at a meaning partly already in nature or in scientific understanding themselves—is for Duncan an almost direct inheritance of Romanticism's (perhaps, above all, Coleridge's and Shelley's) articulations of organic form and its construction of reflective-critical agency, all of which Duncan comes to call "organic-constructivist form."[15]

Poets from Robert Creeley and Denise Levertov to Thom Gunn have noted some of the ways that *Structures of Rime* takes off from Rimbaud's *Les illuminations*, particularly in the formal admixture of verse and prose poem. It might be added that Blake's *The Marriage of Heaven and Hell* seemed also to Duncan to have shown the way, and one might go on to stress Duncan's interest in bringing that Blakean or especially Rimbaudian admixture, in heightened degree, into individual poems themselves (rather than primarily staging this tension between the differentiated verse and prose-poem moments within the overall, predominantly prose-poem, sequence), so that something like movement in and out of different forms or structures of water can be enacted—within the moments of a particular poem—as movement in and out of verse or prose. But Duncan writes this Celan-poem entirely in verse—a relatively rare occurrence within the larger *Structures of Rime*.

It's conventional, even something of a cliché, to say that modern notions of artistic and aesthetic beauty have often left prettiness far behind in order to enunciate the beautiful as being synonymous with the true—at times, as synonymous with the true pain and suffering of specific historical instances of *Being* (as Celan often puts it in partial borrowings from Heidegger, and as Duncan puts it in homage to Celan, Heidegger, and others). And as this essay began by observing, when that's the territory at issue and the discussion assumes a 1945-and-after frame of reference for art and culture in general, and for poetry in particular, the acknowledged or unacknowledged bull in the china shop almost always goes by the name Theodor Wiesengrund Adorno. The usually difficult, sometimes poignant interactions, communications, misunderstandings and tentative apologies between Adorno and postwar German-language poets—Celan above all—hardly needs recapitulation here.[16] Somewhat less known are the echoes outside the German-speaking countries; it is neither accidental nor sarcastically intended when, for example, Antonioni, in his 1961 film *La Notte*, has Marcello Mastroianni and Jeanne Moreau walk grimly into the Milan hospital room of their terminally ill friend—a fellow writer—and try to comfort their dying comrade with words of decidedly postwar reassurance about the value of the doomed patient's just-published essay: his essay, that is, on Adorno.[17]

However much one might expect the United States to have been far removed from such reverberations, things didn't work out quite that way. On the contrary, and for reasons that seem interestingly to have been anticipated by Adorno and various of his Frankfurt colleagues, American poets and critics have in great numbers weighed in, since its 1967 translation, on that 1949 Adorno essay that had offered the first of what, through the decades, would become the various formulations, reformulations, semiretractions, and all-around worryings about *Lyrik nach Auschwitz*, about the alleged barbarism and impossibility of writing a poem after 1945.[18] For his part, Duncan had his Adorno and Benjamin mediated for him largely via the Frankfurt critic who probably more than any other undertook the task of translating Frankfurt aesthetics and critical theory into American oppositional culture and vice-versa: Herbert Marcuse. Some of this mediation occurred through Marcuse's and Duncan's mutual friendship with Norman O. Brown—though Duncan found himself less than pleased when his poetry became an exhibit in an amiable if finally not very enlightening public dispute between Brown and Marcuse about contemporary art's ability to critique commodity culture. And it seems Duncan may have indeed appreciated Marcuse's vociferous defense of Adorno's thoughts about post-1945 poetry, which Marcuse chose to conjoin with his own little-read (and less than generous) analyses of the formal and social weakness, and of the related literary, cultural, and political self-delusions, as Marcuse initially saw them, of Beat and adjacent countercultural or Left poetry.[19] And Duncan seems likewise to have much appreciated Marcuse's vociferous defenses of Adorno's thoughts about the extraordinary challenges facing post-1945 poetry.

Duncan appears also to find sympathetic the way Marcuse really becomes an American. At issue, in significant part, is Marcuse's process of linking, though not insisting on the identity of, Jewish and African American culture, from his difficult 1947 interchanges with his former teacher Heidegger to the early 1970s cover photos on *Time* and *Newsweek* of his and Adorno's perhaps most famous former student, Angela Davis.[20] Not the least important link here is to an earlier stage of Duncan's career. In 1944 he had published, in Dwight MacDonald's journal *Politics*, "The Homosexual in Society," an essay that was simultaneously a sociological analysis, a coming out, and a poetics; the essay had been refused publication by the *Nation*.[21] Among the different but partially converging American histories the essay tries to explore by means of philosophical and aesthetic notions of universality and particularity were those of African Americans, Jews, Native Americans, and gay people. In this, Duncan's work converses intriguingly with someone whom a number of those in his circle periodically felt they could hardly avoid reading, and who happens to present a remarkably similar—and similarly given to further imaginings or reinventions of Romanticism—picture of the value of lyric poetry for the groundwork of critique, historical understanding, and the construction of a critical-progressive culture: W. E. B. Du Bois.[22]

The paeans to Emerson, Whitman, and emancipatory traditions in British and German Romanticism are often remembered in discussions of Du Bois's books on John Brown and his writings on education and sociology, but it's less frequently recalled that Du Bois's 1946 text *The World and Africa: An Inquiry into the Part Which Africa has Played in World History* reserves a special place for Emerson's lyric poetry (characterized by Du Bois as a poetry of resistance), and that Emerson will continue to suffuse Du Bois's most radical texts until the latter's 1963 death. The significance of Emerson's 1854 "Second Address on the Fugitive Slave Law" to both Duncan and Du Bois in their notions of critical aesthetic and critical lyric could hardly be overstated. The address, presented to a mass meeting in New York City, was a ringing, enraged denunciation of the prohibition and criminalization of attempts to assist Black people's efforts to free themselves. In ways that were hardly lost on Du Bois and, later, Duncan, Emerson's address begins with an epigraph taken from a then-signal moment in recent lyric history, Robert Browning's poem decrying Wordsworth's capitulation to Toryism, "The Lost Leader" (a poem important to both Duncan and Du Bois). Browning's poem equates the abandonment of the struggle for social justice with the betrayal of lyric form, modern lyric vocation, and a Romanticism-generated revolutionism ("Just for a handful of silver he left us, / Just for a rib-and to stick in his coat— /... / Shakespeare was of us, Milton was for us, / Burns, Shelley, were with us,—they watch from their graves! / He [Wordsworth] alone breaks from the van and the freemen, / —He alone sinks to the rear and the slaves!").[23]

In any case, it's hardly irrelevant that in *The World and Africa*, and then with more focused attention in his 1952 essay "The Negro and the Warsaw Ghetto," Du Bois undertakes a series of analyses attempting to think recent Jewish and African American history together. At some level one can see Du Bois building on certain moments in his and others' previous writings and experience in this area, including a group of Langston Hughes poems very familiar to Du Bois. Though hardly sharing Du Bois's positive view of the Soviet Union and really existing socialism, Duncan nonetheless partakes of much in Du Bois's rubric and methodology in trying to think about universals and particulars in a manner that might keep both terms alive without either term or group itself being made, as a group, the universal under which other related but distinct groups could be subsumed as mere, already determined particulars whose particularity would thus lack significance.[24] The shadowy reality of universals that exist but are not necessarily right there, empirically available, is prominent among the reasons, Duncan insists, that "I read my Emerson dark"—and it belongs to why Duncan believes this darkness is not an imposition on, but inherent in, Emerson.[25] This was in practice the way Du Bois also approached and relied on Emerson, much as the apparent requirements of Du Bois's characteristically upbeat progressivism might not permit the admission in quite these terms. But these *are* terms that help explain the status and vocation of the lyric work that lend Duncan's final book, volume two of *Ground Work* (first published in 1987), its subtitle: *In the Dark*. The darkness evoked is not that of original, inherited, or assimilated sin, but rather the darkness of beginning in, moving in, inhabiting domains of experience and knowledge not yet lit by what is already known. In that sense, darkness, or working in it, is the precondition or first moment *of* new knowledge, of a poetry, a poetic or aesthetic knowing, of life. It is also an Emersonian condition—found most dramatically in Emerson's essay "Experience" itself—based in grief over a loved one's death, a grief that can be known but never really overcome, calling into question critical commonplaces that present linear advancement as Emerson's (and other Romantics') model for progressive development.

Such a view of darkness—not as the dwelling place of evil, but as containing bedrock layers of pain never ultimately transcendable, so that a recurrent provisionality, incompleteness, jaggedness, or fragmentariness will in some ways characterize all subsequent consciousness, experience, life—bears also on why Duncan tells his friend Levertov that he cannot share her enthusiastic response to "Los dictadores están dentro de nosotros" ("The Dictators Are Within Us"), part of a text by the Nicaraguan poet Ernesto Cardenal (later to become Minister of Culture in the Sandinista-led Nicaraguan government of the 1980s). However grateful Duncan may be for Cardenal's Ezra Pound–inspired poetry in general, and for Cardenal's very important editing and translating work on the 1963 *Antologia de la poesia norteamericana* (which had lent a degree of attention previously unknown in Latin America to the work of the poets in and around Duncan's circle), Duncan nevertheless is fundamentally opposed to following Cardenal's ethic of positing our inherent assimilation of evil or oppression in a manner requiring self-cleansing through a metaphoric leaching, homeopathy, or self-critique (not to mention Duncan's opposition to what seems to him the next, radically intended but self-deluding step, whereby art is recruited to help accomplish this already problematically conceived self-ablation). Duncan links his refusal to a profound, militantly formalist, reinvented Romantic-modernist defense of aesthetic value and provisional aesthetic autonomy (over against what he sees as the misguidedness or delusionality of Left artistic-cultural practices that in effect constitute an aesthetic*ization* dressed up as political commitment in the effort to *identify*—to unite in mutual collapse, in the mutual dissolution of their heretofore provisional autonomy—aesthetics and politics, aesthetics and ethics).[26]

Duncan will go so far—in order to contest what he sees as an inevitably determinist (and hostile to organic-constructivist form), aesthetic*ist* identification of poetic or aesthetic activity with substantive ethics—as to insist on the sheerly formal character, illusion-character, mimetic- or semblance-character (*Scheincharakter*) of poetry's and art's presentation of sociohistorical or ethico-political matters. What's projected is certainly not the condoning of what might seem referentially presented, but the mimesis itself, the presentation-for-apprehension, of aspects of objective reality that have been subjectively called forth, including undesirable, even evil, aspects; and it's the same with beauty or goodness, whose semblance-form (whose formal aesthetic mimesis) isn't meant ultimately to be mistaken for substance (or else, Duncan believes, we're in serious, self-delusionary, ethical and political trouble). Again, in intriguing parallels and sometime-crossings with Adorno and the other Frankfurters, Duncan develops, throughout his life in Left politics and experimental modernist poetics, stances notably similar to the Adornian-Frankfurt distinctions between protocritical aesthetic semblance or *illusion* and the ethical or sociopolitical *de*lusion resulting from attempts to overcome mimesis and provisional aesthetic autonomy. Telling how these poetics and aesthetics evolve in Duncan would require book-length treatment. For our present more limited purposes it'll do to show that—while Duncan hardly needs to crib here from Adorno, or from, say, the more familiar (to Duncan)

Marcusean restatements of Adorno's *Aesthetic Theory* (in, for example, Marcuse's late text *The Aesthetic Dimension*)—this *is* an area of significant overlap with the whole poetry after Auschwitz question, and it's an area where the poetry itself starts to indicate why that now sixty-year-old question and its attendant materials was, and continues to be, such a burning, overarching problem for contemporary poetry, the other arts, and criticism. There are numerous points of entry to the life of this afterlife, even after a provisional narrowing of focus to the American scene; yet it happens that the American poetry and poetics emerging from the Vietnam experience becomes a special crucible. Consideration of some key Duncan contributions to the painting of this collective work will shed significant light on the larger picture.[27]

We noted earlier the double strangeness of William Carlos Williams's 1957 introduction to *Howl*, in which Williams had said absolutely nothing about Ginsberg's formal-technical, indeed about his artistic, abilities, while proceeding virtually to equate Ginsberg's experiences with those of the Jewish people under Nazism. What ought now to be added is Williams's earlier insistence to Duncan, in seminal 1947 and 1950 letters—in other words, in correspondence beginning about a decade before *Howl*—that poetry utterly lacks value if its formal power, and above all, the kinetic movement of its lines, doesn't carry the poem:

> ...THE LINES THEMSELVES. The movement of the lines [in the sixteen pages of poems Duncan has sent to Williams] is the same old monotony. It isn't what the words <u>say</u>, it's what the poem <u>makes</u>. Break it up—somehow.[28]

The genesis of this correspondence with Williams crucially involves the fact that the then twenty-eight-year-old Duncan, a young poet attracting attention in the San Francisco Bay Area and also on the East Coast, had already spent eleven years in and out of UC Berkeley, in Philadelphia, in New York, then *back* in Berkeley and San Francisco and, again, sort of in and out of UC Berkeley. The attention directed toward Duncan stems above all from what seems, to keen observers of both his own age and much older, like abilities and understanding in and about poetic art that far outstrip his years.

Something that *really* catches the eyes and ears of those responding to Duncan's poetry, for better but also definitely, he gathers, for worse in their view, is that the young Duncan seems not have heard the very old news that *modernist* means *anti*-Romantic. Duncan's penchant for having Shelley or Blake or Browning in there cheek to jowl with Pound and Williams is, depending on who's reading or listening, disconcerting or magical and in any case intriguing. Why not, then—Duncan thinks—after these last ten or eleven years, after having already visited and spoken with Pound to mixed result, why not send now, in 1947, sixteen pages of his best work to Williams?[29]

Williams in his response letter holds nothing back; he is semi-apologetic that his critique will seem too intense and explains essentially that's he's spared nothing because he thinks Duncan's own aims and evidence of talent demand no less. As the section quoted earlier demonstrates, Williams's basic critique is that Duncan's lines are monotonous. The poems teasingly suggest, in some of their barest words, what Williams considers genuine "modern mood," but those suggestions of mood, Williams notes, dissipate because the lines don't find ways to *become*, in terms of movement itself, the mood aimed at. In short, Williams emphasizes, too much *saying*, not enough *making*—and the more *making* should make more "*variety.*"[30]

There's insight and justice in Williams's analysis, and generosity in his offering it at some length. Three years later, writing to Duncan again, Williams finds quite a transformation, pronouncing himself especially impressed with Duncan's meter; though, Williams adds, Duncan still seems to want to say too much, to put in too much. Instead, Williams urges Duncan to distill it to, or find, or make, the essential beat.³¹ But there's also some sense in which from the start, Williams in these reading of early Duncan perhaps cannot see or hear part of what Duncan wishes to do with what Williams in the 1947 letter deems the language merely of "reminiscence," and the wrong kind at that, a reminiscence of "past manners rather than perceptions." While clearly having much to learn at every point from what Williams says about prosody, one can almost chart Duncan absorbing, from this critique, as much as he can about line and beat and movement but asking himself how those lessons can be integrated into a language that might for Duncan, if not Williams, evoke historical and imaginative-conceptual perception rather than perception of the more immediate kind. It's of no small interest that the difference between the perceptual and the imaginative-conceptual will replay itself decades later in exchanges between Duncan and poets like Levertov, who had a more extensive correspondence with Williams—and who argue, in a manner parallel to Ginsberg, for poetry's immediate political effectivity (over against Duncan's claim that the immediacy of such intended engagement vitiates poetry's unique abilities to construct, and thus to make available for apprehension as content).

Ironically, there's only one poem in those first sixteen pages of 1947 work that Williams likes; in fact, he gives it real praise, and says it's the one he'd keep, presumably meaning that he'd want published. It's "An African Elegy," a poem with much of Duncan himself in it but also with almost impossible to miss echoes of García Lorca. Apparently unbeknownst to Williams, the poem, under its alternate title of "Toward an African Elegy," had been accepted some three years earlier for publication in the *Kenyon Review* by John Crowe Ransom but was then refused after Ransom read or was notified that Duncan's essay "The Homosexual in Society" had appeared in Dwight MacDonald's journal *Politics*. At any rate, one can hear why Williams thought *these* lines moved, and felt their movement constructing the content: "And I see /

all our tortures absolved in the fog, / dispersed in Death's forests, forgotten. I see / all this gentleness like a hound in the water / float upward and outward beyond my dark hand."[32]

In these 1947 and 1950 typewritten letters to Duncan, Williams seems almost anticipatorily to play with his own later use of the space-period-space [" . "]—and also warns Duncan, in the process virtually punning with the typewriter strokes and spacings, not to try to *be* Williams, valuable as Williams's advice on prosody may be. But Duncan famously takes pride in the originality of what he wanted to claim was his utter derivativeness. The dot or period or point was, it turned out, just waiting to seize on Duncan's imagination or to be seized by it.

And it's almost as if Duncan hears Williams too much and too well, and thus outwaits himself, or lets the dot, the period, the point percolate and grow even beyond what it had been in Williams's own prosody, until Duncan can't keep himself from making it genuinely his own. It begins to appear across the pages of Duncan's 1964 volume *Roots and Branches*, and then is not only exponentially more in use and noticeably thickened and blackened in 1968's *Bending the Bow* (much of which had been written in mid-'60s encounter with the daily experience of opposing the war in Vietnam) but also, in that volume's introduction, explicitly theorized in a way that makes prosody enact in brief the aesthetic's or the imagination's stretching past extant, received boundaries or conceptualizations, likewise exploring (as we broached near the start of this essay via *Ground Work*'s "Some Notes on Notation") silence's role within this stretching:

> The immediate event—the phrase within its line, the adjoining pulse in silence, the new phrase—each part is a thing in itself; the junctures not binding but freeing the elements of configuration so that they participate in more than one figure. A sign appears—" . "—a beat syncopating the time at rest; as if there were a stress in silence. [The poet] strives not for a disintegration of syntax but for a complication within syntax,

overlapping structures, so that words are freed, having bounds out of bound.³³

With that backdrop, it's instructive but hardly surprising that Duncan will come to distinguish his work sharply from that of Ginsberg and his cohort. Add to this Duncan's later disgust with Ginsberg's announcement that "[b]eing a junkie in America today is like being a Jew in Nazi Germany," a statement that nonetheless, for Duncan, had the virtue of capturing what he thought deeply wrong with Ginsberg's and related Beat and/or New Left poetics or nonpoetics. Finally, according to Duncan, though those poets certainly possess the talent to do otherwise, the poetic art—what Duncan calls the organic-constructivist poem or organic-constructivist form—is abandoned for a fused programmatic politicization and media stardom, for Left cultural capital rather than for poetry's undetermined explorations, so that the choice is made for afflatus rather than for making, for linguistic posturing or attitudinizing rather than artistic construction of and with silences, caesuras, periods, points.³⁴ While having cultural-political and, to a certain extent, poetic sympathy for *Howl* and related Ginsberg/Beat/Left experiments, Duncan comes to feel that their seeming reliance on Williams-derived practices and theories (of diction, line, syntax, and, above all, distilled clarity) is, at best, superficial. For even before he's published anything with the Williams dot or period, thickened or otherwise, Duncan begins to argue—in notebook meditations, in some essays, and, perhaps most explicitly, in his remarkable correspondence with Levertov—that Beat and Left poetics too often fail to grasp the irreducibly formal activity (and the Romanticism-articulated, still-present-in-modernism, *agency*) from which the militant experimentalism of a Williamsian democratic poetics actually springs. For Duncan, what Ginsberg and the Beats miss—what they are indeed too often *happy* to miss, because of the difficulties and responsibilities involved—is Williams's and the Romantic-modernist tradition's abiding, agency-related sense of *construction*.

In Duncan's eyes, Beat discussions of, for instance, the breath-line frequently devolve into bad-faith or self-deluding notions of "extending," in superficial "tribute," Williams's ways with the demotic, his feel for phrase and line. The claims about extending Williams, above all through the notion of breath units, quickly become, Duncan believes, an excuse for a unit of poetic articulation not at all *constructed* but—often with no small degree of bombast—*advertised* or *announced* by fiat as somehow having been won for feeling and spontaneity, with the additional suggestion that construction has been begun but then subversively or trangressively undone; Duncan bitterly contests the latter point, believing in such undoing but believing also that it would first require the serious imagining and accomplishment of an initial *doing, making, construction*.[35] For Duncan, an expressivity that earns its keep—that's more than individualist blab, however subversively or transgressively intended—emerges within such construction, is indeed constructed by it.

Though Duncan makes recourse to various formal techniques linked to, if not invented by, Williams and other earlier modernists, that dot or period that Duncan will explicitly theorize in the introductory materials to *Bending the Bow* and in *Ground Work*'s "Some Notes on Notation" understandably becomes an at once almost physical or palpable matter and a constructed thing. It thus simultaneously captures, to reiterate, two things Duncan finds lacking or weak in Ginsberg: construction and silence, which start in Duncan to infuse one another. For Duncan—here following Williams and many other moments of radical experiment in prosody and in poetry's engagements with the social—there's no move toward voice and the song that can stem from speech without a genuine stretching toward the rediscovery of silences, provisional though they may be, in contradistinction to modern culture's antireflective dedication to the noise of pure products that drive America and, increasingly, everywhere and everyone else, crazy.[36] The point of the point, Duncan contends, is to be able to find—that is, to construct our "findings" of—caesuras at their various points within the phrase, line, or sentence, but to do so in a manner that allows first the poet and then the reader to see, hear, feel, and understand where he or she has engaged or re-engaged in the necessary and disciplined yet somehow also play-oriented activity of construction (over against "becoming like Ginsberg" or "breathing like Ginsberg," that is, being encouraged to adopt, memorize, emulate, or imitate rather than *make*).

Hence finally the point, dot, or period's silence potentially can come anywhere within the poem, provided the construction justifies itself expressively. In this sense the point, dot, or period's silence serves as a starting (and restarting, and restarting!) "point" of a theory-practice of constructivist lyric that follows and extends Williams in refusing to make poetic art either sheerly lyric (and hence prone to what Duncan sees as an almost formally inevitable narcissism in Beat poetry) or sheerly constructivist (in a manner that Duncan will come to identify with much in 1970s and '80s Language Poetry's versions of Williams). This silence is thus antithetical to subjectivity's (and radical mimesis's) crucial role in contributing to the further construction of the very ability to express human suffering:

> your feet . sound time in me
> . bells ring in other worlds I cannot see .
> I see . imprint in sound . sound in the imprint . where you
>   have been
> . enduring .
> where you have yet to be.[37]

The point of the dot, the point of the period, the point of the point is first and last the always-again-in-process transformational movement of construction-expression, and first and last the interfusion of musicality (or voiced musicality) and silence. Though the Holocaust will by no means be the only history at issue, Duncan's art may have learned so much from the dot or period or point that at certain moments these may no longer have needed to appear for their work to be accomplished; at any rate, Duncan's poetry in this light cannot help but lead one to reflect on the introduction to *Howl*, for Duncan increasingly engages the question of a particular set of inimical-to-Ginsbergianism silences that will comprehend not only the caesura that is the Holocaust but also the continuing sociopolitical meanings of that suspension and its aftermaths, as poetry attempts to become one with what is simultaneously the point and vanishing point of historical experience.

Yet all this stands as something like an achieved view from near the road's end. The more in-the-moment making—and the polemics, intended and not—in practice often appeared to others as *they* had wished to read it, that is, in line with official countercultural stances that were not quite Duncan's. Take one of Duncan's most famous antiwar poems, "Up Rising: Passages 25," a poem written in 1965 that perhaps not so accidentally melds itself to Ginsberg's great precursor Blake while hearing and voicing a decidedly different Blake than the one drafted into Beat poetics:

> Now Johnson would go up to join the great simulacra of men,
>   Hitler and Stalin, to work his fame
>   with planes roaring out from Guam over Asia
> all America become a sea of toiling men
>   stirrd at his will, which would be a bloated thing,
>   drawing from the underbelly of the nation
>   such blood and dreams as swell the idiot psyche
>   out of its courses into an elemental thing
>   until his name stinks with burning meat and heapt honors
> And men wake to see that they are used like things
>   spent in a great potlatch, this Texas barbecue
>   of Asia, Africa, and all the Americas
>   . . . .

> But the mania, the ravening eagle of America
> > as Lawrence saw him "bird of men that are masters,
> > lifting the rabbit-blood of the myriads up into ... "
> > into something terrible, gone beyond bounds, or
> As Blake saw America in figures of fire and blood raging,
> > ... in what image? the ominous roar in the air,
> the omnipotent wings, the all-American boy in the cockpit
> > loosing his flow of napalm, below in the jungles
> > "any life at all or sign of life" his target, drawing now
> > > not with crayons in his secret room
> the burning of homes and the torture of mothers and fathers and
> > children,
> > > their hair a-flame, screaming in agony, but
> in the line of duty, for the might and enduring fame
> > of Johnson, for the victory of American will over its
> victims,
> > > releasing his store of destruction over the enemy,
> in terror and hatred of all communal things, of communion,
> > of communism   •[38]

Duncan here discovers, in ways distinct from anything in Ginsberg and other Beats, how to use Poundian and post-Poundian prosody to develop further a Blakean ability to *rant* with no holds barred and yet simultaneously to build or formally construct every phrase—indeed, nearly every syllable—with a lyric musicality whose starts and stops, shifts, turns, and circlings are little short of remarkable. (This is evident when, late in the text, Duncan's virtuosic, momentary eruption or fall into and then out of prose poem—in a manner at once unsettling and formally justified—prosaically tells of backroom scenes of weapons laboratories and cocktail-party receptions, as the poem's formal dynamics emerge from the poem's own form-process to reveal a constructed ability to apprehend and express the new content itself.)

At least as remarkable will be the way Duncan comes to realize, through the later 1950s and across the '70s and '80s, that to his own utter astonishment poems like "Up Rising" are being treated, including by some poets, as if they've been produced according to a predetermined Left or oppositional schema, program, or platform: in short, by an abiding, predetermined, and, be it said, ethicopolitical *concept*. Of course for Duncan, the power of poems like "Up Rising," the power of most of Blake, the power of poetry, is precisely that it feels like it knows something beyond what's conceptually predetermined or objective, feels subjectively *as if* its new discovery *is* already there, as if already objectively present and conceptualized, needing only to be reached toward, articulated, specified. That means that for the poem, for an imaginative work, *to work*, its discoveries have to move immanently, spontaneously.[39]

Immense frustration, at times bordering on disbelief, that fellow Left poets appeared to ascribe poems like "Up Rising" to a programmatic or deterministic, already-conceptualized poetry-as-politics finally leads Duncan to what for many seemed the most surprising of sources and connections. What occurs next becomes a later twentieth-century American episode in the long contest between Romantic-modernist provisional aesthetic autonomy on one hand, and overt conceptually predetermined political commitment on the other. In a process too intricate to trace here in detail, the reflections ventured in "Up Rising" and kindred Duncan poems—about how the availability of prodigious scientific technical-technological capability, married to a tendency not to question (particularly in wartime) the use of such capacities (linked especially, in the war at issue, to the ongoing decision and then apparent unthinking nondecision to use napalm) begins to hint at what "after Auschwitz" might mean for Americans. It is hardly an accident that just at this time (the early and mid-'60s), in writings, interviews, and perhaps above all in lectures to students, Adorno and other Frankfurt School figures, in accord with artists, critics, philosophers, and activists from other traditions, begin in earnest to develop an explosive argument they'd previously left inchoate or merely suggestive. They contend not that the contemporary wars in Vietnam, Algeria, and elsewhere directly continue Auschwitz, but rather that they cannot be thought—and that what was happening on the ground could not be taking place—absent the Nazi genocide. Hence Adorno, Horkheimer, Marcuse, and others start to formulate the notion of it being impossible—or reprehensible—simply to identify, as one-with-Auschwitz, later ongoing policies of almost automatically enacted mass atrocities, yet of it being equally barbaric to pretend there could somehow be no historical or ethical link with Auschwitz when the later actions indisputably occur not only in the shadow of "that which happened" but also with acute awareness precisely of how whole cultures could initially, and then subsequently, let anything with such a possible logic happen, even partially, again.[40]

"Hitler and Stalin" in that Blake-inspired "Up Rising" had not been meant rhetorically so much as in deep internal or immanent working-through of infernal historical materials. Reflecting on the failure of others to grasp this—not only in his own poems but also in those of other poets, and in the contemporary situation itself—Duncan begins to feel his way toward one of the most weighty reflections on formal-prosodic, cognitive, existential, and, ultimately, historical caesurae known in English-language poetics. And the Romantic, militantly formalist source text can hardly be coincidental. Puzzling through for the nth time the difference between what he on one hand calls "moralizing" (including, and perhaps especially, Left moralizing) in verse or the prose poem, and what he on the other hand believes organic-constructivist poetry really *does* with materials that are themselves shot through or seeking contact with ethical and political experience, Duncan finds himself reaching for Keats, for negative capability, and for the allied notion of "the camelion poet" in contradistinction to what he sees as an inevitably anti-aesthetic and therefore aesthet*icist* identification of poetic or aesthetic activity with substantive, objective-conceptual, ethics or politics.

In what would become a crucial, mutually painful letter to his dear friend the Left-activist poet Levertov, and later followed through in essays and correspondence with others,[41] Duncan again insists on the sheerly formal character or illusion-character or semblance-character (*Scheincharakter*) of poetry's and art's presentation of ethico-political problematics, declaring in a formulation explicitly indebted to Keats that "the poet's role is not to oppose evil but to imagine it." He then continues Keats's Hazlitt-indebted thought (in Keats's letter about "the camelion poet," the companion meditation to the negative capability letter) about taking equal delight in a Iago and an Imogen: "[W]hat," Duncan queries, "if Shakespeare had opposed Iago?" But Duncan almost immediately emphasizes that the defense of this classically Kantian-Keatsian-Romantic (and, one might add among many analogues, Adornian) notion of the critical value of reflective aesthetic experience does not celebrate formal autonomy for its own sake. Rather, focusing on the decidedly nonutopian, let alone nonescapist, side of the aesthetic autonomy coin, Duncan contends that a conceptually predetermined political stance that dictates or guides the poem actually acts to "forestall any imagination of what the system is." In other words, there are probably more, and perhaps worse, aspects of the particular reality at hand than the sociopolitical system itself makes representionally-conceptually available, more than our existing concepts for that reality can adequately represent. This *more* is something the poem can only get to or toward if it can find its way by subjectively feeling itself negatively capable, capable, as Keats suggests, of "being in uncertainties, mysteries, doubts, without any irritable reaching after fact or reason." Duncan's dwelling—amid the ongoing reality of the Vietnam war—in Keatsian negative capability and indeterminate or ambiguous negation and nothingness, a touchstone for Romantic aesthetic agency and modernist impersonality both—will carry him, in just a few years, toward the revisitation of Celan.[42]

The convergences between Duncan's threading through, over several decades, modes of formal and prosodic experimentation taken from Williams and other modernists and fused with reinvented Romantic and modernist notions of critical agency, and the parallel Frankfurt and especially Adornian meditations on post-1945 lyric, on aesthetic experience more generally, and on how the '60s might be grasped as commanding more rather than less urgency in relation to what had seemed like immediately post–World War II questions, can be quickly sketched.

In a July 29, 1965, lecture to his university students, Adorno had noted—in ways paralleling the meditations on "life," experience, and aesthetic activity that for Duncan had been most located in Emerson and the British Romantics—that

> nothing can be even experienced as living if it does not contain a promise of something transcending life. This transcendence therefore is, and at the same time is not—and beyond that contradiction it is no doubt very difficult, and probably impossible, for thought to go.[43]

The related final sections of Adorno's 1966 *Negative Dialectics* reprise this thinking about transcendence but now explicitly unite it with the workings of art, whose illusion-character or semblance-character (*Scheincharakter*) is conceived as almost synonymous with both its status *as* art and its powerful yet merely formal dynamic:

> Art is semblance even at is highest peaks; but its semblance, the irresistible part of it, is given to it by what is not semblance.... Semblance is a promise of nonsemblance.[44]

Art or semblance is for Adorno as for Duncan critical precisely in its formal character of aesthetic *illusion* as opposed to unknowing aesthetic*ist* *de*lusion. In marking itself as illusion and in advertising its illusion-character to its audience, art's acknowledged and foregrounded formal aesthetic illusion signals the interaction and interdependence of, but also the difference between, itself and the world. (Aesthetic*ist* *de*lusion tends toward the collapse of the different identities—often under the pressure of good-faith, radically intended assumptions of the burdens of responsibility for sociopolitical or ethical engagement, for changing the world, as Marx's celebrated Eleventh Thesis on Feuerbach puts it—and can thus contribute unwittingly to an inability to distinguish at all between the artwork and the world from which the artwork stems but is different, a marking of difference that is actually at the heart of Marx's intentions in his frequently misunderstood Eleventh Thesis). Critical aesthetic illusion and its formal dynamic or dialectic of, to paraphrase Benjamin, *charged distance*—of intense engagement and correspondence with, amid full awareness of difference from, the empirical, sociopolitical, and historical Real—thus turns out to be at the heart of the negative dialectic itself. For semblance is, or inheres in, the possibility of a more than already completely determined life, of more than a life reduced to sheer and dwindling mechanistic immediacy, whose grimmest version—the most dramatic version of complete determination—is the genocidal reduction and elimination of particularity on a mass scale. That's to say that some relationship to a provisional transcendence—to a sense of, or to a sense of a capacity for, an experience of existence that exceeds prior determination—is inextricably related to our opportunity to experience semblance, to undergo the combined thought-and-affect thinking of aesthetic form that surprisingly turns out to be *only* form, to be only semblance, for it ultimately reveals itself to lack the determinate substance or objectivity—cognitively speaking, the already determined *concept*—it had initially felt or seemed to possess. Semblance activity of this kind can exfoliate or construct itself into the feeling-experience, subjective by definition (that is, not predeterminable, not already conceptualized, and thus not capable of objective universality) of life that indeed lives. That is of course the guarded hope for change or reversal implied in Adorno's famous epigraphic recourse, as he begins *Minima Moralia: Reflections from Damaged Life*, to Kürnberger's "Life does not live."[45]

The idea that life absent subjectivity's and agency's animating principle of semblance is "damaged life," "life that does not live," is known to Duncan in its German Romantic, nineteenth-century, and modernist instantiations. But again, for Duncan, the almost instinctively reached-for first markers of the modern version of this idea of life, damaged life, and semblance-enacted living form are Wordsworth, Blake, Coleridge, Shelley, and Keats. Like many artists of his generation, Duncan's access to those poets and then to the modernists themselves is to him hardly a sign of class privilege or class-climbing; it signals instead that a great contemporaneous and future-oriented achievement of Romantic and post-Romantic art has been the ability to address and enable audiences composed of decidedly unprivileged people like himself. Consequently, for Duncan and allied poets, as for Du Bois and Adorno and the Frankfurters, the crucial question on this score hardly concerns what is in any case the mere shadow-fight of "high versus low culture." It turns out rather to concern, in a very Kantian-Romantic manner, whether works or phenomena of art and culture can spur a critical-reflective agency that, through what is initially a semblance-experience, stretches past the extant concepts and conceptual boundaries of reigning status-quo society; or whether aesthetic and cultural works will, on the other hand, merely repeat and echo society's reigning concepts.

Duncan's notion of lyric as "ground work" accords substantially with Frankfurt theorizations of aesthetic and lyric experience; as this essay earlier hinted, in Duncan's—and indeed in Du Bois's—view, just about the most ringing pronouncements on these matters are found in Shelley's *Defence of Poetry*.⁴⁶ Lyric stands for Duncan as groundwork not because it is better or nobler or more right-on than other kinds of literature, art, or cultural works, but because of the otherwise unremarkable fact that, as a formal matter, lyric maintains a special relation to the presumptive medium for significantly communicable conceptuality, language. Each art has its unique character; lyric's is to take language, the presumably bottom-line medium of objectivity (in the Frankfurters' and others' philosophical–theoretical vocabulary, of *conceptuality*) and, first, to subjectivize it, affectively to stretch conceptuality's bounds in order to make something that seems formally like a concept but that does something that ordinary, "objective" concepts generally do not do: sing. For lyric song to reach a significant audience, it must then construct its own form of objectivity or coherence, though the logic is that of art—here especially involving poetic art's relation to musicality—rather than strictly mathematical-conceptual logic. Each of the arts has its mode or modes of semblance. In lyric, semblance primarily involves making speech acts appear, feel, as if their very logic has compelled them somehow to burst—naturally, justifiably, as it were—into song, which suddenly seems necessary but certainly hadn't yet felt predetermined, and which in its bursting (in a manner inseparable from pleasure) the formal contours of extant conceptuality allows for a renewed sense of capacity or agency vis-à-vis *materials* that can eventually, postaesthetically, be grasped as sociopolitical or historical or ethical *content* within the newly stretched form or formal capacity. And while the Frankfurters generally resist the idea that the National Socialist genocide was an inevitable outcome of capitalism, they do stress the importance to "that which happened" of the socioeconomic apotheosis of sheer conceptual determinism represented by decades—if not a century or more—of rule by exchange value, under which subjective valuations made in and toward subjective universality (made from a particular subject's feeling that its pleasure could be noncoercively shared with a potentially universal community) are felt to have become, at best, superfluous vis-à-vis major questions of socioeconomic value. The repeated mass experience of this withering of the importance, and then inevitably the experience itself, of spontaneous, play-oriented thought-activity that contributes toward subjectivity and reflective-critical agency thus becomes crucial in various ways to the notion of damaged life, or to the preconditions that lead to mass damage.[47]

Adorno's point really wasn't that poetry shouldn't be written after 1945, but that its very humanness would in some sense require it to be brutal, "barbaric" in dedicating life-giving semblance-experience—the experiencing of dynamic aesthetic, organic-constructivist form itself—to the attempt to convey that all this, and so much more, had been almost entirely disappeared. The point was to convey as well that far too much had been left, in the aftermath or *nach Auschwitz*, not as life-giving, not as living, but as "life that does not live" in a numbed *survival*, a numbed after-living or beyond-living that thus required an ultimate version of artistic-aesthetic being cruel to be kind, a recourse to and further development of songful lyric semblance precisely to render the genocidal elimination of song's life. The brutal or barbaric point demands, not least because of Celan's inextricable connection to these Adorno-associated questions, to be pushed even further.

For perhaps no poetry has faced as intensely and devastatingly the historical *volta* confronting lyric after the National Socialist genocide. Among the matters Celan so acutely sees and incomparably brings to artistic-aesthetic experience ("brings to life") and that he consistently indicates requires a practice—however reinvented in darker tones—of Romantic-modernist agency *to* bring it to life, is this: The act of remembrance, throughout lyric's long history a crucial starting point in making the dead and the lost live on, must in Celan be radically deferred in favor of what initially seems an inexplicable violence the poem itself commits.

The poem, that is, must murder the victims precisely so that they can then be remembered—known for the first time, so to speak—*as* murdered. Though this verges on the old axiom about artworks killing their victim-subjects all over again, it verges there only to establish its crucial difference. The rub is the "killing them all over again"; the poem somehow clarifies that though the *killing* certainly already occurred, its status and meaning as *murder* has to an astonishing degree remained—against the wishes of countless people seeking to come to terms with the event, and hence as if in infernal, perverse accord with the original perpetrators' professed intent—unassimilable. The poetry therefore ruthlessly and as if for the first time brings into being, as the particular murder after particular murder after particular murder it surely was, "that which happened." Whatever remembrance the poem can then with prodigious effort turn toward attempting in semblance to spark in the reader will be, to put it mildly, earned and hard won. The poem's fearlessness—its willingness not only to risk but also to immerse itself brutally or barbarically in a necessary ruthlessness—acts as a self-administered inoculation against the potential ease of familiarity or final comfort that so often attach to consolatory and redemptively oriented art, and indeed to the genuinely humane intent that tends to drive them but that can arrest exactly the corrosive experience Celan's poetry senses has already been suppressed and that needs voiced reconstruction.

Celan grasps that the genocide's vast, totalized, mass-industrial character has more often than not made it seem, in the aftermath, strange or difficult to conceive in terms of *murder*. Murder as a cultural, ethical, and legal concept develops historically to apply to certain kinds of forbidden destruction of *human* life, to unjustifiable *homicide*, the unlawful and usually conscious taking of ineradicably individual, particular lives, even when victims were marked collectively or en masse. This characterization differentiated murder from, among other things, historical practices (understandable or nefarious, as one may view them) of finding mass killings and eliminations of other living beings (nonhuman animals, for example) to be something other than murder. To get back behind the phenomenon wherein the very scale of mass murder starts to make it difficult to apprehend *as* murder, Celan's poems rediscover "the language of the stone"; in their breathtaking formal dance, their deftness and nimbleness and indeed beauty they nonetheless gravely articulate or starkly sing "the thousand darknesses of deathbringing speech"; they transform the nurturant image of milk into a sullied liquid that, with still another recognitional shock-twist, reveals itself as an apostrophic beseeching of the addressee-beloved to imbibe and assimilate what the body would otherwise reject as rotten, spoiled, polluted, as this willingness to take in the address to "black milk" becomes the process of interacting with or provisionally becoming one with—finally, of loving—the poem's beseeching speakers, its suffering subjects: "Gestern / kam einer von ihnen und / tötete dich / zum andern Mal in / meinem Gedicht" (Yesterday / one of them came and / killed you / once more in / my poem).[48]

Apprehending the enormity and singularity of Celan's achievement, Adorno clearly felt—in ways that were contrastively illuminated by his readiness to write about the form-and-content difficulties and virtuosity of Beckett almost on first encounter and to continue doing so for decades thereafter—that a criticism even beginning to do justice to Celan's poetry would assume a responsibility almost as "impossible" and "barbaric," and as barbaric *not* to risk, as the poetry itself. Adorno famously died leaving in his desk the notes toward what by then—1969, the year before Celan's suicide—was evidently about to bear fruit in the writing of the long-intended and certainly long-awaited essay on Celan. Yet it's easy enough to see that a kernel of the imagined essay appears in *Aesthetic Theory*'s "Paralipomena" fragment on Celan as the artistic and sociohistorical apogee of the Baudelairean line most profoundly understood, Adorno emphasizes, by Benjamin. Significantly in terms of the question of lyric and life, the "Paralipomena" fragment starts by threading its way through the poetry, history, and theory constellated in Benjamin's seminal articulation of Baudelaire's imaginative-artistic ability to convey, through aesthetic experience, a particular experience of the loss *of* particular experience itself (and the loss in consequence of a precondition for reflective-critical subjectivity and agency). Adorno begins to suggest how Celan incomparably understands and enacts the ways that lyric poetry's attempts to take the measure of the National Socialist catastrophe raise to the most extreme degree imaginable the fundamental problems Baudelaire delineates for an earlier modernist poetics: how, artistically, to bring experience, particularity, and/or *life* to materials that at their core evince the sociohistorical "withering" or elimination of those phenomena.[49] This too rarely remarked inability of Adorno finally to write the piece on Celan has everything to do with the question of modernism, of whether it has a postwar life or afterlife. For Adorno is in one special and rare way not alone in his predicament concerning how to approach Celan; one might go further and speculate that Adorno's reticence involves an extra charge precisely because of his sense of something that among other critics and commentators hardly registers if it registers at all: Celan's modernism, indeed, his radical—his necessarily barbaric—modernism. For while the critical literature has been happy to talk at length about Celan's modernist sources and sympathies, in practice criticism hasn't even bothered to ask whether he might indeed still be modernist, whether Celan himself might regard modernism as the *only* way to make poetry after 1945. Criticism has tended either entirely to ignore the question and its difficulty, in effect treating Celan as an unnamed Movement of One, or as if he stands just past the end of modernism (though Celan's poetry and prose actually gives little evidence of such a stance). In this way, Celan criticism and poetry criticism more generally—joined here with the even broader phenomenon and overwhelming interest, for the last four decades, in establishing a poetics of *post*modernism characterized especially by the alleged superannuation of aesthetic autonomy and its Romantic-modernist critical agency and subjectivity—strangely recapitulates in criticism the seeming nondiscussion in art itself of modernism's mass murder.[50] That is, what if Celan is grasped—as it in fact should be impossible to *avoid* trying to do—as unique and brilliant but still modernist? It would then be hard to avoid wondering whether the death of modernism—in art and in art's attendant critical literature—stems in significant part from an understandable wish to interrupt brutality and barbarism, the brutality and barbarism that would make poems and other artworks pivot on the murders modernism would perforce symbolically seem to commit all over again in engaging "that which happened." Modernism itself is murdered so that the murderousness it would instance can be sidestepped. It will be among the special contributions of Duncan and American poetry to manifest that their participation from a remove—their *not* being saddled with all the special pathos adhering to Celan and later European poets—helps illuminate the after-modernism question.

The foregoing at any rate helps us see why, nearing the last pages of *Negative Dialectics*, Adorno appears apologetically to shift the question from poetry after Auschwitz to "the question of whether you could go on living after Auschwitz." All too conscious that across three decades his words, not intended to harm anyone, nonetheless—in part due to his own naivete—have caused great pain, he doesn't add what's nonetheless true: The two questions, poetry and life, are to him, as to Celan and, as we'll further see, to Duncan, the same question. They are the same question, that is, so long as *life* is understood to include the experience of an ineradicably intellectual-affective activity, a stimulus to critical agency and subjectivity allowing one to sense, and in semblance to feel the possibility of acting with, a capacity beyond what's already been conceptually determined: a phenomenon that in modernity has tended to be called *aesthetic experience*.[51]

Lyric *song, songfulness,* and *musicality* is, in Duncan's Romantic later modernism as in Celan and in so much Frankfurt School writing, the aesthetic's ground-form or foundational modality and is thus cognate with expressive capacity—with an activated sense of being *alive* in feeling and thought, capable of constructing, exercising, articulating, and developing critical agency—itself. Informed by the strains of poetics and aesthetics discussed earlier, something nonetheless weird and perhaps irritating immediately asserts itself in "A Song from the Structures of Rime Ringing As the Poet Paul Celan Sings." In its apparent withholding of imagery and related concretizations, and its concomitant apotheosis of abstraction, Duncan's poem brilliantly enacts the tensions and questions before us. Engaging its materials and content via lyric's song-semblance, "A Song" paradoxically constructs itself, for all its evidently humane intentions, into and as extreme abstraction, in a manner that in its remoteness finally can seem brutal, if not barbaric. Concrete particulars—specific images of beauty or, for that matter, specific images of just about anything—are suppressed; it is almost unnecessary to add that this abstractionist suppression of imagery and other concrete particulars at once dramatizes and mourns the historically genocidal elimination of human particularity that, via "Celan," is surely among the poem's primary referents. And this emphasis contributes to what initially and for perhaps many readings thereafter disturbs or unsettles the poem's audiences: the text's excessive abstraction can simply seem too much, too one-sided, obsessive, even fanatical. (It may well be that Duncan's elaborate, very specific instructions for the French chapbook edition of the poem was an attempt to balance the scales—or, on the other hand, numerically to heighten the text's abstractionist tension.)

Yet it begins to dawn upon the reader that the poem's commitment to intense formal abstraction works through to the other side of the looking glass, because ultimately this heightened abstraction becomes inseparable from concretion itself. For what, as the canonical axiom of lyric has long (and especially since Romanticism) intoned, is simultaneously more abstract and more concrete than the sensuous but utterly ephemeral, invisible substance of music or musicality? In its homeopathically ruthless suppression of the imagistic or visual, Duncan's poem not only becomes exponentially ideational, intellectual, and philosophical but its very abstractness also turns itself into one large sound-image through Duncan's extraordinary way with the structuring, the sound-building, the architectural casting into musical phrase-units that come to comprise one living sound-form. This sound-image (to return to the governing tension-paradox of concretion and abstraction) is finally the apparent semantic blankness but also literally the concretely felt-and-heard *sound* of both music and, as the poem consistently puts it, "nothing" (for the poem tends toward the enactment of an ultimate sonic palpability of sheer sound that, exactly via such excessive or heightened concretion, seems to move *away* from concretization as it abstracts itself from any fully conceptualized or determined reference or content). This amplified abstraction allows the poem and its audiences to discover anew, but with terribly raised stakes, how lyric at once embodies and distills or disembodies into abstraction both language and music (or musicality).

Duncan's masterful sound-sculpting can be recognized in, for example, the poem's felt-as-spontaneous cadences and precise but apparently unprescribed, not-predetermined metrics, its inescapable, ever so slightly changing repetitions and phrasings made quasi-fugally to thread through, inside, behind, and ahead of one another, which are hauntingly redolent of Celan's probably most celebrated poem, "Todesfuge" ("Deathfugue"). ("Todesfuge" was ultimately rejected by Celan himself because of his perception that the poem had become comforting to those it should have continued to unsettle.) When we recognize that Duncan's stark abstraction has been shaped to be at-one-in-process with a complex, concretized rhythmics and micromelodics (so that what results is the creation of one grand, monumental yet self-dissolving and mobile image of lyric musicality itself, constructed from the interchange of over-insistent, mechanized or steamroller abstraction and fleeting, encased-in-silencing-marble songfulness), then we recognize as well that Duncan has somehow integrated brutality, even barbarism, with beauty and made them sequential or ultimately inseparable in the experiencing of the poem. He thereby reinforces how and why it is that here lyric's song-semblance must capture that which is least evidently beautiful, the materials most sociohistorically and ethically resistant to songful particularization because songful particularization was precisely what had been arrested and abstracted away toward liquidation. The poem packs all of this into the sign "Paul Celan" through the irreducible particularity and, in its own way, the almost-too-painful-to-admit gorgeousness (painful because of the hardly beautiful content this gorgeousness genuinely aims to realize) of the entire text itself, of "A Song." The poem's difficult but haunting song almost blasphemously particularizes the after-experience of history's recent nightmarish attempt to liquidate particularity itself; the blasphemy stems from the artwork's having followed through and enacted the Adornian insight, the Celanian realization, that such creation of particularity, such creation of songful engagement, necessarily risks the purveyance of at least semicomforting untruth. This would be untruth not only in the sense that the memorialization of the dead and their suffering can suggest something redemptive where, as here, redemption is hardly the poet's aim and is questionable in any case. It would also be untruth because the very particularization that is art's play-work of stretching toward undetermined universals (dramatized in lyric as the initial subjectivization/particularization of our medium *par excellence* for already-universalized and determined objectivity, language) here particularizes—voices—precisely those people for whom the truth of historical experience was not only to have been murdered but also to have been "eliminated" in a manner meant to extirpate all traces of individual and collective particularity, of individual and collective voice. In a manner honoring and following but hardly copying Celan, lyric beauty or lyric particularization—raised in Duncan's cultural and temporal remove to an even higher, more forbidding level of stylistic abstraction—nonetheless here concretely enacts or names, in a gesture meant ultimately as loving conjuration-memorialization, a historically mass-scale murder whose very massiveness had tended to abstract its character as the murder of individual after individual after individual after individual, and so on.

To write a poem of ethical and political engagement thus again casts itself as necessarily barbaric. On one level, the assertion that must always appear to be lyric song's definitional assertion—its assertion of musical or songful capacity, of capacity for voice, of the relative freedom and availability of the play-work necessary *for* such voicing—appears brutally insensitive to the victims' experience, to the liquidation *of* their experiences and lives; or worse: in the poem, song kills. In other words, everything modernity has associated with robust subjectivity, and with subjectivity's presumed apotheosis in art's conceptually free or undetermined play-experience (whose effect can be the discovery and naming *of* not yet known or articulable experience), has in fact been incinerated with the incineration of the subjects themselves, in their millions. So the attempt to convey all this *in* poetic-aesthetic subjectivity, *in* lyric poetry's continued experimental construction of particularity, is where not only the poem but also its barbarism, and its historical truth, begins. Lest we miss this binding, Duncan from the get-go cross-threads into the poem's style, mode, and content another register of formal dynamic, namely, the virtuosic handling of the pronominal shifter, its weaving into the song-circulation that makes apparently propositional statements move toward being mere alternative propositional soundings on the way toward perhaps becoming *simply* soundings: "Something has wreckt this world," "I think I have wreckt this world," "Nothing has wreckt this world" "Nothing has wreckt this world I am in," and so forth. Thus the poem's circling movements of song-speculation, the play with different angles of responsibility and relationality and interchange (of self/subject for world, world for self/subject, both for nothing and nothing for both) are—at this most basic yet sophisticated level of form's work—a profound homage to Celan's much-discussed virtuosity with the shifter.

In fact, the homage is startlingly immediate, more so than has been known. No critic has yet discussed it—probably because it was only recently catalogued in Duncan's archive—but Duncan wrote out the one-page manuscript of "A Song from the Structures of Rime Ringing [As] the Poet Paul Celan Sings" on the verso of a one-page, old-fashioned blue-ink mimeographed copy of the German of Celan's "Todesfuge" (fig. 1). It is not known if the copy had been given to Duncan or if he made it himself.[52] Duncan's handwritten text, in black ink, makes up the reverse side of the mimeographed page (fig. 2).[53] Fascinatingly, the manuscript's caret-mark reveals that the words "Paul Celan" are added to the title as a second thought or afterthought.

Duncan had already worked on the *Structures of Rime* across some three decades when he composed "A Song from the Structures of Rime Ringing As the Poet Paul Celan Sings." Throughout that time, he had made a practice of titling each individual poem of the sequence simply by number: "The Structure of Rime I," "The Structure of Rime II," and so on. The only variations were that, at times, the series' title lost the definite article and was written simply as "Structure of Rime," or it was titled in the plural, "The Structures of Rime VI" or "Structures of Rime X"; or a particular book's table of contents would also give the individual poem's first words or first line: "Structure of Rime XX: "The Master of Rime told me ... " But "A Song from the Structures of Rime Ringing As the Poet Paul Celan Sings" marks the first time that a poem within the series is not numbered, that it carries a full title, and that it explicitly mentions "song" (though here it is the absent

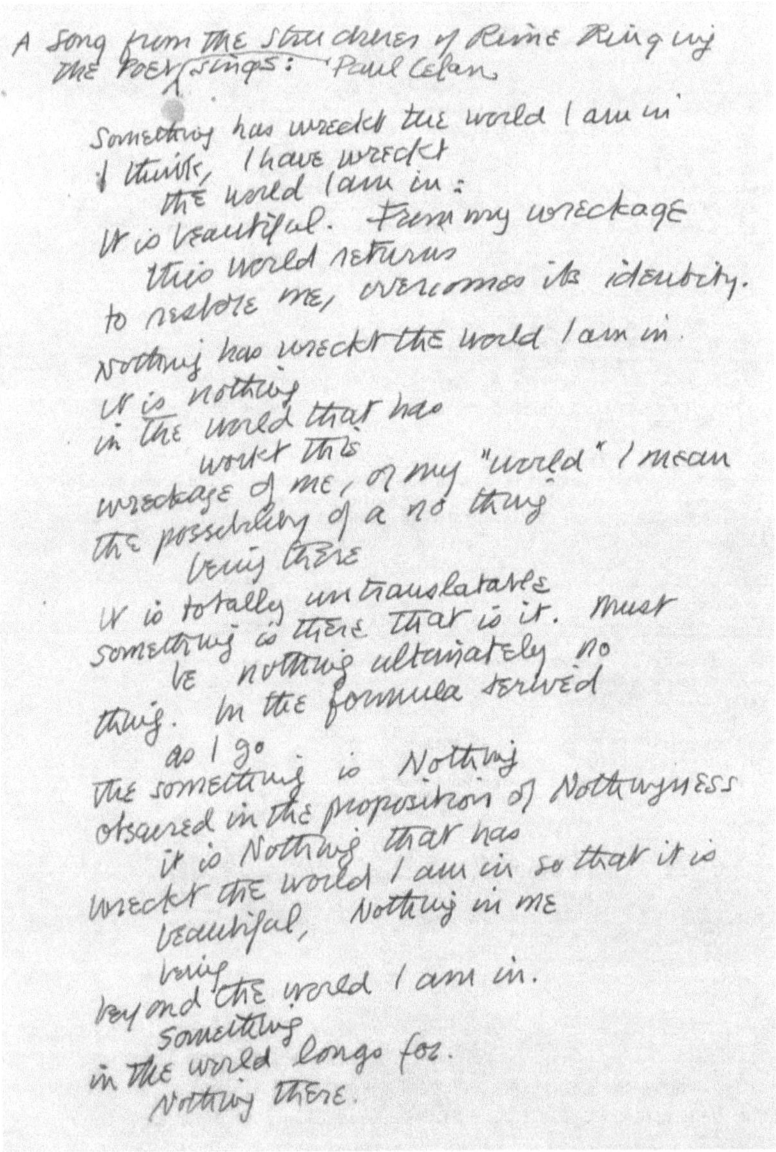

> A Song from the Structures of Rime Ringing
> the Poet sings: Paul Celan
>
> Something has wreckt the world I am in
> I think, I have wreckt
>   the world I am in:
> It is beautiful. From my wreckage
>   this world returns
> to restore me, overcomes its identity.
> Nothing has wreckt the world I am in.
> It is nothing
> in the world that has
>   wreckt this
> wreckage of me, or my "world" I mean
>   the possibility of a no thing
>   being there
> It is totally untranslatable
>   something is there that is it. Must
>   be nothing ultimately no
> thing. In the formula served
>   as I go.
> the something is Nothing
> obscured in the proposition of Nothingness
>   it is Nothing that has
> wreckt the world I am in so that it is
>   beautiful. Nothing in me
>   being
> beyond the world I am in.
>   something
> in the world longs for.
>   Nothing there.

Figure 1. Image of Robert Duncan's undated holograph manuscript of his poem "A Song from the Structures of Rime Ringing As the Poet Paul Celan Sings," Robert Duncan Collection, courtesy of the Poetry Collection, University at Buffalo, the State University of New York. © 2010 by the Jess Collins Trust and reproduced by permission.

Paul Celan

Todesfuge

SCHWARZE Milch der Frühe wir trinken sie abends
wir trinken sie mittags und morgens wir trinken sie nachts
wir trinken und trinken
wir schaufeln ein Grab in den Lüften da liegt man nicht eng
Ein Mann wohnt im Haus der spielt mit den Schlangen der schreibt
der schreibt wenn es dunkelt nach Deutschland dein goldenes Haar Margarete
er schreibt es und tritt vor das Haus und es blitzen die Sterne er pfeift
                          seine Rüden herbei
er pfeift seine Juden hervor läßt schaufeln ein Grab in der Erde
er befiehlt uns spielt auf nun zum Tanz

Schwarze Milch der Frühe wir trinken dich nachts
wir trinken dich morgens und mittags wir trinken dich abends
wir trinken und trinken
Ein Mann wohnt im Haus und spielt mit den Schlangen der schreibt
der schreibt wenn es dunkelt nach Deutschland dein goldenes Haar Margarete
Dein aschenes Haar Sulamith wir schaufeln ein Grab in den Lüften da
                        liegt man nicht eng

Er ruft stecht tiefer ins Erdreich ihr einen ihr andern singet und spielt
er greift nach dem Eisen im Gurt er schwingts seine Augen sind blau
stecht tiefer die Spaten ihr einen ihr andern spielt weiter zum Tanz auf
Schwarze Milch der Frühe wir trinken dich nachts
wir trinken dich mittags und morgens wir trinken dich abends
wir trinken und trinken
ein Mann wohnt im Haus dein goldenes Haar Margarete
dein aschenes Haar Sulamith er spielt mit den Schlangen

Er ruft spielt süßer den Tod der Tod ist ein Meister aus Deutschland
er ruft streicht dunkler die Geigen dann steigt ihr als Rauch in die Luft
dann habt ihr ein Grab in den Wolken da liegt man nicht eng

Schwarze Milch der Frühe wir trinken dich nachts
wir trinken dich mittags der Tod is ein Meister aus Deutschland
wir trinken dich abends und morgens wir trinken und trinken
der Tod ist ein Meister aus Deutschland sein Auge ist blau
er trifft dich mit bleierner Kugel er trifft dich genau
ein Mann wohnt im Haus dein goldenes Haar Margarete
er hetzt seine Rüden auf uns er schenkt uns ein Grab in der Luft
er spielt mit den Schlangen und träumet der Tod ist ein Meister aus
                                        Deutschland

dein goldenes Haar Margarete
dein aschenes Haar Sulamith

Figure 2. Image of Robert Duncan's mimeographed reproduction of Paul Celan's poem "Todesfuge" (Death Fugue), Robert Duncan Collection, courtesy of the Poetry Collection, University at Buffalo, the State University of New York. © 2010 by the Jess Collins Trust and reproduced by permission. German text from Paul Celan, *Mohn und Gedächtnis*, © 1993 Deutsche Verlags-Anstalt, a part of Verlagsgruppe Random House GmbH, Munich, and reproduced by permission.

Celan who sings, while Duncan's poem appears to allow itself only the chiming or echoing role of "ringing").

"A Song from the Structures of Rime Ringing As the Poet Paul Celan Sings" is published, after its 1984 appearance in *Ground Work: Before the War*, twice more before Duncan's death. The poem appears in an anthology published by Emmanuel Hocquard and Raquel Levy (who in 1977 had published the poem's original edition of the nine palm-size chapbook copies). The chapbook and anthology printings added a great deal to Duncan's reception and importance in French poetry, poetics, and aesthetics, where his significance has only grown with the passage of time (so that a very recent and much-discussed French meditation on Kant's ethics begins with three epigraphs: from Benjamin; from the French poet Jean Daive—a friend, colleague, and translator of Celan, who in turn translated Daive's poetry into German; and from Duncan).[54] Then, gravely ill in 1987, Duncan gives permission—through the writer David Levi Strauss—for the poet Benjamin Hollander to include the poem as the inaugural page of a special issue of the journal *Acts* titled "Translating Tradition: Paul Celan in France" that Hollander is editing.[55]

Only three more poems enter *The Structures of Rime* before Duncan's 1988 death; two follow the Celan poem in *Ground Work: Before the War*; they are prose poems and are titled simply by number, though the second also announces that it is written "In Memoriam Wallace Stevens." In *Ground Work II: In the Dark* one last stunning contribution is made to the series, and it makes retrospectively clear that "A Song from the Structures of Rime Ringing As the Poet Paul Celan Sings" had been a final turning point, wherein the series moved into a new level of fully accessed songfulness. It becomes clear too that that turn had been inseparable from the exploration undertaken in "A Song" of how an American poet and American poetry might continue to bring into its fields of formal construction and expression the incomparable artistic achievement and unspeakable sociohistorical and ethical materials of Celan's work, and to find ways to constellate them—to make them feel necessarily, rather than contingently or additively connected—with an American sociocultural history of Emersonian darkness, with Du Boisian presentation of the glory but also the suffering of Africa. These are presumably the materials least amenable to song-making within the whole content-range of twentieth-century poetry and culture, while formally, Celan's extreme difficulty makes it seem as if his might perhaps be, among the great post-1945 poetic oeuvres, the least available to the wide circulation or echoing *of* its hazarded song.

Yet Duncan's unique technical abilities and deep insight tend to demonstrate otherwise, and it is significant that Duncan can and does rely not only on his reading of Celan and the German and French traditions informing Celan but also on a particularly American way of inheriting British Romanticism's allied figurings of voice, agency, reflection, and the like. These abilities enable Duncan, at any rate, to compose "A Song" and, as a result, to go on to write and publish, almost at the end of *Ground Work II: In the Dark*, the astonishing and influential "Structure of Rime: The Five Songs," which will be the concluding song sequence within the series as a whole, a concluding song sequence that Duncan inaugurates with the following notes or prose poem preface, "Of The Five Songs" (while the immediately following "Five Songs" themselves are all in verse):

> Not having found *The Five Songs*, a sound and then an other is sent out to search meaning. But *The Five Songs* is not hidden there. In the sounding alone there is a rumor of *The Five Songs*. They, the Five, are earth, air, fire, and water, and an other. They are four suites—hearts, diamonds, clubs, spades, and another. Spring, summer, fall, winter—four seasons and one other. They are the five vowel-letters and each one is an other.[56]

Among the apparent kinds of otherness that Duncan here imagines, one surely is the otherness—ostensibly other to the determined elements of nature and matter themselves—of human agency, spirit, *anima*. Whatever term is used from among these, its expression for Duncan is, or begins in, song's elemental musical phrasings, which—in Duncan's extensions of Pound's thinking about the undetermined yet still somehow *metrical* modernist experimental practice of poetic "composition by musical phrase"—require the voice of maker and reader to "lead with the vowel tones" (and hence those vowels are themselves—"each one is"—already "an other" in its distinctness).

>   we are
>   almost there   but O,   Dear
>   as I sang then
>
>   I have always been   here
>
>   where you were   I sound my refrain the "Sea"
>   releases, the "heart"
>   in the earliest poem awaited,
>
>   Again I have arrived.
>
>   "Wind" and "Fire"
>   take up the signature
>
>   beyond   naming.[57]

Duncan's commitment to lyric and to our aesthetic experience of it is, explicitly and repeatedly, a reinvented and remodernized American negative-Romantic and modernist commitment to the nothing that is in fact the yet-to-be determined, the yet-to-be-conceived; the perception and engagement of this field as such is the apprehension-construction of it as living form. Following Celan and indeed Adorno in the poetry after Auschwitz imbroglio, Duncan contributes to the making of a poetry after poetry after Auschwitz, and among its effects are the reopening of the question of modernism and its afterlives, perhaps simply its life. The poem in Duncan is the commitment to an imagined and made space of aesthetic illusion or semblance that keeps determination and ethico-political possibility open, *alive*, for exploration, over against the *de*lusion that the poem itself is already an ethical or political act. More severely, the poem is a commitment to the exploration, through a projected illusion-space, of the twentieth century's, if not modernity's, most "wreckt"—because utterly, grimly, determined—world, in which semblance and thus life has, or at least appears to have, no further place. It's no minor thing that "A Song from the Structures of Rime Ringing As the Poet Paul Celan Sings" makes this happen in a trajectory that allows at least a distillation of Romanticism's famously full-throated lyric songfulness to help later twentieth-century American modernist poetry find a way to voice a relation to a devastating historical watershed without presuming to have assimilated or directly identified with the experience itself. "Yet the need in thinking is what makes us think," Adorno writes as the curtain comes down on *Negative Dialectics*. It bears repeating one last time that Duncan's ringing of Celan's song likewise lets us know, in further understanding of what semblance-enactment of living form makes possible, how and why it is that

> beyond the world I am in
>   something
> in the world longs for
>   nothing there.

Endnotes

For their responses to earlier versions of this essay, I am indebted to Tony Cascardi, Norma Cole, Jean Day, Stephen Fredman, Bob Hass, Brenda Hillman, Benjamin Hollander, Chana Kronfeld, Francine Masiello, James Maynard, Michael Palmer, Eric Sundquist, Ross Wilson, and Alex Woloch. Any errors are the author's alone.

[1] Theodor W. Adorno, "Kulturkritik und Gesellschaft" (written 1949; first published in *Soziologische Forschung in unserer Zeit: Leopold von Wiese zum 75. Geburtstag* [1951]; subsequently published in Theodor W. Adorno, *Prismen. Kulturkritik und Gesellschaft* [Berlin, 1955], pp. 7–31), p. 31; the English translation of the essay is Theodor W. Adorno, "Cultural Criticism and Society," in *Prisms*, trans. Samuel and Shierry Weber (1967; reprint, Cambridge, MA, 1981), pp. 17–34, p. 34 (translation emended). The original sentence:

> Kulturkritik findet sich der letzten Stufe der Dialektik von Kultur und Barbarei gegenüber: nach Auschwitz ein Gedicht zu schreiben, ist barbarisch, und das frisst auch die Erkenntnis an, die ausspricht, warum es unmöglich ward, heute Gedichte zu schreiben. (p. 31)

The *Prisms* English translation:

> Cultural criticism finds itself faced with the final stage of the dialectic of culture and barbarism. To write poetry after Auschwitz is barbaric. And this corrodes even the knowledge of why it has become impossible to write poetry today. (p. 34)

[2] Elsewhere I've tried at length to rehearse and interpret the history of what Adorno, Celan, and others did and didn't say, what their criticism or poems did or didn't demonstrate, about poetry, art, culture, and criticism's post-1945 barbarity or impossibility, as well as the overlapping story of partial understandings and pained miscommunications. While necessarily threading modern poetry's history—and key poetry texts—into itself, that account aimed mostly to offer a historical-theoretical view of the relevant poetic-aesthetic, ethical, and critical issues. See Robert Kaufman, "Poetry's Ethics? Theodor Adorno and Robert Duncan on Aesthetic Illusion and Sociopolitical Delusion," *New German Critique* 97 (Winter 2006): pp.73–118.

[3] William Carlos Williams, introduction to Allen Ginsberg, "Howl," originally in *"Howl" and Other Poems* (San Francisco, 1956); reprinted in *"Howl" on Trial: The Battle for Free Expression*, ed. Bill Morgan and Nancy J. Peters (San Francisco, 2006), pp. 19–20.

[4] For discussion of Hamletian poetics in relation to aesthetic experience more generally, and to the question of aesthetic experience's possible relations to sociopolitical analysis and interpretation, see Robert Kaufman, "Negatively Capable Dialectics: Keats, Vendler, Adorno,

and the Theory of the Avant-Garde," *Critical Inquiry* 27, no. 2 (Winter 2001): pp. 354–84, esp. pp. 372–77, and "The Sublime as Super-Genre of the Modern, or, *Hamlet* in Revolution: Caleb Williams and His Problems,"*Studies in Romanticism* 36, no. 4 (Winter 1997): pp. 541–74.

5   See Percy Bysshe Shelley, *A Defence of Poetry*, in *Shelley's Poetry and Prose*, ed. Donald H. Reiman and Sharon B. Powers (New York, 1977); Muriel Rukeyser, *The Life of Poetry*, with a new foreword by Jane Cooper (1949; reprint, Ashfield, MA, 1996); and see Susan Stewart, "What Praise Poems are For," *PMLA* 120, no.1 (2005): pp. 235–45; and see too Denise Gigante, *Life: Organic Form and Romanticism* (New Haven, 2009); on Rukeyser, see the especially illuminating discussion in Susan Schweik, *A Gulf So Deeply Cut: American Women's Poetry of the Second World War* (Madison, 1991).

In what might otherwise prove unjustifiably idiosyncratic use of the terms *organicism, expressivism, constructivism,* and *later modernist,* this essay, while sketching the formal and historical case for such usage, relies largely on what I've tried elsewhere to establish by sustained argument from evidence; the notes point throughout to published versions of the fuller showing. Briefly, I assume here that the work of construction is everywhere present in what Romanticism or Romantic vocabularies in the twentieth century call "organic form," and that this is fully understood by most of those who invoke artistic-aesthetic (as opposed to political) "organicism." By the same token, a significant number of modernist constructivists follow and extend Hölderlin's and other Romantic poets' understanding that expression or mimetic affinity, far from needing to be banished from advanced art, is precisely what experimental construction constructs (or coaxes toward renewal) in the attempt to strengthen capacities for experience, reflective judgment, and critical agency. Finally, *later modernist* in this essay generally refers to poetry of what's usually called the postmodern period. I use *later modernist* descriptively, correctively, and polemically to designate a post-1945 poetry that, for all its departures from the modernist poetry that precedes it, has more in common—in terms of formal dynamics and provisionally autonomous artistic-aesthetic experience, and in terms of militant commitment to lyric genre or modality—with earlier modernism than with what becomes the canonical version of postmodernist poetics. As the essay itself indicates, this later-modernist poetry's conjoined rethinking of Romanticism and modernism has everything to do with its abilities to see past postmodernism, and to allow the apprehension of later-twentieth century histories incapable of being grasped via postmodernist poetics.

6   On Duncan's romantic later modernism more generally, see Michael Palmer, "Robert Duncan and Romantic Synthesis," *American Poet* (Spring 1997), reprinted at http://www.poets.org/viewmedia.php/prmMID/15949, and Robert Kaufman, "Lyric's Constellation, Poetry's

Radical Privilege," *Modernist Cultures* 1, no. 2 (Winter 2005): pp. 209–34, http://www.js-modcult.bham.ac.uk/backissues.asp?issue=22&issue_name=Volume+1%2C+Issue+2+%28Winter+2005%29.

7 See Robert Duncan, *Ground Work: Before the War* (New York, 1984), p. 8. Unless otherwise noted, all further citations to "A Song from the Structures of Rime Ringing As the Poet Paul Celan Sings" and to *Ground Work* are to the recently published book combining *Before the War* with *Ground Work*'s 1988 second volume, *In the Dark*; see Duncan, *Ground Work: Before the War, In the Dark*, intro. Michael Palmer, ed. Robert J. Bertholf and James Maynard (New York, 2006), p. 12.

8 Paul Celan, "Psalm," in *Gesammelte Werke in sieben bänden*, ed. Beda Allemann, Stefan Reichert, and Rolf Bücher (Frankfurt am Main, 2000), 1: p. 225; see too *Poems of Paul Celan*, trans., with an introduction and postscript, Michael Hamburger (1972; reprint, New York, 2002), pp. 152–53:

Psalm

Niemand knetet uns wieder aus Erde und Lehm,
niemand bespricht unsern Staub.
Niemand.

Gelobt seist du, Niemand.
Dir zulieb wollen
wir blühn.
Dir
entgegen.

Ein Nichts
waren wir, sind wir, werden
wir bleiben, blühend:
die Nichts-, die
Niemandsrose.

Mit
dem Griffel seelenhell,
dem Staubfaden himmelswüst,
der Krone rot
vom Purpurwort, das wir sangen
über, o über
dem Dorn.

Psalm

No one moulds us again out of earth and clay,
no one conjures our dust.
No one.

> Praised be your name, no one.
> For your sake
> we shall flower.
> Towards
> you.
>
> A nothing
> we were, are, shall
> remain, flowering:
> the nothing-, the
> no one's rose.
>
> With
> our pistil soul-bright,
> with our stamen heaven-ravaged,
> our corolla red
> with the crimson word which we sang
> over, O over
> the thorn.

9 For a succinct introduction to a good deal of these reading, translation, and reception histories, see Matthew Hofer's excellent "'Between Worlds': W. S. Merwin and Paul Celan," *New German Critique* 91 (Winter, 2004): pp. 101–15. See also *Poems from the Floating World* 1 (1959): pp. 11–12, and *New Young German Poets*, trans. and intro. Jerome Rothenberg (San Francisco, 1959), esp. introduction and pp. 16–24.

10 See Paul Celan, *Speech-Grille, and Selected Poems*, trans. Joachim Neugroschel (New York, 1971), and *Poems of Paul Celan*.

11 For this publication and reception history, I am indebted to May 2005 conversations in Paris with Emmanuel Hocquard and Claude Royet-Journoud and subsequent correspondence with Royet-Journoud.

12 Duncan, "Some Notes on Notation," in *Ground Work*, pp. 3, 4.

13 Duncan seems also in Paris to have for the first time come across Celan's astonishing translations of Dickinson into a German that somehow managed further to compress Dickinson's already incomparably condensed thought; the translations proved so remarkable that they led a number of French poets to begin translating into French Celan's German translations of Dickinson.

14 Palmer's own developing thoughts about the poem, ventured for years in discussions with other poets and critics, have found their way into his introduction to the new edition of *Ground Work*, xii.

15 For some key instances of Duncan's later-modernist rewritings of what are nonetheless still Romanticism-identified notions of organic form—which for Duncan usually means, in practice, Coleridgean notions

before all else—see "Ideas of the Meaning of Form," in *Robert Duncan: A Selected Prose*, ed. Robert J. Bertholf (New York, 1995), pp. 23–37, and two astonishing letters in *The Letters of Robert Duncan and Denise Levertov*, ed. Robert J. Bertholf and Albert Gelpi, intro. Gelpi (Stanford, CA, 2004), pp. 404–8. For a brilliant treatment of the poetics of "rime" and condensation—and adjacent issues—in relation to scientific understanding in the Enlightenment and Romanticism, see Joann Kleinneiur's doctoral dissertation "The Chemical Revolution in British Poetry, 1772–1822" (PhD diss., Stanford University, 2007).

[16] For extended discussion see Kaufman, "Poetry's Ethics?"

[17] See *La Notte* (1961), dir. Michelangelo Antonioni, screenplay Antonioni, Ennio Flaiano, and Tonino Guerra (1961); for the braiding of Adorno with the film's primary, almost immediately projected concerns, see the screenplay text in Michelangelo Antonioni, *Sei film: Le amiche, Il grido, L'avventura, La notte, L'eclisse, Deserto rosso* (Turin, 1964), pp. 304–5, and in *Screenplays of Michelangelo Antonioni: Il grido, L'avventura, La notte, L'eclisse*, trans. Roger J. Moore and others (New York, 1963), pp. 214–15. Antonioni and his collaborators further load the dice by making Mastroianni's character—Giovanni, a novelist—quickly admit that, although he has roundly praised his dying comrade Tommaso's article on Adorno, he's actually only skimmed the piece (and is thus, the audience sees, incapable of thinking and talking meaningfully about it with Tomasso). Tommaso's imminent death and Giovanni's dedication to skimming generate much of what follows in *La Notte*.

[18] For the full passages, contextualizations, examination of what Adorno did and didn't say across three decades about poetry after the Holocaust, and about what it all may have meant, see, again, Kaufman, "Poetry's Ethics?"

Within American poetry, art, and criticism themselves, and to some extent in public liberal and Left American culture more generally, polemics over Adorno's controversial aphorisms have been unceasing, even entering television news magazines' debates centering on Bosnia, Kosovo, and Rwanda. Influential contributions to the discussion have been made by a range of American poets and poet-critics, including recent meditations by Lyn Hejinian, Joan Retallack, Susan Stewart, and Susan Gubar. See Lyn Hejinian, *The Language of Inquiry* (Berkeley, 2000), *passim* and at, e.g., pp. 31–32, 40–58, 89, 147–48, and esp. 318–36; Joan Retallack, *The Poethical Wager* (Berkeley, 2003), *passim* and esp. at pp. 1–62, 88; Susan Gubar, *Poetry After Auschwitz: Remembering What One Never Knew* (Bloomington, IN, 2003), *passim*; and Susan Stewart, "On the Art of the Future," in *The Open Studio: Essays on Art and Aesthetics* (Chicago, 2005), pp. 15–27, 259–60 n. 3, 260 n. 7, citing her earlier *Poetry and the Fate of the Senses* (Chicago, 2002).

[19] See Herbert Marcuse, *Negations: Essays in Critical Theory* (Boston, 1968), p. 245.

20   See the discussion in Kaufman, "Poetry's Ethics?" pp. 84–86, 92–94.

21   See Duncan, "The Homosexual in Society," published originally in Dwight Macdonald's journal *Politics* 1, no. 7 (August 1944); republished in *Robert Duncan: A Selected Prose*, pp. 38–50.

22   On Du Bois's relationship to British Romanticism, see Robert Kaufman, "Intervention and Commitment Forever! Shelley in 1819, Shelley in Brecht, Shelley in Adorno, Shelley in Benjamin," *Romantic Circles Praxis Series* (May 2001), http://www.rc.umd.edu/praxis/interventionist/kaufman/kaufman.html, and "The Madness of George III, by Mary Wollstonecraft," *Studies in Romanticism* 37, no. 1 (Spring 1998): pp. 17–25.

23   Excerpted from Robert Browning, "The Lost Leader," in *Robert Browning's Poetry*, ed. James F. Loucks and Andrew M. Stauffer (New York, 2007), pp. 124–25.

There's a line of concern here that leads to the contemporary poet-critic Nathaniel Mackey's ongoing championing of Duncan's work in various forums, including in the Mackey-edited journal *Hambone*, which has featured not only poets but also other figures in the arts speaking—perhaps most notably the jazz composer and pianist Cecil Taylor—about what Duncan has meant to their work, and to their understandings of lyric's place in African American culture. See, e.g., Nathaniel Mackey, "Gassire's Lute: Robert Duncan's Vietnam War Poems," "Editing *Hambone*," and the plethora of weavings in and out of Duncan's thought in *Paracritical Hinge: Essays, Talks, Notes, Interviews* (Madison, 2005), pp. 71–178, 244–48, and *passim*, and Nathaniel Mackey, "The World-Poem in Microcosm: Robert Duncan's 'The Continent'" and "Uroboros: Robert Duncan's *Dante* and *A Seventeenth Century Suite*," in *Discrepant Engagement: Dissonance, Cross-Culturality, and Experimental Writing* (1993; reprint, Tuscaloosa, 2000), pp. 49–65, 66–103, and *passim*.

24   See W. E. B. Du Bois, "The Negro and the Warsaw Ghetto," *Jewish Life* (May 1952): pp. 14–15, reprinted in *The Oxford W. E. B. Du Bois Reader*, ed. Eric J. Sundquist (New York, 1996), pp. 469–73. It's worth adding that as late as the 1940s, Duncan can think of Lenin as one whose impulses toward an at least kindred and ostensibly noncoercive theory of universals had been muted and then outright eliminated in the Soviet Union's development. That sympathetic, quite Du Boisian image of Lenin still explicitly animates Duncan texts like "The Homosexual in Society."

25   Robert Duncan, "The Self in Postmodern Poetry," in *Fictive Certainties: Essays by Robert Duncan* (New York, 1985), p. 226.

26   See *The Letters of Robert Duncan and Denise Levertov*, pp. 540–46; and *Antologia de la poesía norteamericana*, trans. and ed. Jose Coronel Urtecho and Ernesto Cardenal (Madrid, 1963). See too, for extended discussion of the underlying issues of poetics, aesthetics, ethics, and politics, Kaufman, "Poetry's Ethics?"

27 See Theodor W. Adorno, *Aesthetic Theory*, ed., trans., and with a translator's introduction by Robert Hullot-Kentor (Minneapolis, 1997), *Ästhetische Theorie*, vol. 7 of *Gesammelte Schriften*, ed. Gretel Adorno and Rolf Tiedemann (Frankfurt am Main, 1970–86), and Herbert Marcuse, *Die Permanenz der Kunst: Wider eine bestimmte marxistische Ästhetik* (1977), in vol. 9 of *Schriften* (Frankfurt am Main, 1987), trans. and rev. Herbert Marcuse and Erica Sherover under the title *The Aesthetic Dimension: Toward a Critique of Marxist Aesthetics* (Boston, 1978).

28 William Carlos Williams to Robert Duncan, June 2, 1947 (underlinings in original). My thanks to the Robert Duncan Archive of the Poetry Collection, University at Buffalo, the State University of New York, and to curator James Maynard, as well as to the Estate of Robert Duncan for permission to reprint this passage.

29 Such mixed results included Pound's later, semi-amiable complaints about Duncan's reinvented Romanticism, and, as Duncan will later tell it on various occasions, the anti-Semitic pamphlets so graciously given to Duncan by Mrs. Pound that were, Duncan said, among the most hair-raising things he'd ever seen. See the discussion and citations in Thom Gunn, "Adventrous Song: Robert Duncan as Romantic Modernist," *PN Review* 17, no. 4 (March/April 1991): pp. 14–23.

30 Williams to Duncan, June 2, 1947, Robert Duncan Archive of the Poetry Collection, University at Buffalo, the State University of New York.

31 Williams to Duncan, February 23, 1950, Robert Duncan Archive of the Poetry Collection, University at Buffalo, the State University of New York.

32 From Robert Duncan, "An African Elegy" (written as "Toward an African Elegy," 1942; republished in Robert Duncan, *The Years as Catches* [Berkeley, 1966], pp. 33–35).

33 Robert Duncan, introduction to *Bending the Bow* (New York, 1968), p. ix.

34 For his quotation of and response to Ginsberg's comment, see Duncan's 1959 note-commentary "The Homosexual in Society," pp. 46–47 n. 7.

35 Consider, for example, Duncan's response to Ginsberg's *Howl*-period "Siesta in Xbalba and Return to the States" (1954); first published in *Evergreen Review* 1, no. 2 (1957): pp. 137–47, then published in Allen Ginsberg, *Collected Poems, 1947–1980* (New York, 1984), pp. 97–110. The poem begins:

> Late sun opening the book,
>
> > blank page like light,
>
> invisible words unscrawled,
>
> > impossible syntax
>
> Of apocalypse—

> Uxmal: Noble Ruins
>
> No construction—
>
> > let the mind fall down.

After reading the poem in *Evergreen Review,* Duncan writes to Levertov (May 8, 1958): "Take Ginsberg's 'Howl' or the earlier 'Xbalba' that appeared in *Evergreen*: with the proposition 'NO construction—let the mind fall down.' My sense that there could be a poem is whetted. But then there is no dis-construction in it—only lazy lines, loose talk that gets looser and soon he's asking 'what love in the cafes of God' which is both exalted and gassy"; *The Letters of Robert Duncan and Denise Levertov,* p. 119.

Cf. Duncan's May 25, 1959, comments: "Last Saturday we had a group reading for *Measure*—where Ginsberg read from his 'Kaddish' for his mother—and for the first time I heard him read 'with emotion'; once you grasp that the poem—like 'Howl' is designed in order to wind up an hysterical pitch (at the close of the poem he was shouting like Hitler or an evangelist, so that the audience having risen with him on wave upon wave of momentous lines ROARD). As the seizure of the poem increased, the content became disorderd, then idiotic and finally disappeard. But no wonder it is impossible to attack his work as bad writing—it is almost exactly calculated to be an agency for such a frenzy. And what we see (hear) when it is not used to arrive at the seizure, is like the funny expressions of a face separated from the terrifying fit it is going thru.

"I dislike *using* a poem, and that's the crux of the matter"; *The Letters of Robert Duncan and Denise Levertov,* p. 172 (italics in original).

36 The allusion is to "Spring and All":

> The pure products of America
>
> go crazy—
>
> . . . .
>
> It is only in isolate flecks that
>
> Something
>
> is given off
>
> No one
>
> to witness
>
> and adjust, no one to drive the car

Excerpted from "Spring and All" (1923), Poem 18, in *The Collected Poems of William Carlos Williams,* ed. A. Walton Litz and Christopher MacGowan (New York, 1986), 1: pp. 217–19.

37 Duncan, *Ground Work,* "An Eros/Amor/Love Cycle: 3. Structure of Rime,"

Ground Work: Before the War, In the Dark, p. 223.

[38] From Duncan, "Up Rising: Passages 25"; written 1965, first published under title "Up Rising" in the *Nation* 201 (September 13, 1965): pp. 146–47; subsequently published as part of Robert Duncan, *Passages 22–27: Of the War* (Berkeley, 1966), and in Duncan, *Bending the Bow*, pp. 81–83.

[39] See Duncan's December 16, 1966, comments to Levertov about even a poem like "Up Rising" not being "personal witness" but rather poetic-imaginative: "Even 'Up Rising' is not this kind of witness [wearing a button, talking about war]; for ultimately [what's constructed and then expressed in "Up Rising"] ... belongs to the reality of that poem and a vision of Man. And I do not answer for myself in my work but for Poetry"; *The Letters of Robert Duncan and Denise Levertov*, 563.

[40] See, e.g., Theodor W. Adorno, "Lecture 13" (13 July 1965) and "Lecture 14" (15 July 1965), in *Metaphysics: Concept and Problems* (London, 2000), pp. 101–2, 103–4, 106–9, 177 n. 5, 179 n. 12; Theodor W. Adorno, *Metaphysik: Begriff und Probleme* (Frankfurt, 1998), pp. 159–62, 166, 169–70, 274 n.187, 276–77 n. 195.

[41] Such correspondence included, very significantly, the then-young poet and critic Michael Davidson.

[42] *The Letters of Robert Duncan and Denise Levertov*, 669; John Keats, letter to George and Tom Keats, 21, 27 (?) Dec. 1817 (the "negative capability letter) and letter to Richard Woodhouse, 27 Oct. 1818 (the "camelion poet" letter), in *The Letters of John Keats,* ed. Hyder Edward Rollins, 2 vols. (Cambridge, MA, 1958), 1: pp. 193, 386–87. For extended discussion of Frankfurt and other modernist inheritings of negative capability and the "identitlyless" or "camelion" poet, see Kaufman, "Negatively Capable Dialectics," pp. 354–84.

[43] Adorno, "Lecture Eighteen" (July 29, 1965), in *Metaphysics: Concept and Problems*, pp. 144–45 (italics in original translation); *Metaphysik: Begriff und Probleme*, p. 226 (italics in original German).

[44] Theodor Adorno, *Negative Dialectics*, trans. G. B. Ashton (1966; reprint, New York, 1973), pp. 404–5; *Negative Dialektik* (1966), vol. 6 of Adorno, *Gesammelte Schriften*, pp. 396–97.

[45] Theodor W. Adorno, *Minima Moralia: Reflections from Damaged Life*, trans. E. F. N. Jephcott (London, 1974), 19; *Minima Moralia: Reflexionen aus dem beschädigten Leben* (Frankfurt am Main, 1951), p. 13. Among *Minima Moralia*'s best-known aphoristic reflections are those that play variaions on Kürnberger, including, "Our perspective of life has passed into an ideology which conceals the fact there is life no longer," so that "life has become the ideology of its own absence" (Leben ist zur Ideologie seiner eigenen Absenz geworden; pp. 15–16, 190; 7–8, 252).

[46] See Robert Kaufman, "Legislators of the Post-Everything World: Shelley's

Defence of Adorno," *English Literary History* 63, no. 3 (Fall 1996): pp. 707–33.

47 See Robert Kaufman, "Lyric Commodity Critique, Benjamin Adorno Marx, Baudelaire Baudelaire Baudelaire," *PMLA* 123, no. 1 (January 2008): pp. 207–15. And see Ross Wilson, *Subjective Universality in Kant's Aesthetics* (Oxford, 2007).

48 See Paul Celan, "Todesfuge," in *Gesammelte Werke*, 1: pp. 39–42, "Wolfsbohne," in *Gesammelte Werke* 7: pp. 45-49, and "Ansprache anlässlich der Entgegennahme des Literaturpreises der Freien Hansestadt Bremen," in *Gesammelte Werke*, 3: pp. 185–86; "Death Fugue" and "Wolfs'-Bean" in *Poems of Paul Celan*, pp. 31, 33, 340–45; Paul Celan, "Speech on the Occasion of Receiving the Literature Prize of the Free Hanseatic City of Bremen," in *Collected Prose*, trans. with an introduction by Rosmarie Waldrop (New York, 2003), pp. 33–35 (trans. emended). On the relation of this suffering to lyric expressivity, and on why the formal experimentation necessary to construct such expression becomes part of lyric's content (becomes, in fact, lyric's form-content), see the discussion of Brecht, Michael Palmer, and Frankfurt School aesthetics in Robert Kaufman, "Lyric's Expression: Musicality, Conceptuality, Critical Agency," in *Adorno and Literature*, ed. David Cunningham and Nigel Mapp (London, 2006), pp. 99–16. For a profound consideration of how Celan's poetry must radically re-image and rework nature itself to make the suffering at issue apprehendable, see Rochelle Tobias, *The Discourse of Nature in the Poetry of Paul Celan: The Unnatural World* (Baltimore, 2006).

49 Adorno, *Aesthetic Theory*, pp. 321–22; *Ästhetische Theorie*, pp. 475–77.

50 For a representative example of these tendencies—in this case, assuming and asserting but never really showing that Celan is at most modernism's traumatized swan song, see the otherwise fine discussion of Celan in Ulrich Baer, *Remnants of Song: Trauma and the Experience of Modernity in Charles Baudelaire and Paul Celan* (Stanford, 2000).

51 See Kaufman, "Poetry's Ethics?"

52 I am profoundly indebted to James Maynard, Assistant Curator at the Poetry Collection, University at Buffalo, the State University of New York, which houses the Duncan materials, for bringing to my attention the existence of Duncan's mimeograph of Celan's "Todesfuge" and the verso's holograph of "A Song."

Besides knowing the poem in German, Duncan was also very familiar with Michael Hamburger's translation of Celan's most famous poem, in *Poems of Paul Celan*, 30–33:

Death Fugue

Black milk of daybreak we drink it at sundown
we drink it at noon in the morning we drink it at night

we drink and we drink it
we dig a grave in the breezes there one lies unconfined
A man lives in the house he plays with the serpents he writes
he writes when dusk falls to Germany your golden hair Margarete
he writes it and steps out of doors and the stars are flashing he whistles
    his pack out
he whistles his Jews out in earth has them dig for a grave
he commands us strike up for the dance

Black milk of daybreak we drink you at night
we drink in the morning at noon we drink you at sundown
we drink and we drink you
A man lives in the house he plays with the serpents he writes
he writes when dusk falls to Germany your golden hair Margarete
your ashen hair Shulamith we dig a grave in the breezes there one lies
    unconfined.

He calls out jab deeper into the earth you lot you others sing now and
    play
he grabs at the iron in his belt he waves it his eyes are blue
jab deeper you lot with your spades you others play on for the dance

Black milk of daybreak we drink you at night
we drink you at noon in the morning we drink you at sundown
we drink you and we drink you
a man lives in the house your golden hair Margarete
your ashen hair Shulamith he plays with the serpents
He calls out more sweetly play death death is a master from Germany
he calls out more darkly now stroke your strings then as smoke you will
    rise into air
then a grave you will have in the clouds there one lies unconfined

Black milk of daybreak we drink you at night
we drink you at noon death is a master from Germany
we drink you at sundown and in the morning we drink and we drink you
death is a master from Germany his eyes are blue
he strikes you with leaden bullets his aim is true
a man lives in the house your golden hair Margarete
he sets his pack on to us he grants us a grave in the air
he plays with the serpents and daydreams death is a master from
    Germany

> your golden hair Margarete
> your ashen hair Shulamith

53 As can be seen, Duncan's holograph of the poem fails—as an oversight, or perhaps intentionally—to include the word "As" in the title. However, the poem's typescript does include "As"; see the undated typescript in the Robert Duncan Archive of the Poetry Collection, University at Buffalo, the State University of New York. The typescript also adds some punctuation marks absent from the holograph. Duncan made additional changes—primarily involving spacing, the choice of capital or lowercase letters, and hyphens or dashes within words—for the version of the poem as published in France by Orange Export Ltd. and in *Ground Work* (reproduced earlier in this essay); Duncan also personally proofread and approved both publications.

54 For the French publication of Duncan's poem, see *Orange Export Ltd.: 1969–1986*, ed. Emmanuel Hocquard and Raquel Levy (Paris, 1986), pp. 111–12; as printed in the anthology, the section breaks reproduce the page divisions of the original chapbook's layout. For the epigraphs from Benjamin, Daive, and Duncan, see the opening page in Michèle Cohen-Halimi, *Entendre Raison: essai sur la philosophie pratique de Kant* (Paris, 2004).

55 See "Translating Tradition: Paul Celan in France," ed. Benjamin Hollander, *Acts* 8/9 (1988). The issue features Celan's poetry, translations of it, and work by a number of French and American poets and critics (including John Felstiner's almost moment-by-moment recreation of Celan's astounding, aforementioned translations into German of Emily Dickinson).

56 Duncan, "Structure of Rime: Of the Five Songs," in *Ground Work*, p. 256.

57 Duncan, "Structure of Rime: The Five Songs," *Ground Work*, p. 262.

Credits

The following publishers and individuals have graciously granted permission to include the indicated material in this volume.

Deutsche Verlags-Anstalt: German text of "Todesfuge" by Paul Celan, from *Mohn und Gedächtnis*, © 1993 Deutsche Verlags-Anstalt, a part of Verlaggsgruppe Random House GmbH, Munich,

The Robert Duncan Archive of the Poetry Collection, University at Buffalo, the State University of New York, curator James Maynard, and the Estate of Robert Duncan: Images of Robert Duncan's manuscript poem "A Song from the Structures of Rime Ringing As the Poet Paul Celan Sings" and mimeographed reproduction of Paul Celan's poem "Todesfuge" (Death Fugue), copyright © 2010 by the Jess Collins Trust and reproduced by permission. Passages from William Carlos Williams to Robert Duncan, June 2, 1947, and February 23, 1950, copyright © 2010 by the Estates of Paul H. Williams and William Eric Williams. Used by permission of New Directions Publishing Corp.

S. Fischer Verlag and the heirs of Paul Celan: "Psalm" by Paul Celan, copyright © 1963 by S. Fischer Verlag, Frankfurt am Main.

New Directions Publishing Corp.: "A Song from the Structures of Rime Ringing as the Poet Paul Celan Sings" by Robert Duncan, from *Ground Work: Before the War, In the Dark*, copyright © 1988 by Robert Duncan. Passages from William Carlos Williams to Robert Duncan, June 2, 1947, and February 23, 1950, copyright © 2010 by the Estates of Paul H. Williams and William Eric Williams. Excerpt from the introduction to *Bending the Bow* by Robert Duncan, copyright © 1968 by Robert Duncan. Excerpt from "An Eros/Amor/Love Cycle: 3. Structure of Rime" by Robert Duncan, from *Ground Work: Before the War, In the Dark*, copyright © 1988 by Robert Duncan. Excerpt from "Up Rising: Passages 25" by Robert Duncan, from *Bending the Bow*, copyright © 1968 by Robert Duncan. Excerpts from "Structure of Rime: Of the Five Songs" and "Structure of Rime: The Five Songs" by Robert Duncan, from *Ground Work: Before the War, In the Dark*, copyright © 1988 by Robert Duncan. Excerpt from "Spring and All" by William Carlos Williams, copyright © 2010 by the Estates of Paul H. Williams and William Eric Williams.

Persea Books, Inc.: Translations of "Psalm" and "Death Fugue" by Paul Celan, translations by Michael Hamburger; translation copyright © 2002 by Michael Hamburger.

Routledge, Taylor & Francis Group: Excerpts from an earlier version of this essay, entitled "AfterNach: Life's Posthumous Life in Later-Modernist American Poetry," in Ross Wilson, ed., *The Meaning of "Life" in Romantic Poetry and Poetics* (New York, 2009).

Aleš Erjavec

Aesthetics and the Aesthetic Today: After Adorno

> *What is this instant that is ours?*
> —Michel Foucault

AESTHETICS, AS ADORNO often remarked, has lagged behind developments in art. Since its articulation as a field of inquiry, aesthetics has often been unable to accomplish its aim of offering an explanation, evaluation, or identification of its object, which remains predominantly art. Furthermore, it was often the artists who were suspicious of the role of aesthetics, asking, "Why do you waste your time and mine by trying to get value judgments? Don't you see that when you get a value judgment, that's all you have?"[1] They warned: "The danger to be avoided lies in aesthetic delectation."[2] In brief, for the artists, often the maximum that aesthetics was considered capable of achieving for art was, according to Barnett Newman, what ornithology is for the birds. A similar view is shared by much of philosophy: "The dominant opinion...shows that the glorious sensible presence of art is devoured by a discourse *on* art which tends to become its own reality."[3]

If these views are accurate, why continue to carry out aesthetic analysis except for historical, documentary, and purely intellectual purposes? Adorno himself offered a persuasive answer: "What is essential to art is that which in it is not the case, that which is incommensurable with the empirical measure of all things. The compulsion to aesthetics is the need to think this empirical incommensurability."[4]

In Adorno, the aesthetic theory—as opposed to aesthetics as an academic discipline or division of philosophy and a segment of a philosophical system—is necessary not only because of the desire to know and to reflect but also to have an effect on artistic practice.[5] The philosopher is an authority for practitioners of art and those who contemplate it.[6] As Adorno claims in *Aesthetic Theory*, "Every artwork, if it is to be fully experienced, requires thought and therefore stands in need of philosophy" (*AT*, 262). In this respect he is unlike the analytic aesthetician—but very much like the Dantoesque theorist of art who appears to have achieved the impossible, namely, a conflation of the analytic and the Hegelian lines of reasoning. Adorno in his turn succeeds in bringing together an insightful analysis of high modernist art without succumbing to the temptations of a Hegelian totalizing mindset.

Traditionally, aesthetics targets the gray realm on either side of the borderline of art *qua* art, aims at the object at the dividing line between art and not-art, be it temporally synchronous or historically diachronous, whether what is at issue is the inclusion of a work or a body of works within the changing realm or "class" called art. "Art is no fixed set of boundaries but rather a momentary and fragile balance" (*AT*, 300). The identity of art is determined with the aid of borderline cases that are then included within the parameter of art. What is therefore at stake are borderline cases: instances of works that are candidates for aesthetic and/or artistic appreciation but have not yet attained such status within the current art world. While past art has often met with the designation of not-art or bad art, in contemporary art all such production purportedly falls within the realm of "art." Even more: once a work is admitted into this parameter of "art," with the encircled realm being the institution called art, it may lose its artistic or aesthetic worth, but it hardly ever loses its status as a work of art.

But this is only one side of the coin; on the other side, precisely such borderline cases can be regarded as the *only* authentic cases of art. Jean-François Lyotard introduced the unusual designation of artworks being first "postmodern" and then "modern"—postmodern when they are still outside the parameter of the institution of art and modern when they enter it and lose their nature as "events."[7]

From designations such as Lyotard's (one of whose historical roots being anarchist aesthetics) arises a conflict and a contradiction between works that are already a part of the institution of art, works that are potential candidates for such an inclusion, and works that, by not yet being members of this institution, function as authentic art. A major factor in the development of art is precisely the disagreement over whether something is art or not.[8] On its own terms, this disagreement reveals the conflict between art as a part of the institution of art and art as an event.[9]

In Adorno the "negativity" of art prevents its utopian realization, since this realization would cause its end. In this thought, Adorno distances himself from Schiller in his *Letters on the Aesthetic Education of Man* where the latter claims that if we are to resolve the problem of politics in practice we must approach it through the aesthetic. "It is Schiller's idea that precisely because it renounces all direct intervention in reality, art is suited to restore man's wholeness,"[10] namely, by bringing together the halves of man represented by sensousness and reason. Schiller's view was not isolated, or at least not for long; witness Saint-Simon's 1825 statement about the artists who "will develop the poetic aspect of the new system."[11] The artistic avant-garde is from its historical beginnings linked to its political double, causing—Baudelaire was the first to note[12]—the artistic avant-garde to accept, in spite of its infinite desire for freedom, the militaristic discipline of the political avant-garde. Adorno sees the characteristic feature of avant-garde art in the concept of the "new" rather than in "the intent of the avant-garde movements to reintegrate art in the praxis of life" (*TA*, 87), which, for him, would suffer precisely the consequences of such a discipline.

The notion of the avant-garde is crucial to an understanding and interpretation of modernism in the last two centuries. Adorno also sympathizes with the notion of the avant-garde, but the aspect that would be of interest to him would today more appropriately be called modernist. This aspect is exemplified by the concept of the new and by the dissonance that prevents facile consumption of an authentic artwork in bourgeois society. The radical—the politicized—avant-gardes partly overlap with Adorno's notion of modern art, but in their central features they represent a very different form of artistic dissonance. Their avant-garde aesthetic intent in the culture of the thirties and forties no longer meets with a supportive or indifferent social environment, which is why they cease to be considered worthy of discussion by Adorno. Around World War I their utopian potential is still present, but even then they are subversive not in the artistic manner propounded by Adorno, but in staking out another path of dissonance: that of *aesthetic* militarism. Nevertheless, that their aesthetic procedure is not alien to Adorno can be seen in his frequent remarks on Dadaism, as when he states that hermetic poetry (and that of Mallarmé) converges with its political counterpole, Dada (*AT*, 321).

In the debates preceding postmodernism, the notion of avant-garde art attains a variety of designations, from those that associate the debates with, or dissociate them from, the political avant-garde organizations to those associated with "classical" avant-gardes (Stefan Morawski); Bürger's almost eponymous "historical" avant-gardes; Greenberg's "avant-garde"; and post-, trans-, and retro-gardes.

Contrary to the notion of autonomous art defended by Adorno, the avant-garde in art was conceived as art that transcends the confines of its autonomy. In Adorno, autonomous art of course cannot be subsumed under the category of Kantian disinterestedness, which, for him, is in fact pleasure masquerading "beyond recognition" (*AT*, 13), very much resembling the effects of *l'art pour l'art*. Modern art has eliminated the universal, but the excluded is retained through its negation. It is the specificity of this negation that is "constitutive of the modern" (*AT*, 351). The other feature of modern art—of any authentic art—is, for Adorno, its existence as a mediated form between the historical society and the work: the "constitutive immanence of the aesthetic sphere is at the same time the ideology that undermines it" (*AT*, 349). This mediation is a theme for philosophical aesthetics. In Adorno's opinion, the social aspect of art is its opposition to society by way of its immanence and not its political stance: by being partisan, art negates its autonomy and becomes reducible to a particular interpretation. Since society is thoroughly instrumentalized—everything is but a means for something else, has value only in relation to something else and not to itself—autonomous art is one of the few instances of human activity and existence that does not succumb to the demands of the capitalist system. Still, as noted in the case of Dada, Adorno's aversion to partisan art (and the "kitsch of the Soviet bloc"—*AT*, 349) should not be confused with his implicit support for some aspects of the activities of the classical avant-gardes.

In accordance with the prevailing dichotomy of the first half of the twentieth century, Adorno perceives authentic art of his epoch as that which achieves the subversion of content by form, offering as examples works by Kafka and Beckett, and Picasso's *Guernica*. Works of artists such as these allow for the experience of the autonomy of an artwork in its relation to the heteronomy of society.

In the opinion of Wolfgang Welsch, in Adorno "the autonomy of the artistic work criticizes the heteronomy of society."[13] Welsch points to Adorno's accentuation of what he calls "work-internal heterogeneity" (*Undoing*, 71), namely, Adorno's opinion that a work contains a heterogeneity of the sensible that is to be understood not as "raw" but as a sensible diversity. In Welsch's view, a similar interpretation must be applied to the "work-external heterogeneity": the variety and divergence in artistic paradigms regarding different artworks, as well as a divergence in the sphere of art on the whole, must be acknowledged. Welsch concludes that modern works no longer comply with one general canon, but each develops its own. "Thus two things are self-evident for aesthetic awareness from the modern stance: that one must discover the idiolect in a singular work; and that one must be aware of the fundamental plurality of paradigms in regard to art as a whole" (*Undoing*, 72).

Welsch's assessment of Adorno is preceded by his critical view of the latter as an adherent of traditional aesthetics. It attests to Welsch's opinion regarding the recent philosophical and historical situation—that of *Unsere postmoderne Moderne*, "our postmodern modernity," as proclaimed by the title of his influential work from 1987. His views could, nonetheless, be regarded from that (and as that) borderline between modernity and modernism and postmodernity (the postindustral epoch, the epoch of multinational capital, the epoch of information society, and so on) and postmodernism, the latter pair being specified by the emergence of the novel questioning of the possible *Ausgang* of modernity.

Some of the questions implied by Welsch's observation are: How do we organize our understanding of what art is? How is the history (consciously viewed from the present vantage point) constructed or interpreted, and how does art change through history, especially recent history? In brief, is today's art essentially art of Adorno's modern time, or is it essentially different?

The questions raised are of course fundamental questions of aesthetics understood in a plethora of ways. Let me attempt to offer some minor hints as to how they could be answered. In what follows I shall briefly discuss some views concerning these issues, occasionally turning to Adorno and concluding with some observations regarding contemporary art.

Let me begin with Peter Bürger. Bürger posited as the telos of the European avant-garde movements an "attack on the status of art in bourgeois society" (*TA*, 49), thereby offering, in the seventies, a novel interpretation of avant-garde art of the previous century. The deep and broad influence of this study continues into the present. While the avant-gardes discussed by Bürger actually represented, as he argued, a historic break with previous bourgeois art, early modernism included, it must be noted that Bürger's empirical and historical data did not fully support his theoretical positions. Thus, for example, the many provocative, revolutionary, and original gestures, procedures, devices, and inventions of the avant-gardists often owed more to Georges Sorel than to German Romanticism.

Dada presents a similar case: Bürger proclaimed it "the most radical movement within the European avant-garde" for no longer criticizing "schools that preceded it, but [criticizing] the art as an institution" (*TA*, 22). In fact, Tristan Tzara (highlighted by Bürger in his study) and the Romanian circle of Tzara's Zürich friends had been deeply influenced by their native Romanian cultural background—the Jewish tradition; the Dadalike performances and events; poetry and prose in prewar Bucharest; and the futurism of Marinetti, whose initial *Futurist Manifesto* appeared in Bucharest a day before it was published in *Le Figaro*.[14] Much of what Bürger called "criticism of art as an institution" may have been in fact a consequence of the transposition of a foreign culture to a West-European ambiance. In short, many of the procedures and ideas of Zürich Dada may have had more in common with cultural practices and specifics in that distant part of the European East than with a conscious attack on autonomous bourgeois culture.

A very similar criticism could be raised in regard to Italian futurism (designated by Bürger as yet another historical avant-garde movement), for Marinetti's prefuturist artistic practices in Paris and then his early futurist activities in Italy had much in common with anarchist aesthetics,[15] with Gustave Kahn's *esthétique de la rue*, and with the bourgeois carnivalesque culture of European (and later American) metropolises at the turn of the century and in the period that ended with the end of the First World War.[16] What is even more important is that it was within *il primo futurismo* (1909–1915) that the really radical and subversive ideas arose concerning art as an institution, making the early futurism a much better example of a critical stance toward "art as an institution" than Dada.

What remains of import in Bürger's study is that the previously mentioned avant-gardes had attempted to breach the border between art and life, although they may have realized this to a lesser degree than we would tend to conclude from Bürger, less consciously than is usually thought, and more due to a "cunning of reason" than by a conscious adherance to Romanticist suppositions of the historic role of art as regards the realization of humanity. In Bürger, the Hegelian interpretation of the history of art remains a potent factor that, while offering a totalizing view of artistic history, nonetheless distorts the more site-specific artistic, aesthetic, and historicaly specific events and acts surrounding the war—acts of the kind highlighted by Welsch.

The "aesthetic"—in the guise of freedom, "the order of disorder," the realization of art, the breaking down of the barrier separating "life" and art, and so on—remains an essential feature of the art and broad historical human action (or *praxis*) of much of the first half of the previous century. In different terms, this characteristic (or trend) was the cause of a continual introduction of new works into the institution of art, endowing such artifacts with the aura of historical authenticity and consequently aesthetic value.

Bürger's analysis is valid insofar as it points out that the historical avant-gardes were a cultural provocation not with the simple aim of *épater le bourgeois*, but with the intention to transform the whole artistic and human—perhaps the correct term would be "existential"—domain into a utopian event, a dynamic state of things created according to desires, proclamations, manifestos, and often actual actions of individual avant-garde artists ("persons" would perhaps be a more suitable term). In their final stages of development, these avant-garde projects and acts mostly descended (or ascended) into the realm of the institution of art: the historic role of the avant-garde was lost, but the institutional role was recaptured and it blossomed.

Bürger's narrative could thus be regarded as one story of the recent history of art. Still, Bürger himself saw his story as objective. He thus claimed that "self-criticism" of art (as carried out by Dadaism, for example) allows for objective understanding: "[O]nly when art enters the stage of self-criticism does the 'objective understanding' of past periods of the development of art become possible" (*TA*, 22). Bürger added that this "objective understanding" does not mean that the understanding is "independent of the place in the present of the cognizing individual"; instead, "it merely means insight into the overall process insofar as this process has come to a conclusion in the present of the cognizing individual" (*TA*, 22). If this claim had been true, then Bürger's attempt to fix the course of the development of avant-garde art within the twentieth century would have originated from a privileged historical position: that at which the process of development of the avant-garde has come to an end.

Aside from some previously noted factual weaknesses, Bürger's position is made less tenable by a further limitation, namely, the more recent appearance of new avant-garde art, that is, the politicized postmodern art of the transitional period from socialism to postsocialism,[17] to which we could easily ascribe features characteristic of avant-garde art,[18] making Bürger's (somewhat Hegelian) claim about the "conclusion in the present of the cognizing individual" questionable. In brief, Bürger's narrative is limited by its modern and culture-specific framework.

Aesthetics as a discipline is destined to be incomplete and to promise an impossible outcome, for it attempts to make commensurable what cannot be. This initial and incessant transgression of its own domain prevents it, argues Adorno—and even today we cannot but accept his point—from achieving its aim of grasping theoretically its continually transformed object of reflection. Such reflections are always circumscribed by historical and often also cultural specifications of their vantage points. The plethora of the latter, on the one hand, and their dialectical linkage with the object of their reflection—what Adorno called "the philosophical insight that fact and concept are not polar opposites but mediated reciprocally in one another" (*AT*, 343)—on the other, is what makes the task of aesthetics an incessant procedure.

It could be objected that we should not search for borderline cases but limit ourselves to perspicuous instances of great art, where no doubt exists as to their artistic credentials. Martin Heidegger's analysis of Van Gogh's painting *A Pair of Boots* could serve as an example of such a perspicuous instance. In *The Origin of the Work of Art*, Heidegger proclaims the decline of modern art but praises this painting as a case of "great" art: a contemporary (modern) work is offered as an example of "great art" in spite of all modern art being proclaimed in decline.

It is within this philosophical horizon, charted by Heidegger and appertaining to modernism, that the issue of truth is situated. Adorno acknowledges: "Only he understands an artwork who grasps it as a complex nexus of truth" (*AT*, 262). Like Heidegger, Adorno too accentuates the role of truth in art. In Heidegger's own words from *The Origin of the Work of Art*, "Beauty is one way in which truth essentially occurs as unconcealedness.... In the work, the happening of truth is at work."[19] For both, truth is the basic ontological precondition for art and its exemplary status (and, in

Heidegger, position) in modernism and modernity. "Emphatically, art is knowledge, though not the knowledge of objects" (*AT,* 262). Truth, appearing *via* a specific form of knowledge—art—is the fundamental category of a modernist philosophy of art. Within this horizon, philosophy offers the self-reflection of art that the latter, in spite of all its significance, by definition cannot articulate in a purely abstract way, for in that way it would reach into the realm of philosophical concepts. It is the philosopher who explains, reflects, and *judges*: "The idea of a value-free aesthetics is nonsense" (*AT,* 262). And "[a]rtworks, especially those of the highest dignity, await their interpretation.... Grasping truth content postulates critique" (*AT,* 128). For some time aesthetics retains the evaluative faculty; later, with the advent of pop and conceptual art, all that remains to be discussed is the position of such art within the institution of art, for "there really is no art more true than any other, and ... there really is no one way art has to be: all art is equally and indifferently art."[20]

In juxtaposing Adorno and Heidegger regarding truth, some essential differences must be noted: Heidegger's position on past and contemporary art changes significantly over decades. Early on, he endorses Hegel's theory of the end of art and the elevated position ascribed to Greek art as the most authentic, when art purportedly provided guidance as to how to live. Art of the modern epoch "is designed to provide 'aesthetic experiences.'"[21] Such an experience offers no more than repose and relaxation, for it accentuates beauty, not truth. The later Heidegger acquired an affinity for modern artists such as Rilke, Le Corbusier, Stravinsky, Braque, Klee, and Cézanne; it appears that he wanted to write a sequel to *The Origin of the Work of Art* (1935–36) that would refer to Klee and Cézanne.[22]

In Adorno's view, great art characteristically overcomes historical limitations: not as an atemporal entity, but as a transient, but therefore no less crucial, crystallization of truth:

> Authentic art of the past that for the time being must remain veiled is not thereby sentenced. Great works wait. While their metaphysical meaning dissolves, something of their truth content, however little it can be pinned down, does not; it is that whereby they remain eloquent. A liberated humanity would be able to inherit its historical legacy free of guilt. What was once true in an artwork and then disclaimed by history is only able to disclose itself again when the conditions have changed on whose account that truth was invalidated. (*AT*, 40)

This could be called Adorno's interpretation of the historical transformation of a work of art and therefore of art as such: works have their historical moment in which they adequately relate to their broader historical frame and thereby express and present its truth. Since this truth does not lie on the surface of a work, it must be grasped by interpretation and critique. The artistic experience meets with resistance that mirrors the resistance of the work to its historical conditions of authenticity.

"Great works wait." They are reborn when historical circumstances reenact the situation in which they achieved their role as exceptional artworks. It is also for this reason that "a univocal construction of the history of art" is impossible (*AT*, 210): art is not a dead entity, but a potentiality that in the case of a great work awaits its rebirth. In his correspondence with Walter Benjamin, Adorno agrees that "the aural element of the work of art is declining."[23] In the same breath he distances his own notion of the autonomy of a work of art from the notion of "auratic" art as suggested by Benjamin. It would thus be incorrect to claim that Adorno envisioned an "end of art." Nonetheless, in his opinion art is undergoing some kind of a decline: he speaks of Rimbaud anticipating "art's decline" (*AT*, 4). To make matters more complicated, Adorno refers also to "the progress of art," a general judgment that "has to do with a difficulty presented by the structure of [art's] history." (*AT*, 209). The problem with the notion of progress in art arises from the specific nature of art. In art, progress develops through forgetting: past works ("great works") become alive after a period of waiting and reemerge as "contemporary" in spite of their origin in the past. Progress in art emerges only if past works are forgotten and some theme or artistic device, to use a different terminology, is invented anew or brought forth from oblivion. What exists in art are parallel presents: different historical lines run parallel to each other, interrelate, and are separated. This is why in Adorno's opinion art's essence "cannot be deduced from its history" (*AT*, 2). "The concept of art is located in a historically changing constellation of elements; it refuses definition" (*AT*, 2). If art were susceptible to a definition, that definition would always arise from a particular work or limit its scope to the present. It would thus exclude future instances of art, for which the main characteristic is that it cannot be deduced from the past to be applied to them. Art's characteristics change incessantly, and much of the issue of art remains the question of whether a certain work is a work of art at all. It is because of this uncertainty that "[a]rt can be understood only by its laws of movement, not according to any set of invariants" (*AT*, 3).

If we were to translate Danto's claim that "there is a kind of a transhistorical essence in art, everywhere and always the same, but it only discloses itself through history,"[24] into Adorno's conceptual frame, we would have to describe such "essence" as a rule or principle that generates the constellation called art.

At the end of his "Draft Introduction" to *Aesthetic Theory*, Adorno makes this far-reaching Marxist proposition:

> The principle of method here is that light should be cast on all art from the vantage point of the most recent artworks, rather than the reverse, following the custom of historicism and philology, which, bourgeois at heart, prefers that nothing ever change. If Valéry's thesis is true that the best in the new corresponds to an old need, then the most authentic works

are critiques of past works. Aesthetics becomes normative by articulating such criticism. (*AT,* 359)

The immediate interpretation of this statement would be, of course, that we should look at past art from our own vantage point—something that cannot be avoided. Adorno furthermore claims that the role of aesthetics is to criticize works of the past since contemporary works are also critiques of past works, thereby privileging such contemporary criticism. But let us interpret the statement somewhat differently and claim that the most recent artworks put all past works into a different light, thereby transforming these same most recent works.

Which works of art do we bring forth from oblivion and which do we resuscitate because they "waited" and awaited the repetition of specific circumstances or a condition that is ours? Which are the determining factors the making visible of which allows us to grasp similarities between historical epochs? And which works of today become petrified and lose their life because they no longer correspond to our *vision du monde*? The issue is worthy of scrutiny not only for historical reasons, not only for being an essential issue for aesthetics as philosophy of art, but also because of its import for our contemporaneity, for shedding some light on the issue of "what is this instant that is ours"[25] as regards art, aesthetics, and the aesthetic.

It was of course Hegel who first persuasively presented a response to this question. Hegel grasped the essential issue of art in the epoch of the pervasive notion of development. He interiorized the question, exposing it for what it remains today: the question of our perception and reception of past art from our proper vantage point *for* our vantage point. This is also true of the "instant that is ours": Hegel's concern and its articulation address our own concerns today: while he may be concerned with classical art of the past, his depiction of the situation regarding past art relates also to art of our own time and our relation to the art of the past.

> The statues set up are now corpses in stone whence the animating soul has flown, while the hymns of praise are words from which all belief is gone.... They are themselves now just what they are for us—beautiful fruit broken off the tree; a kindly fate has passed on those works to us, as a maiden might offer such fruit off a tree. Their actual life as they exist is no longer there, not the tree that bore them.... Our action, therefore, when we enjoy them is not that of worship, through which our conscious life might attain its complete truth and be satisfied to the full: our action is external; it consists in wiping off some drop of rain or speck of dust from these fruits, and in place of the inner elements composing the reality of the ethical life, a reality that environed, created and inspired these works, we erect in prolix detail the scaffolding of the dead elements of their outward existence,—language, historical circumstances, etc. All this we do, not in order to enter into their very life, but only to represent them ideally or pictorially [*vorstellen*] within ourselves.[26]

The issue raised by Hegel concerns the impossibility of authentically experiencing past artworks. This impossibility also determines our proper possibilities; it witnesses to a change in our sensibility and a change in our vantage point that arises from our proper historical circumstances. The past is closed to us in the artistic forms that were open to people of a past epoch. Hegel's position is similar to Heidegger's in the *The Origin of the Work of Art*, where the perception offered by past art is also changed in contemporaneity. Contemporary art, on the other hand, is also a path not to truth, but to sheer enjoyment. It has become beautiful and has therefore lost its potentials *qua* art: it no longer allows for immediacy of truth and its unconcealedness; it is an accessory to concealment. The artistic has become the aestheticized; it no longer allows for the aesthetic.

A related issue is raised by Marx in the introduction to the *Grundrisse* where he notes that

> [t]he difficulty we are confronted with is not, however, that of understanding how Greek art and epic poetry are associated

with certain forms of social development. The difficulty is that they still give us aesthetic pleasure and are in certain respects regarded as a standard and unattainable ideal.[27]

Here Marx echoes Hegel's views regarding classical art. His thought can be divided into two related statements:

First, Greek art and epic poetry are creations of their own time and dependent upon historical and other site-specific circumstances. In many respects—the stage of development of the means of production, the import of mythical thought on the thematics of Greek art, the determining role of pagan religion and its influence on epic poetry—all these features shape and determine the artistic nature and the aesthetic ("pleasurable") effect of such art. What, then, do Adorno's words, "[g]reat works wait" (*AT*, 40), say in relation to or in light of Marx's observation that these works (epic poetry) "still give us aesthetic pleasure"? Obviously, claim both Marx and Adorno, some works remain alive, actual, and relevant in epochs that transgress their historical circumstances and places of origin. Such works are "great works."

Second, Marx claims, as does Hegel, that Greek art and epic poetry "in some sense" remain for art of his time—this is the year 1857—the rule and unreachable example. As S. S. Prawer showed in his reconstruction of Marx's epoch as regards literary knowledge, influence, and tastes,[28] in Marx's time knowledge of Greek art and epic poetry were still very much considered obligatory for educated men. But Prawer's study also shows that Marx was quite ignorant of art (especially fine art) that was not in the mainstream art of his time. He was thus interested in Eugène Sue and Honoré de Balzac, Balzac being one of the few popular writers among his contemporaries who still remains part of the literarary canon today.[29]

Of course, Karl Marx may not have been an art connoisseur of his time, and his tastes may have been average and rather traditional. Still, it is fair to consider that, as regards Greek art and epic poetry, he shared the tastes and appreciation of his contemporaries. Today, by contrast, hardly anyone will claim that poetry remains a part of the actual cultural canon of the present. It most probably wasn't part of the mainstream literature even in Adorno's time. Still, once a work has been admitted into the perimeter of "art," with the encircled realm being the institution called art, it may lose its artistic or aesthetic worth, but it hardly ever loses its status as a work of art. This is what has happened in our time to epic poetry and probably also to much of Greek art—a fact intuitively manifested by Marinetti's irreverent mockery and disregard for Nike of Samothrace in his 1909 *Futurist Manifesto*.

Something important has occured between Marx's lifetime and "this instance that is ours." The diminution, if not outright disappearance, of contemporary appreciation of epic poetry signals that our own positions regarding our contemporary art have been transformed.

Which art has emerged in recent decades? This most certainly was not an art familiar to Marx or his contemporaries. This new art was then in its nascent stage. In a majority of cases it was the art of European modernism. But perhaps even the art of modernism, regarded by Adorno as paradigmatic of the modern epoch and at the same time as an instance of art in its form of critical negativity, was not the art that changed the cultural paradigm of the early twentieth century. If we turn to Georg Lukács as a central defender of critical realism of the first half of the previous century, we recognize his choices as those Marx himself would probably readily have accepted as instances of great art.

What represented a central turning point were not the parallel currents of realism and modernism (with the avant-gardes representing a radical part thereof) but the advent of postmodernism, arising from European modernism, with Marcel Duchamp's readymades representing the first instance of postmodern art. If Peter Bürger, when referring to Dadaism, had had Duchamp in mind, his analysis would be much more persuasive.

Although Fredric Jameson was correct in claiming that "cultural forms of postmodernism may be said to be the first specifically North American global style,"[30] that the *logic* of postmodern culture—its functioning, dissemination, distribution (as a symbolic and as a financial commodity), and institutionalization within the frame of historical and cultural archives—arose from the United States, the roots of this functioning are to be found in European modernism. In (continental) Europe art retained its special status—arising from the tradition of Romanticism and the *fin de siècle*—well into the twentieth century, and this status assigned to art the special locus of creativity (as promoted by most European authors, ranging from Karl Marx to Maurice Merleau-Ponty) as opposed to repetition of industrial labor. With the passage into the postindustrial society, the paradigmatic role of art as the highest form of creativity has withered away, a process having as its side effect the diminution of the previous privileged role of art. This change in the role of art is noted by Gérard Genette in his observation that in Heidegger and Adorno a symmetery exists between "two antithetical forms of overvaluation" of art,[31] a fact revealed also by the ready-made nature of the readymade.

A similar gesture—arising from a critique of Bürger, but through him from a critique of Adorno—is to be found in Benjamin H. D. Buchloh's reevaluation of his own views regarding American neo-avant-garde art. In his opinion,

> [t]he first of Bürger's many delusions (and my own as well) was of course to situate neo-avantgarde practices in a perpetual, almost Oedipal relation to the accomplishments of the parental avant-garde of the twenties.... The second and equally fatal delusion, shared by Bürger and this author to some extent ... was the assumption that the criteria for aesthetic judgment would have to be linked at all times, if not to models of an outright instrumentalized political efficacy, then at least to a compulsory mode of critical negativity.[32]

By diminishing the import of classical avant-gardes and by elevating the neo-avant-gardes to a higher status—by discarding the requirement that neo-avant-garde art possess the predicate of negativity—the placement of pop art also changed: the same author persuasively argued (complementing in this Arthur Danto's claim that pop art effectively transgressed the division between high and low in culture) that Andy Warhol successfuly transformed himself from a commercial artist into a fine artist, aiding in this way pop art's replacement of abstract expressionism as the leading American art of the period.[33]

As Jameson has demonstrated in his comparision of Heidegger's hermeneutic analysis of Van Gogh's painting *A Pair of Shoes* with his own analysis of a Warhol work, the contemporary issue regarding art is no longer that of truth, but meaning. In other words, contemporary art predominantly aspires to create meaning, not to reveal truth. As Boris Groys argues,

> It turns out that this question [of the value of a product] cannot be answered by reaching back to reality and that the truth of the product cannot be the basis of its value. The question about the value of a product thus remains the question about its relation to tradition and other cultural artifacts.... Neither innovative art nor innovative theory can be described or argued in their signifying relationship to reality or, which is the same, in their truth. The question therefore is not are they true but are they culturally precious.[34]

This means that works of art do not relate to their referents (the truth of which they establish, reveal, and disclose) but form a system of equivalences within which they function according to a grid of mutually dependent meanings. Neither Adorno nor Heidegger see art forming such a system of significations. For both of them, art still reveals the truth of the referent, be it society, an epoch, or an existential artistic expression. For art arising from Duchamp's readymades and continuing with Warhol, Groys's description is more valid, for the Duchampian and postmodern art that Groys has in mind does actually function very much according to the principles of the institutional theory of art: this art no longer discloses existential or other truths, it functions exclusively within the institution of art it incessantly recreates. It is within such a framework that the previously mentioned passage from Wolfgang Welsch acquires additional significance: although Welsch was referring to modern art, he was in fact relating to the postmodern, this art being exemplified by the borderline, a borderline determining the essence of the center. Art as an institution has replaced art as part of the aesthetic, and great art of the past has been turned into marketable commodities for the culture industry. Adorno may have sensed this when he expressed his harsh criticism of the cinema.

The transformation from modernism to postmodernism is global, yet it is the art of modernism—much more than the art of the classical avant-gardes—that is still being universally disseminated, acquiring on its way across the globe local and hybrid forms. These hybrid forms, often considered postmodern products of culture (and not necessarily art) within their place of origin, apparently contradict Adorno's claims for the universalism of modernism and his value judgments regarding works that represent a negation of the bourgeois frame of reference. If in the recent past there existed a belief that the decline of art, as diagnosed by Arthur Danto, Gérard Genette, Gianni Vattimo, and so on, did not exist to the same extent in the postcolonial countries as it does in the most developed parts of the world, this hope today seems obsolete. As a Latin American theorist notes,

> Aesthetic innovation is of declining interest in the museums, in the publishing houses, and in film; it has been shifted instead into electronic technologies, into musical entertainment and fashion. Where there were painters or musicians, there are now designers and disc jockeys.[35]

The decline of art is universal. What Adorno sensed as the negativity of art of his time, and which found its authentic manifestation in the opposition between content and form, no longer applies. Descriptions and judgments such as this one from Latin America are today enunciated across the globe, from China to Slovenia. While the art markets are booming, the symbolic capital of art is rapidly diminishing. One way of explaining this phenomenon is to suggest that it is a consequence of the global proliferation of art, of its increased production, of the merging of the high and the low (as in the previously mentioned case of pop art), and of the general acceptance of the idea that all art is equally art. The art of high modernism, appreciated by Adorno, has become a historical style; contemporary art in its various forms relates not so much to modernism as to the art of the historical avant-gardes with their mixing of genres, techniques, procedures, and different realms of life, these ranging from science to politics.

"Walter Benjamin claimed that the creation of mechanically reproduced images tends to diminish the 'aura' of the original. In fact the opposite is true. The existence of the reproduction, in all its manifold copies, actually hightens a sense of the uniqueness of the original."[36] This statement says something about the auratic potentials of the extant original works vis-à-vis those that are devoid of Benjamin's aura, but, as Adorno had already pointed out in his correspondence with Benjamin, the issue of auratic art does not really touch upon the issue of the autonomy of art as conceived by Adorno himself. It says something relevant, though, about the *changed* mode of art.

The theory of the avant-garde developed by Peter Bürger and discussed at the beginning of this essay has been one of the important analyses of the development and broader framework of art and the aesthetic. Bürger's theory can be regarded within the framework of modernism and as a theory that has, as Bürger claims, become possible when the development of the avant-garde reached its end. The fact that Bürger has not envisioned other "parallel" modernities does not refute the argument of this 1974 book. To this same modern framework Heidegger and Adorno also belong. Their position toward truth is essential, for they both view it refracted through or existing in art. This "overvaluation of art" is also typical for both—as it is for Bürger, who links his historical avant-gardes to the historic, albeit unsuccessful, attempt to overcome the division between art and life and between the sensible and the rational.

Walter Benjamin offered a different narrative concerning art and its meaning within the recent historical framework, especially in his essay *The Work of Art in the Age of Mechanical Reproduction*. Disputed by Adorno and generating very little interest for decades, the essay (like its author) became influential with the advent of postmodernism. Benjamin claims that, with the technological developments represented mainly by photography and the cinema, a new artistic and aesthetic sensibility has arisen.

> During long periods of history, the mode of human sense perception changes with humanity's entire mode of existence. The manner in which human sense perception is organized, the medium in which it is accomplished, is determined not only by nature but by historical circumstances as well.[37]

Regarded in conjunction with Adorno's observation about the necessity of viewing past works from the position of recent art, Benjamin's statement attains additional relevance, for it foreshadows from a historical distance of several decades a drastic change in, and an essential modification of, the human and social import of art beginning in the sixties. Contemporary art no longer offers a path to truth and is not historically, socially, or existentially relevant to the extent it still was in Adorno's time. Modernist art, just as epic poetry, has today increasingly turned from a truth-revealing document of its time into its monument.

Benjamin believed that this change has to do with collective experience. He claimed that "[p]ainting simply is in no position to present an object for simultaneous collective experience, as it was possible for architecture at all times, for the epic poem in the past, and for the movie today."³⁸ He noted that collective experience is dialectically linked to our mode of sense perception. Not only is the creation of certain art forms no longer possible but these forms are also perceived differently or, as the epic poem attests, not at all. This process had already begun in Marx's time, with the advent of technical advancements in representation and the emergent "plurality of paradigms in regard to art" that Welsch speaks of.

From our contemporary position, in "this instant that is ours," past art has been more quickly and radically than ever incorporated into the present or more recent art, and is being viewed accordingly—following Hegel's description from *The Phenomenology of Mind* as the paramount work of the modern philosophy of art. Within the framework of more recent art, art of the past has become aestheticized to provide, in Heidegger's words, "aesthetic experiences" and has ceased to be "emphatically knowledge," that is, truth, as Adorno claimed. Instead of truth, contemporary art offers meaning. Art has become but another commodity. Attempts to subvert the extant art system are few and far between. There is no longer the possibility of conflict between content and form and hardly the possiblity of conflict between an individual and the society or politics.

In the highly developed part of the world, art no longer serves as an expressive means for social, national, and religious minorities—or if it does, it is practiced for some time (before it joins the institution of today's popular culture) in subcultural forms such as rap and ethnic music, grafitti, fashion, and lifestyle.³⁹ It is in such ways that the aesthetic today has been retained: to a small extent, on a limited scale, and without the hope of bringing together the divided halves through art. In Rancière's view, to which no persuasive alternative has yet been offered, "[t]he postmodern reversal had as its theoretical foundation Lyotard's analysis of the Kantian sublime, which was reinterpreted as the scene of a founding distance separating the idea from any sensible presentation."⁴⁰

Peter Bürger's statement from his *Theory of the Avant-Garde* had a premonitional value. There he said that what was at stake in early avant-gardes was the notion of art, namely,

> an attack on the status of art in bourgeois society. What is negated is not an earlier form of art (a style) but art as an institution that is unassociated with the life praxis of men.... The demand is not raised at the level of the contents of individual works. Rather, it directs itself to the way art functions in society, a process that does as much to determine the effect that works have as does the particular content. (*TA*, 49)

In postmodernity, total commercialization and thus commodification has permeated all segments of society, including Adorno's autonomous art. The proof of this permeation lies in the fact that not only are we no longer able to experience epic poetry, but that autonomous art that Adorno had in mind is becoming aesthetically opaque and is equally intensively being replaced by mass and popular culture. It is within this popular culture and within the new forms of emergent art that a dedifferentiation seems to be occurring, bringing together previously isolated domains of knowledge and creativity—bioart and technology-based art as well as other new forms of experimental art—that art may be "finding a way" to continue its life in the aesthetic domain (the utopian, the avant-garde) and not so much in that of aesthetics, within which a work is viewed only as an aesthetic resource. What currently exists in much art of the past may thus be more akin to what Slavoj Žižek has called, in regard to politics, the complete "commodification of politics."⁴¹

Art has undergone a similar commodification that is linked to another development in art, diagnosed as early as 1984 by Arthur Danto:

> The age of pluralism is upon us. It does not matter any longer what you do, which is what pluralism means. When one

direction is as good as another direction, there is no concept of direction any longer to apply. Decoration, self-expression, entertainment, are, of course, abiding human needs. There will always be a service for art to perform, if artists are content with that. A subservient art has always been with us. The institutions of the art world—galleries, collectors, exhibitions, journalism—which are predicated upon history and hence marking what is new, will bit by bit wither away. How happy happpiness will make us is difficult to foretell, but just think of the difference the rage for gourmet cooking has made in common American life. On the other hand, it has been an immense privilege to have lived in history.[42]

Somewhat paradoxically, contemporary art, then, very much resembles contemporary politics: both are commodified, in their contemporary forms most probably devoid of a future, and both remain in need of the political and the aesthetic. Perhaps the resuscitation of this pair today requires an effort no less demanding than that suggested two centuries ago by Friedrich Schiller, and a task as relevant—for aesthetics as philosophy of art, and for art—as that carried out by Adorno half a century ago, for today too, "[e]very artwork, if it is to be fully experienced, requires thought and therefore stands in need of philosophy."

Endnotes

1. John Cage, quoted in Tony Godfrey, *Conceptual Art* (London, 1998), p. 63.
2. Marcel Duchamp, quoted in Arthur C. Danto, *The Philosophical Disenfranchisement of Art* (New York, 1984), p. 13.
3. Jacques Rancière, *Malaise dans l'esthétique* (Paris, 2004), p. 11. Unless otherwise noted, all translations are my own.
4. Theodor W. Adorno, *Aesthetic Theory*, trans. Robert Hullot-Kentor (Minneapolis, 1997), p. 335. (Hereafter *AT*.)
5. "Aesthetics presents philosophy with the bill for the fact that the academic system degraded it to being a mere specialization"; ibid., p. 262.
6. Adorno's continuing influence on and import for music studies is attested, for example, by the fact that in many continental music academies his *Introduction to the Sociology of Music* remains part of the syllabus.
7. "Une œuvre ne peut devenir moderne que si elle est d'abord postmoderne. Le postmodernisme ainsi entendu n'est pas le modernisme à sa fin, mais à l'état naissant, et cet état est constant"; Jean-François Lyotard, *Le Postmoderne expliqué aux enfants* (Paris, 1988), p. 28.
8. See Andrew Bowie, "Adorno, Heidegger, and the Meaning of Music," *Thesis Eleven* 56 (February 1999): p. 4.
9. The more recent theorists of the "event" range from Lyotard and Gilles Deleuze to Jean-Luc Nancy and, esp., Alain Badiou.
10. Peter Bürger, *Theory of the Avant-Garde*, trans. Michael Snow (Minneapolis, 1999), p. 46. (Hereafter *TA*.)
11. Quoted in Matei Calinescu, *Five Faces of Modernity: Modernism, Avant-Garde, Decadence, Kitsch, Postmodernism* (Durham, NC, 1987), p. 103.
12. See ibid., esp. pp. 110–11.
13. Wolfgang Welsch, *Undoing Aesthetics* (London, 1997), p. 69.
14. See Tom Sandqvist, *Dada East: Romanians of Cabaret Voltaire* (Cambridge, MA, 2006).
15. "From political theorists Arturo Labriola and Georges Sorel [Marinetti] borrows the Marxist concept of transforming the world; in anarchist thinkers, such as Max Stirner, Bakunin and Peter Kropotkin he emulates especially the protesting stand towards art and cultural institutions of the past"; Noëmi Blumenkranz, "Une poétique de l'héroisme. L'esthétique de Marinetti," in *La Présence de F. T. Marinetti* (Lausanne, 1982), p. 51.
16. Could we not view Marcel Duchamp's irreverent gesture of exhibiting

Fountain in New York in April 1917 as an act resembling many of the futurists' activities?

[17] See Aleš Erjavec, ed., *Postmodernism and the Postsocialist Condition: Politicized Art Under Late Socialism* (Berkeley, 2003).

[18] "Post-avant-garde" art of the former socialist countries visibly displayed all the pertinent features of the neo-avant-gardes and many of the historical avant-gardes. See Aleš Erjavec, "The Avant-Gardes: From Modernism to Postmodernism," *Journal of Contemporary Thought* 22 (Winter 2005): pp. 65–85.

[19] Martin Heidegger, *Basic Writings*, ed. David Farrell Krell (San Francisco, 1976), p. 178.

[20] Arthur C. Danto, *After the End of Art: Contemporary Art and the Pale of History* (Princeton, 1997), p. 34.

[21] Julian Young, *Heidegger's Philosophy of Art* (Cambridge, 2001), p. 9.

[22] See ibid.

[23] Theodor Adorno et al., *Aesthetics and Politics* (London, 1980), p. 122.

[24] Danto, *After the End of Art*, p. 28.

[25] Michel Foucault, *The Politics of Truth*, ed. and trans. Sylvère Lotringer and Lysa Hochroth (New York, 1997), p. 158.

[26] G.W.F. Hegel, *Phenomenology of Mind*, trans. J. B. Baillie (New York, 1967), pp. 753–54.

[27] Karl Marx, introduction to *A Contribution to the Critique of Political Economy*, trans. S. W. Razanskaya (Moscow, 1970), p. 217.

[28] Sigfried S. Prawer, *Karl Marx and World Literature* (Oxford, 1976).

[29] Fredric Jameson notes that Balzac, although an author of "best sellers," escapes the designation of being a part of the culture industry, for "no contradiction is yet felt in his time between the production of best sellers and the production of what will later come to be thought of as 'high' literature"; Fredric Jameson, *The Political Unconscious* (Ithaca, 1981), p. 208.

[30] Fredric Jameson, *Postmodernism, or, The Cultural Logic of Late Capitalism* (London 1991), p. xx.

[31] Gérard Genette, *L'œuvre de l'art. La relation esthétique* (Paris, 1997), p. 11.

[32] Benjamin H. D. Buchloh, *Neo-Avantgarde and Culture Industry: Essays on European and American Art from 1955 to 1975* (Cambridge, MA, 2000), p. xxix.

[33] See ibid., esp. pp. 463–81.

34 Boris Groys, *Über das Neue. Versuch einer Kulturökonomie* (Frankfurt am Main, 2004), pp. 18, 19.

35 Néstor García Canclini, *Hybrid Cultures: Strategies for Entering and Leaving Modernity*, trans. Christopher L. Chappari and Silvia L. López (Minneapolis, 2005), p. xxxix.

36 Paul Crowther, *The Transhistorical Image* (Cambridge, 2002), p. 138.

37 Walter Benjamin, "The Work of Art in the Age of Mechanical Reproduction," in *Illuminations*, ed. Hannah Arendt, trans. Harry Zohn (New York, 1968), p. 222.

38 Ibid., pp. 234–35.

39 See Aleš Erjavec, "Die neuen Vorzeichen der Kunst. Eine Fallstudie zu Mittel- und Osteuropa," in *Zurück aus der Zukunft. Osteuropäische Kulturen im Zeitalter des Postkommunismus*, ed. Boris Groys, Anne von der Heiden, and Peter Weibel (Frankfurt am Main, 2005), pp. 508–35.

40 Jacques Rancière, *The Politics of Aesthetics*, trans. Gabriel Rockhill (London, 2004), p. 29.

41 Slavoj Žižek, "A Leninist Gesture Today," in *Lenin Reloaded*, ed. Sebastian Budgen, Stathis Kouvelakis, and Slavoj Žižek (Durham, NC, 2007), p. 85.

42 Arthur C. Danto, "The End of Art," in *The Death of Art*, ed. Berel Lang (New York, 1984), p. 35.

J. M. Bernstein

"The Demand for Ugliness": Picasso's Bodies

*Indeed, it is for the sake of the beautiful that there is
no longer beauty: because it is no longer beautiful.*
—Adorno

*[T]he demand for ugliness, the older Hellenes' good, severe will to
pessimism, to the tragic myth, to affirm the image of all
that is fearsome, wicked, mysterious, annihilating and fateful
in the very foundations of existence—where must the origins
of tragedy have lain at that time?*
—Nietzsche

*[T]his is the tremendous power of the negative;
it is the energy of thought, of the pure "I," death....
Beauty hates the understanding for asking of her what it cannot
do. But the life of Spirit is not the life that shrinks from death, and
keeps itself untouched by devastation, but rather the life
that endures it and maintains itself in it. It wins its truth only
when, in utter dismemberment, it finds itself.*
—Hegel

1907: An Axial Rotation in Painting

Arguably, after emphatic adumbrations and anticipations, modernist painting arrived at its exemplary realization in 1907 with Picasso's *Les Demoiselles d'Avignon* (fig.1). The *Demoiselles* finally gave modernist painting an axial turn away from the constituting subject and toward the object. The turn toward the object in Picasso's practice hinges on his handling of the role of the human body in painting; beginning with the *Demoiselles* and then, after the interlude called cubism, returning to it in the 1920s, the body is not so much a representational object (as it is for nearly all previous painting), but a condition for pictorial space. Only by thus conceiving the body-object could Picasso so radically transform modern art.

This somewhat opaque way of articulating Picasso's achievement—the only terms through which the full extent of that achievement can be understood—depends upon the philosophical framework of Adorno's critical theory. Let me quickly sketch the relevant background. The well-known phrase from the preface to *Negative Dialectics*—"by critical self-reflection to give the Copernican revolution an axial turn"[1]—is a useful one for summarizing Adorno's critical project as a whole. Kant's Copernican revolution consists in the idea that categorical features making experience possible—substance, causality, space, time, and so on—which previously had been located in or identified with features of things-in-themselves, were now to be transferred to the faculty of cognition, to reason itself, to what has come to be called transcendental subjectivity. Empirical subjectivity refers to the subject of everyday experience, with its pains and pleasures, perceptions and ideas; the transcendental subject refers to the abiding structures of subjectivity responsible for providing the framework of concepts within which all empirical experience is to be understood; the abstract concepts spontaneously employed by the transcendental subject provide the necessary conditions for the possibility of experience—without them the world would

Figure 1. Pablo Picasso, *Les Demoiselles d'Avignon*, 1907. Oil on canvas, 8' x 7'8". © 2010 Estate of Pablo Picasso / Artists Rights Society (ARS), New York.

be nothing but a blooming, buzzing confusion. Reason thus becomes the lawgiver to nature, providing the very idea of a natural, law-governed world.

Adorno employs Kant's conception of transcendental subjectivity to summarize and model the historical rationalization of reason through which the reason that was to be the instrument of freedom and reconciliation with nature on becoming total drives out all other forms of reasoning, and consequently reverts to its opposite, a source of domination and separation: "The doctrine of the transcendental subject faithfully discloses the precedence of the abstract, rational relations that are abstracted from individuals and their conditions and for which exchange is the model."[2] Adorno is contending that Kant's idea of transcendental constitution is, while philosophically false, socially and historically true; what is consolidated in the idea of the transcendental subject is the socially mandated precedence of abstract categories (of exchange) over their objects. Hence, the idea of providing the Copernican turn with an axial rotation—toward the object—as the programmatic movement of negative dialectics means demonstrating how the object of cognition is more than, different from, and nonidentical with how it appears in the context of rationalized reason; how subject is also object; how subject depends upon what it assumes to dominate and control.

Modernism is the operation of negative dialectic in art; it is that art practice that criticizes abstract rationality by remaining a repository for an alternative—mimetic—rationality. Modernism thereby becomes the voice of sensuous particularity against abstract rationality. In brief, this is the core thesis of *Aesthetic Theory*. It is also what Picasso accomplishes in *Les Demoiselles d'Avignon*, giving painting an axial turn toward the object.[3] Modernist painting lives or dies by its acknowledgment of and fidelity to this moment, for only the *Demoiselles* self-consciously demonstrates what might be asked of painting if it is to sufficiently acknowledge its object-dependence, its role as vehicle for the disclosure of irreducible sensuous particularity and the demonstration of what is more than and beyond exchange, above all, of its revelation of the inner affinity binding social sign (the practice of painting itself) and material nature (say, that practice's—and thereby any cognitive practice's—material conditions of possibility).

For theoretical and practical reasons, evaluating and demonstrating the stakes of the *Demoiselles* is usually a retrospective affair. Although from the outset, Picasso conceived of his brothel painting as a defining, statement-making effort (he filled sixteen sketchbooks with preliminary studies), it was almost uniformly reviled by friends and followers who visited his studio in the autumn of 1907. It appeared aggressive, fragmented, incoherent, ugly. So indigestible was it that Daniel-Henry Kahnweiler, Picasso's dealer and an excellent commentator on his work, contended ever afterwards that it was unfinished. Certainly, at that moment it was unshowable, unseeable. It was first publicly exhibited in 1916 in a small, brief show, but its true life or afterlife did not begin until it was acquired and shown by the Museum of Modern Art in New York in 1939.

The *Demoiselles'* ugliness provides a useful starting place for understanding its stakes. I will certainly want to argue that something of the *Demoiselles'* ugliness is internally related to the work's performing an axial rotation in modernist painting. Its ugliness is also connected to its difficulty in being seen at all, and hence to its coming, only retrospectively and very late, perhaps not until now, to define how modernist painting can and must mean. But this is also to say that the *Demoiselles*, as Picasso's first ugly painting, along with the numerous ugly paintings he did throughout the 1920s and 1930s, stand at the crossroads of a core debate about Picasso and modernist painting. The matter is immensely complex, but for the purposes to hand I want to risk limning it as if it were direct and simple. This abbreviated, partial telling of the story is meant to demonstrate how getting clear about the *Demoiselles* is a, if not *the*, necessary condition for getting clear about the history of modernist painting as it presses on our artistic present: only a sufficient elaboration of the *Demoiselles* can address what art or aesthetics after Adorno might be, since only through placing it do we adequately clarify what modernist painting from an Adornoian perspective was in the first instance.[4]

On what has become the dominant theory of modernist painting, Picasso's defining artistic achievement is, with Braque, the invention of cubism. One might think of cubism as a version of enlightenment rationalism in which the magic of perspective and illusionism that allows an as-if view into a world spatially and temporally removed from our own is replaced by a threefold gesture: first, the frank acknowledgment of the picture plane, its shallow depth and delimited space as "where" a painting occurs, as the site of painterly meaning; second, the systematic replacement of mimetic forms by geometric forms, especially squares and rectangles whose two-dimensional form mimics and repeats that of the canvas on which they are painted; hence, third, the incremental displacement of representation and significant iconic content by abstraction and formal content. So much might be regarded as the common elements shared by most accounts of cubism, but it does not say quite enough to tell us how the cubist moment reorients painting in a way that prefigures our postmodern situation. On this more radical reading of the cubist trajectory, cubism, in formalizing painterly practice, involves the deskilling of artistic technique in the direction of mechanical technique as part of a general critique of subjectivity in art, that is, as part of a critique of all that went under the honorifics of individuality, originality, genius, and authorship—all art's prizing of painterliness, touch, and style. Cubism, continuing the scientism and rationalizing efforts of earlier modernisms, sought to move painting in the direction of a formally purified and shareable practice; for Picasso, sharing the development of cubism with Braque was, at least in part, what constituted it as formally anonymous and impersonal, and thereby as truly social and objective. Cubism's intended divorce from the shadows of a forever private subjectivity is what called up the claim that it was to be the true language of painting, painting's own autonomous language.

Conceiving of cubism as a procedural and formal language, as painterly syntax or method, can itself be retrospectively construed as entailing that the ambition of painting cannot be to distinguish itself from photography—as its nearest competitor and threatening avatar of technological rationality—but rather to perform a rapprochement with it. Assume that cubism is the defining breakthrough that allows painting to progress toward a reconciliation with photography; it would then follow that Picasso's own postcubist work, more and more, and certainly from, say, 1918 on, becomes a series a defensive strategies to save painting, which for Picasso was not that different from saving himself, his sense of the authority of his painterly performances, from the mechanical denouement that cubism itself had definitively launched. If the advance to cubism and what can be deciphered as following from it deserves recognition as painterly achievement, then all else—and especially Picasso's ugly paintings—is reaction and defense, the vanity of subjectivity reasserting itself once more. Here is Rosalind Krauss saying exactly this:

> In Picasso's practice, classicism ... is merely the sublimated face of a more powerful and threatening force, the automation of art through the linked logics of the photomechanical, the readymade, and abstraction. And if Picasso acted phobically against automation, deskilling and serialization—erecting the defense of classicism, uniqueness, and virtuosity—this was not because the mechanical was simply an external threat to cubism but rather because it stood as a logical conclusion that could be drawn from within.[5]

It would be fatuous to argue that the mechanical did not stand as *a* logical conclusion to be drawn from cubism. And if it is the case that a dialectical strategy in which *only* the spear that wounds can save, then the abstract, deskilling, mechanical conclusions drawn from cubism are truly necessary: they mark out the only path painting could take if it, or the burden of human significances that the practices of painting espouse and elaborate, are to survive. Prima facie, whatever the temptations here, above all that painting should progress through being at one with technological modernity, this sounds a wildly implausible strategy: to save painting only through its rapprochement with abstraction and the photomechanical, painting in a manner that, by the slightest and almost invisible gesture of difference, does not collapse into what at every moment threatens to absorb, devour, and extinguish it. The reason this Scheherazade version of modernism fails is that *finally* it can make *nothing* of the difference between painterly mechanism and real-world mechanism.[6] Clearly, the danger has not been avoided—the dialectical strategy has manifestly failed; painting's survival is patently being threatened, its emphases and meanings dissolving, the artful enemy of the photomechanical absorbing and extinguishing them at every turn.

What is disappointing in the cubism-is-automation view, however, is not that modernism fails, but that it possesses no content apart from what it borrows from its nearest antagonist. It is that thought, above all, that licenses the counterclaim that cubism was not the great breakthrough moment for modernist painting, that, rather, the "breakthrough" of *Les Demoiselles D'Avignon* can be reinscribed so that it can be seen to adumbrate both what modernism became (at its best) and still might become, and that for these purposes something in the range of Picasso's ugly paintings deserves further consideration since they are in part a response to and upshot of his own disillusionment with cubism. We thus need another way of figuring modernism, one in which cubism becomes a detour in a project whose force field lies elsewhere.[7] My hypothesis is not, of course, that ugliness defines this alternative approach, but that by tracking the deployment of ugliness as a painterly strategy we can prize open an alternative trajectory for modernism, a trajectory emphatically opposed to the mechanical, the geometric, the antirepresentational, and the deskilling, whose hegemony has proved no more beneficial to art than Greenberg's formalist one of which it is the direct descendent.

For the purposes of this paper, I want to claim an ugly, materialist Picasso in opposition to the beautiful, idealist Picasso. Here, then, in just a few sentences, is my hypothesis: There are two irreducible transcendental schemas for the representation of space—geometry and the human body; since the representation of space is a necessary condition for the representation of the world in general, then geometry and the human body are, in the setting of modern painting, competing transcendental frameworks for making perceptual experience of the world possible. Cubism, and all that follows from it, adopts the geometric paradigm. Picasso's ugly paintings are part of a wider attempt to demonstrate that the human body is a material a priori for the space of painting, and hence for perceptual experience generally. Picasso could not conceive of giving up representation not because of hubris or sentimentality, but because he took the human body as providing the necessary conditions for the intelligibility of painting in general.[8] The human body is not merely an object to be represented, grasped, captured, depicted; it is simultaneously the necessary condition of representation. Ugliness is, at a certain moment in our history, the necessary means for disclosing this truth about the meaning of painting; it is a skeptical operator, the force of the negative dismantling the illusory positivity of beauty. In this setting, ugliness is on the side of materiality and truth, and beauty on the side of ideality and illusion.

Ugliness and the Beauty System

From *Les Demoiselles d'Avignon*, Picasso is not merely risking ugliness by transgressing existing aesthetic norms but also contesting what he had come to regard as the shallow illusoriness, the emptiness of modern art as premised on female beauty, female beauty as the figure and bearer of art beauty. That at least some (intense) forms of aesthetic pleasure have their source in the desiring/possessive male gaze on the female form was not even news when Freud stated it.[9] As Laura Mulvey famously elaborated the thesis in relation to cinema:

> In a world ordered by sexual imbalance, pleasure in looking has been split between active/male and passive/female. The determining male gaze projects its phantasy on to the female figure which is styled accordingly. In their traditional exhibi-

tionist role women are simultaneously looked at and displayed, with their appearance coded for strong visual and erotic impact so that they may be said to connote *to-be-looked-at-ness*. Women displayed as sexual object is the leit-motif of erotic spectacle.[10]

For Picasso, this "beauty system," as I shall call it, was fully operative in the art world he inhabited. Beauty as anchored in the male gaze was the way in which the repressive regime of identity thinking sustained itself, its power and ideality, in modern painting. What struck Picasso about the beauty system, however, was not its moral impropriety, but rather its dependence on unacknowledged fantasies and idealizations, hence on the perpetuation of illusion—values simply incommensurable with modernism's self-conscious rigor. Nothing authentic or honest or authoritative could be built on such illusion-driven foundations. Hence, ugliness becomes for Picasso a means of disenchanting art, of seeking an authenticity for painting not dependent on either the easy attractions of the female form or the seductions of pictorial illusion. As Elizabeth Cowling nicely states the thesis: "[H]is revolutionary purpose [in the *Demoiselles*] was to claim the right to regenerate contemporary art through harshness, brutality, fearsomeness, disharmony."[11] The *Demoiselles* was, again, originally too brutal and fearsome to be seen at all; but after the failure of cubism, Picasso returns to this impulse: he would learn how to make irrevocably ugly paintings as no one had before him: *The Dance* (1925), *The Kiss* (1925), *Head of a Woman with a Self-Portrait* (1927–29), through to the weeping woman series of 1937, extending into, say, *Man with a Lollipop* (1938). Picasso's explicitly ugly works are internally related to the pictures of, or meant to cause, horror, especially *Guernica* (1937). My sense that only through retrospection can the impact of the *Demoiselles* be gathered will mean, finally, elaborating it from the perspective of the 1929 *Nude Standing by the Sea*.

It is worthwhile quickly reminding ourselves of what Picasso thought he needed to subvert if modern painting was to continue:

not only the sublime examples of Ingres, who was never far from Picasso's mind, from the more or less discrete early paintings like *The Valpincon Bather* (1808) and *La Grande Odalisque* (1814), to the extravagance of late paintings like *The Source* (1856) and *The Turkish Bath* (1862), a work evidently on Picasso's mind as he painted the *Demoiselles*,[12] but equally the now hard to take and almost absurd Renoir nudes, from the faux discretion of *Bather Arranging Her Hair* (1885) to what looks from our coign of vantage like the paradigm case of the male gaze, the exorbitant fantasizing, idealizing of female sexual availability in *La Dormeuse* (*La baigneuse endormie*; 1887).

Closer to home, Picasso was explicitly attempting to distance himself from Matisse's recent efforts: *Bonheur de vivre* (1905–6), which Cowling describes as "rapturously sensual and joyous,"[13] welcomes the male spectator in as emphatically as Ingres invited him into his Turkish bath or Renoir invited his libidinous gaze to devour the sleeping bather. If Matisse denaturalizes the invitation, the rule of beauty and idealization remain. A year later, in 1907, Matisse will outrage and puzzle visitors to the Salon des Indépendants with *Blue Nude: Memory of Biskra*. Through distortion, sculptural modeling, a posture of uninhibited exposure, and the adoption of a muscular, compact, self-possessed female form whose bodily contours are repeated by the surrounding landscape, Matisse's partially realized ambition was to invoke an "explosive sexuality"[14]—his presumption doubtless being that the more flagrant the sexuality, the more honest or truthful the work. It is this equation that fails here: Matisse's painting is evidently fantasized, a Western nostalgic mythologizing of a primitive North Africa; not only is the painting's primitivism and pastoral vision an overcooked fantasy but it is also impossible now to ignore how that fantasy remains essentially a vehicle for the elaboration of male desire: the nude exhibits herself in all her self-possessed sexuality—her far from ugly upper torso, her long and rounded belly beneath ample breasts—for the sake of the desiring spectator, the hopeful male viewer. Because the presumptive ugliness of this painting results in a heightened exhibition of sexual candor, finally little in the rule of beauty will have been changed; on the contrary, Matisse's effort at debeautification lasts only as long as it takes us to catch up with him, his distortions a declension of beauty, not a departure from it. Candor here translates not into truth, but into a more satisfying illusoriness. And if Matisse loosens the hold of certain formal and naturalistic strictures with *Blue Nude*, one would nonetheless be hard pressed to discover anything definitive in the language of painting that is won by it.

It is the overwhelming power of the beauty system at work in even the most advanced art of the time that reveals why ugliness cannot be a side issue for Picasso, why it must become a constitutive element of what modern painting, hence modernism, must want for itself. Yet, ever since Lessing's *Laocoön*, it has been presumed that the plastic arts, and especially painting, are bound by the rule of beauty: the plastic artist cannot ignore the demands of beauty because an object's beauty is the harmonious effect of its various parts absorbed by the eye at a glance; but because the syntax of the plastic arts is one of part to whole, the material syntax of painting directly converges or overlaps with the logic of beauty.[15] How can ugliness belong to painting if the syntax of painting overlaps with the at-a-glance harmony of parts and whole constituting physical beauty? Part of Picasso's technical answer to this will be to loosen the at-a-glance, providing the apparently static with a complex sense of movement, hence temporality, and relocating the placement of wholeness from canvas to spectator. Such technical answers nonetheless slide past the philosophical conundrum. It is no accident that after setting up the question of the relation of art and aesthetics, and limning their situation, Adorno leads into the heart of his aesthetic theory with a section entitled "On the Categories of the Ugly, the Beautiful, and Technique," a discussion that precedes his accounts of natural beauty, art beauty, semblance and expression, and so on. Ugliness, which for the musically fixated Adorno means dissonance, comes first.

That said, the discussion of ugliness is among the least satisfying, the ugliest, in *Aesthetic Theory*, the one I imagine Adorno reworking the most brutally for a final draft.[16] Yet the leitmotif of the section is plain: ugliness must be shown to have a meaning that is not simply the absence of beauty if its role in modernist art is to begin to be comprehended. Here are four theses that I think are vindicated, at least in part, by the example of the *Demoiselles*. First, "Inner coherence shatters on what is superior to it, the truth of content.... The utmost integration is the utmost semblance and this causes the former's reversal."[17] The second sentence first: Integration generates the appearance of a work *being* self-sufficient, whole, complete, and unique. This is semblance because the condition of such apparent completeness is an item being outside the demands of empirical experience, of being isolated in an art world. It is further the case that it is only apparently true that parts are realized or fulfilled in their placement within the whole. Although the authority of artworks as wholes depends on fully absorbing and integrating their materials and only thereby becoming fully self-realized, this always occurs at the cost of dominating the materials integrated. One feature of beauty—for which the model of the human form is insistent—is the harmonious integration of materials. Because art is form, then at least in the case of modern autonomous art, the integrity of the materials formed must be sacrificed to the whole; the more formally powerful the art, the more thoroughly are the parts dissolved into a functionally assigned place. It is precisely awareness of this dissolution that marks the shift from classical modern art to modernism: as formal integration perfects itself, the sacrifice of that which has been integrated is noted and released. (Adorno locates the emergence of this movement toward disintegration in Beethoven's late style.) This shift presages a reversal in the logic of the artwork: instead of its material parts being for the sake of the ideal whole, the now no longer ideal whole becomes a vehicle for the disclosure of its sensuously particular parts. Dissonance, disunity, fragmentariness as forms that underline that disintegration of authoritative wholeness, of harmony and resolution, hence appear originally as ugly.

Second, Adorno claims that inner coherence, perfected wholeness, must, in time, shatter before a higher value: the truth of content. To the degree that aesthetic wholes become vehicles for the disclosure or authorization of their parts, the goal of art shifts away from beauty to, well, something like truth or authenticity or rigor or consistency—some appropriately quasi-cognitive notion that reveals the stakes of an artwork apart from just being beautiful and delivering pleasure, however difficult. To some extent, this has always been true of modern art: shorn of its role of legitimating religious and political ideals external to itself, artistic autonomy demanded an art that obeyed only those laws immanent to its practice. But this entails that a necessary condition for aesthetic authority is that works self-consciously come to bind themselves to laws immanent to their possibility of existence. And this requires that artworks come to have as one of their constitutive goals the advance of art itself, the advance in the development and purification of the laws constitutive of the practice. Modernism is the self-conscious adoption of this entailment and requirement. But this is as much as to say that not only is there a protest against the beauty system (thesis one) but also, even formally, that modernist art possesses goals fully independent of the beauty of harmonious resolution. It is this fact that leads Adorno to claim that the "deaestheticization of art is immanent to art" (*AT*, 59).

Theses one and two motivate an espousal of the ugly and ground an art that can be rationally indifferent to the claim of beauty. Neither demonstrates the falsity of the idealist theorem that makes ugliness nothing but a lack of beauty. Third, then, Adorno claims that "what appears ugly is in the first place what is historically older, what art rejected on its path toward autonomy, and what is therefore mediated in itself. The concept of the ugly may well have originated in the separation of art from its archaic phase: It marks the permanent return of the archaic, intertwined with the dialectic of enlightenment in which art participates" (*AT*, 47). These formulations are more than usually condensed and qualified, but there can be little doubt that Adorno is here employing genealogy in order to make conceptual space for the emergence of primitivism in modernist art in a manner that is not intrinsically regressive—as he originally thought was the case with respect to Stravinsky.[18]

If art is itself historical, then a conceptual space is opened for a historical consideration of beauty and ugliness too. In claiming that ugliness is what appears historically older, with one swipe Adorno displaces the idealist reification of beauty. What came first on Adorno's account were the cultic masks whose terrified looks were intended to be expressive passively and actively; archaic masks express both being terrified at all-powerful nature and, in the look of terror to express, that is, to cause, terror and thus to appropriate for oneself the power of the very thing that is terrifying. Masks are primitive mimetic forms, art before there was art, art as still submerged in magic. Art as mimetic comportment can only emerge fully if it separates itself from the magical heritage implied in its archaic forms. Art beauty, the beauty of form, Adorno appears to be claiming, is the sublation, the negation and preservation of the archaic ugly; or rather, what we now call ugly becomes so as art distances and separates itself from the cultic response to terrifying nature (in part because, with the advance of civilization, it has stopped being terrifying). Beauty belongs to the dialectic of enlightenment because as a series of mechanisms for *forming* nature, not merely as a means but as an end (which is what beauty signifies for Adorno), it both brings nature within the ambit of the civilizational process of release from bondage to natural ends and, simultaneously, dominates and represses those items it forms.

An immediate inference from this historical understanding of beauty is that the archaic or primitive is a disowned stratum of the artwork (what art repudiated in becoming art), whose recurrence in modernist art should thus be viewed not as an importation of the exotic, but as a return of the repressed. Almost certainly thinking about the *Demoiselles*, Adorno says just this about Picasso: "Not all advanced art bears the marks of the frightening; these marks are most evident where not every relation of the *peinture* to the object has been severed, where not every relation of dissonance to the fulfilled and negated consonance has been broken off: Picasso's shocks were ignited by the principle of deformation" (*AT*, 287).

Fourth, what goes along with the identification of the archaic as ugliness is the survey of specific kinds of contents that are condemned as ugly. Adorno conceives of ugly contents in a variety of ways: ugliness entered art as the lower classes became objects of artistic representation; their suffering and deformation at the hands of society was expressed by ugliness. Equally prohibited as ugly are simply all those items condemned by art: "polymorphous sexuality as well as the violently mutilated and lethal" (*AT*, 47). Finally, as a kind of summation or elaboration of these contents, Adorno contends that the aesthetic condemnation of the ugly is "dependent on the inclination...to equate...the ugly with the expression of suffering, and by projecting it, to despite it" (*AT*, 49). Evidently, this account of ugly contents merges easily with theses one and three.

Les Demoiselles d'Avignon mobilizes all four theses on ugliness—protesting repressive harmony through dissonance, promoting artistic advance, the return of the archaic repressed, the expression of suffering—in its ambition of expressing the primitive and irresolvable ambiguity of human sexuality, where human sexuality is taken, via the beauty system, to be internally related to the very idea, the formal logic of modern painting. Hence, elaborating these four aspects of the beauty system is what painting must do if it is to overthrow that system, where overthrowing the beauty system will amount to giving the Copernican turn an axial rotation toward the object. It is this overthrow I now want to demonstrate.

Picasso's Parataxis

Leo Steinberg summarizes the *Demoiselles'* accomplishments thus: "The picture breaks the triple spell of tradition—idealization, emotional distance, and fixed-focus perspective—the tradition of high-craft illusionism which conducts the spectator unobserved to his privileged seat." Notice how for Steinberg the triple spell of tradition operates in order to place the unobserved spectator in a privileged position: contemplator, beholder, possessor of what is beheld. In order to break the spell of the beauty system the beholder must himself become beheld; in being beheld he must become undone (losing the privilege of emotional distance); in order to become beheld and undone the pictorial surface must become disordered, not incoherent, but emphatically *not* arranged for the sake of licensing the privileged seeing of one contemplator looking in on the depicted scene (hence breaking the rule of fixed-focus perspective); in becoming beheld, undone, and the locus of an order rather than the contemplator of it, the viewer must be corralled into the material world of painterly representation rather than the ideal world of beauty: he must undergo ugliness.

It will prove useful to employ the disordering of fixed-focus perspective as an interpretive wedge. My hypothesis here is that Picasso deploys what is best thought of as the painterly equivalent of parataxis in order to accomplish this systematic disordering, a disordering into a new conception of pictorial order. Literally, parataxis is a form of syntax in which semantic units—words, clauses, sentences, paragraphs—are ordered by sheer juxtaposition rather than through logical/conceptual subordination that is signposted by the familiar connectives of hypotactic syntax: if x, then y; x because y; x necessitates y; and so on. With parataxis there are just the items set next to one another—*xy*—with the character of their relation to be elicited through reflective consideration of their respective semantic/material contents. Adorno argues for parataxis being one of the central mechanisms of modernist art since it opens up the possibility of a different relation between concept and object, unity and multiplicity.[19]

Here then is my analogical hypothesis: what Steinberg calls the spell of the tradition leading the spectator to his privileged seat is the equivalent in the history of painting to what Adorno identified as the spell of the unifying ego subordinating the multiplicity of the world to its instrumental ends by conceptual synthesis, by, that is, unifying the complex many under a system of hierarchical subordination. This, recall, is his conception of transcendental subjectivity as the fullest expression of the Copernican turn. Since in painting it is high-craft illusionism that lends the spectator his privileged position, this illusionism can usefully be considered as equivalent to painting's version of transcendental idealism: *the ideal spectator replaces the transcendental ego, the three mechanisms of idealization, emotional distance, and fixed-focus perspective thus become the forms of synthesis subordinating pictorial space to ideal unity that make the position of privileged contemplation possible*. The female body is the fundament—both in terms of form and affect—supporting the entire system. The female form in its what-is-to-be-looked-atness is technically, at least in part, the mechanism of idealization itself; however, this feature of the beauty system, like causality in the conceptual system, can be considered the pivot of the system as a whole.[20] Hence, as the upshot and support of the threefold synthesis, the female form expresses the beauty system's concept of an object in general. Conceptual synthesis understood hypotactically deprives the units ordered of their particularity and material density because it subordinates them all to what will satisfy the ego, what will accord with its needs for order and control—knowledge as domination. The tradition of high-craft illusionism with its threefold synthesis subordinates the female form to the contemplating gaze of the male ego for the sake of aesthetic-sexual pleasure—beauty as sexual availability. The harmonization of truth and beauty, their exchangeability or translatability into one another is the way in which art has been complicit with the long reign of instrumental reason even as it has worked against it, even as it meant to be offering an alternative, noninstrumental rationality, even as it has sought to reveal a domain of ends beyond the sway of instrumental need and want. *The beauty system is what prevents beauty from being beautiful.*

By dropping connectives and ordering devices, parataxis ends the rule of subordination, forcing or permitting each element or unit to become a concrete particular whose relation to what is placed against it, adjacent to it, side-by-side with it to become no longer given but what is to be worked out by the reader/observer. Painterly parataxis, I want to argue, is one of the keys to Picasso's art; parataxis is to Picasso's art what overallness (decorative order) is to Matisse's. The *Demoiselles* is the founding instance; parataxis is its orienting formal device. In a way, that this is what Picasso is up to should be obvious: if the project is to move away from deep illusionist space, then the action of a painting must press up to the picture plane itself. The obvious question then arises: how does one carry on with significant representation while simultaneously acknowledging the authority of the picture plane? Picasso's answer, or at least one of his answers, which he kept revising and refining for the remainder of his life, was, instead of subordinating the parts to the whole—the parts of the painting to the whole of the painting, and the parts of the human body to the ideal whole of the human body—he would set the parts next to one another, juxtapose them, place them side by side. (Even the terms necessary to describe parataxis—"setting," "juxtaposing," "placing"—lend to the parts so placed independence and solidity, with the act of painting itself coming to be depicted as acknowledging that independence, a mastering through a letting go of mastery.)

In claiming parataxis to be Picasso's organizing gesture in the

Demoiselles, I am doing no more than giving a procedural and aesthetic name to what Steinberg critically described in his remarkable essay "The Philosophical Brothel"—a title referring to the painting's own first name. Steinberg summarizes the upshot of Picasso's paratactic practice as being, exactly, an axial rotation in virtue of which the viewer, rather than having a privileged seat, the scene for his sake, becomes the painting's "object."

> In the *Demoiselles* painting this rule of traditional narrative art [the threefold synthesis of the beauty system] yields to an anti-narrative counter-principle: neighboring figures share neither a common space nor a common action, do not communicate or interact, but relate singly, directly, to the spectator. A determined dissociation of each from each is the means of throwing responsibility for the unity of the action upon the viewer's subjective response. The event, the epiphany, the sudden entrance [of the student into the brothel in the preparatory drawings for the painting] is still the theme—but rotated through ninety degrees toward a viewer conceived as the picture's opposite pole.[21]

My procedure in what follows is to track Steinberg's account sufficiently, including various divergences from it, to reveal how Picasso's parataxis entails the axial rotation, and how that axial rotation amounts to giving painting as a whole a turn toward the object—by which I will mean not the turn toward the spectator as object, although that too, but rather what Steinberg fails to grasp: the emergence of the body-object, the form of the human body itself as the transcendental condition for the possibility of pictorial space. Confirming this final move will require going beyond the *Demoiselles* to Picasso's 1929 *Nude Standing by the Sea*.

Let me begin by considering a small but obvious instance of Picasso's paratactic procedure: the far left figure's left hand, which appears to float disconnected above her head, without the—organizing, syntactical—mediation of arm length and distance. What are we to make of this? Steinberg thinks we should assume "that

Picasso here wanted an oblique recession, pursued by an implied outstretched arm raised at thirty degrees. The disconnectedness of the hand at the visible terminus of the stretch then becomes emblematic of the maximum distance" (25). Steinberg then lays out what it means to be employing a paratactic formula at this juncture: "The aim is to express the recession of this upper flap not through linear or aerial perspective, not by way of color or physical clues such as overlaps, but through the suasion of gesture, the supposed necessity of an omitted arm between head and hand—a saccadic leap offered only to our anatomic intuition" (26). Our "anatomic intuition" here does the work formally done for us by linear perspective; in making sense of her gesture in this way, *we* become responsible for the integrity of her body and its spacing, its integrity "up to us," up to the viewer, and achieved only through the viewer rather than offered up to him. Further, to underline the obvious, insofar as it is the "suasion of gesture" that ignites our anatomic intuition, our judgment must be operating through mimetic recapitulation rather than constructive elaboration: we grasp her position not through observation but, finally, through identification. This is central for Adorno's claim that art forms a repository for mimetic, thinglike rationality, a rationality that both acknowledges the precedence of the thing and returns the seeing eye to its bodily habitation.

The next nude presents even more ferocious problems. Her left leg does not appear to reach down to the ground; rather, the left foot appears draped over her right shin, with the right leg simply disappearing. Given the slight bend of her right knee, we are forced to conclude that she is not, in fact, standing. At one point in the preparatory studies she was sitting in a chair with her left leg crossed over her right; in "subsequent studies her chair dissolves and she sinks back, disposing herself at last, like an odalisque. She ends up recumbent ... but seen in bird's eye perspective" (27). The idea of verticalizing a supine figure has precedents. What nonetheless makes the idea so difficult to hold in place here is that she is given to us as nearly vertical to the picture plane while placed in utter adjacency to the, in fact, vertical nudes on either side of her. Everything about how Steinberg goes on to describe her heightens the extraordinary paratactic formulation Picasso is working: "She rests recessive but still extended, insulated in her own rocking space capsule. Adjacency without nearness; withdrawal without attenuation of presence. The full-length projection of her, claiming undiminished scope in the field, makes the beholder work harder; one has to push mental levers to keep an erected *gisante* lying down" (28).

Once we are alerted to her posture and the disposition of her limbs, we *know* that the second nude must be lying down; but given her location in the painting, the lack of recession from knee to head, and her consequent vertical relation to the picture plane, we are never going to *see* her as fully recumbent (a point Steinberg worries and fudges); we cannot ascend to the aerial view implied without losing our viewing perspective altogether. Being unable to see her as she must be seen automatically buckles illusionist pretense; illusion is just what we are missing here. But that is also what we are missing in her relation to the nudes on either side of her: her apparent verticality in relation to their actual verticality splinters or fragments the demoiselles' space of habitation, so that each possesses her own space as defined by posture and gesture, a bodily space (without any of the other clues that normally provide spatial depth), without there being any space they are emphatically *in*. They are truly juxtaposed one to the other across the picture plane. Said differently: each nude possesses her own space in light of her bodily being; hence each nude provides orientation and structure for the picture as a whole, which is as much as to say that none does—the idea of "picture as a whole" must now go into scare quotes. Each nude is a center, a place, and an orientation; hence each demands acknowledgment separately from her companions. Each nude becomes related to her companions through literal adjacency on the picture plane, on the one hand,

and through being related by the observer to the space implied by bodily posture. In the same way that in the case of the floating hand the observer must, through "anatomical intuition," connect hand to body, so generally, through the possibilities of bodily orientation, the observer now becomes responsible for making room for and spacing the nudes in relation to one another.

However, and here is Picasso's move beyond the containing logic of part and whole, *this effort will fail* because the bodies provide clues sufficient only for the *possibility* of their spatial relation one to the other without enough systematic detail or systematic relating of one bodily amplified space to another to turn possibility into actuality; this scene can be registered but not surveyed or reconstructed. This is as much as to say that these bodies *are* the space of this painting, it emerges from them and collapses back on them.[22] These bodies are not in space; they spatialize, give it and hold it open in just the way the far left demoiselle opens the curtain onto the scene and the back demoiselle parts the curtains that allow her to be seen. Both these figures, I am suggesting, demonstrate the difference between body-spatiality and high-craft illusionism of the kind where the curtain really is an entry into deep space, as in Vermeer's *Artist in His Studio* or *Allegory of the New Testament*. Picasso's overturning of this is patent in his making the figures presumably furthest away—the center demoiselle and the right-hand figure emerging from the curtains—pictorially the tallest.

The impossibility of eliciting an overall spatial structure and the power of each of these bodies to give space by being its source achieve a fierce and wildly disorienting realization with the squatting nude on the right. While it is natural to read her as sitting with her back to the viewer, her head rapidly swiveling around at his entrance, there is sufficient counter-evidence in the other direction, above all that she casts both eyes on the intruder, her head hence so frontal as to make a back view improbable; a hypothesis underlined by the way her "boomerang hand" cups her face mask. Conversely, the hint of backbone and disappearing pigtail press in the opposing direction. Picasso's elision of thumbs, the purely angular thrust of arms and elbows, the odd extra flat plane of flesh adhering to the "left" arm resting on her knee, and, Picasso's paratactic coup, no neck, her head simply sitting atop the body, leave the position of this nude systematically ambiguous. As Steinberg rightly comments, her flattened impress "orients itself simultaneously inward and outward" (58), which is to say, Picasso is here pursuing not flatness but a spatiality that emanates from her body alone. While Picasso is not yet quite explicitly offering multiple perspectives of the body all at once—that will have to await *Large Nude by the Sea* (1909), with her sternum and backbone both equally present—he does make her bodily orientation systematically ambiguous so that on the picture plane itself are implied competing perspectives and orientations, which in turn imply the necessity for imaginatively elaborating spatial structures concomitant with each perspectival take. Yet, in remaining systematically ambiguous, all these implied spatial possibilities themselves remain irresolvable and unmasterable—they are "hinted at," "implied," "invoked," the "sense" of them "palpable," all without even the glimmer of a corresponding fulfilling intuition; hence these spatial possibilities are in fact incapable of being inspected; which entails that there is, in fact, *no place from which she can be seen*. I almost want to say that she possesses all the conditions for see-ability while not being actually seen. And, of course, this final twist is no accident: for all her outrageous exposure, explicitness, and savagery, she sees more than is seen—as do they all. Thinking through what is at stake here is complex.

In a typically crescendo-building passage, in his "Resisting Cézanne, Part 2: The Polemical Part," Steinberg summarizes what he takes to be the formal character and innovations of the *Demoiselles* under the heading of Picasso's "discontinuity principle." What is perfect in this reprise of the painting for our purposes is that nearly every word or phrase Steinberg uses to designate features that are either components of or contribute to the painting's "discontinuity" could, with more right be said to be aspects of or features contributing to its paratactic structuring.

> Comparison with the numerous studies for the *Demoiselles* revealed how tenaciously Picasso pursued this end; he was resolved to undo the continuities of form and field which Western art has so long taken for granted. The famous stylistic rupture at the right turned out to be merely a consummation. Overnight, the contrived coherencies of representational art—the feigned unities of time and place, the stylistic consistencies—all were declared to be fictional. The *Demoiselles* confessed itself a picture conceived in duration and delivered in spasms. In this one work Picasso discovered that the demands of discontinuity could be met on multiple levels: by cleaving depicted flesh; by elision of limbs and abbreviation; by slashing the web of connecting space; by abrupt changes of vantage; and by a sudden stylistic shift at the climax. Finally, the insistent staccato of the presentation was found to intensify the picture's address and symbolic charge: the beholder, instead of observing a roomful of lazing whores, is targeted from all sides. So far from suppressing the subject, the mode of organization heightens its flagrant eroticism.[23]

The advantage of thinking of what is depicted in the passage in terms of parataxis rather than discontinuity is that the latter term is merely negative, while the former concerns the liberation of material or semantic elements from their embedding in logical, abstract, or grammatical forms that, finally, are discovered to be indifferent to the material they bear, or worse, are an arrangement of those materials for purposes wholly extrinsic to them. I should not want to say that classical forms delivering beauty were, historically, only forms of domination (on the contrary, again, beauty bore an indefatigable emancipatory meaning), but they can become predominantly so, and had done for modern painting.

As Steinberg pointedly concludes, the upshot of Picasso's fragmentary style in the *Demoiselles* is the dislocation of viewer from his privileged position until he becomes "targeted from all sides," the painting's "subject," that is, who or what is subject-ed, done and undone by the nudes' piercing, freezing looks: abandon all hope, ye who enter here. If there is a place where Steinberg's reading seems inappropriate it is in his claim of "flagrant eroticism." In the viewer losing the privilege of viewing subject and becoming subjected to the cool or harassing views of these women, the meaning of body alters radically. Begin with the obvious: these bodies do not invite possession: none are stereotypically feminine, none invites touch, and, if sight is the erotic extension of touch, then none even quite invites being seen, or welcomes it; none is presented as expressly passively sexual. These are large, mannish women with thick thighs; angular, narrow-waisted bodies; breasts, when present at all, more often than not pointed rather than round. The three on the left have small, slit mouths, while the mouths of the two masked figures open in tight surprise to hoot an unreadable denigration of the interloper. If the posture of two central nudes—the one on the left with one arm reaching behind her head, her partner with both arms reaching back—acknowledges a sexual situation, acknowledges their in-principle sexual availability, their eyes, bolted on the intruder, bespeak a saturnine indifference, as if nothing about their bodies, above all their nakedness, their exposure, should be taken as wanting or welcoming or needing—on the contrary.[24] These bodies and the space they carve out for themselves refuse "entry."

The first and most obvious conclusion to be drawn from this reversal from invitation to refusal is a generalization of the conclusion already drawn about body and spatiality: because these bodies cannot be possessed, because of their implacable character, their unavailability, together with their possession of their own objectifying gaze, the natural link between seeing and erotic, possessive desire is severed. The desire to see that is the paradigmatic sublimation of the desire to sexually possess, which itself was classically fulfilled through the ecstatic vision of female beauty is here emphatically broken. But since the classical vision of beauty was a fantasy—and no less fantastical in Matisse's *Blue Nude* than in Ingres's *The Turkish Bath*—Picasso's painting, precisely in its implacableness, its nonsurveyability, and its interruption and dismantling of the possessive gaze, strikes out toward truth against fantasy. Its overcoming of illusion is the mark of its truthfulness, its authenticity. The *Demoiselles* is the first "true" painting of the twentieth century—it impels truthfulness or authenticity in place of beauty as the locus of painterly authority. Ugliness, in its unmasking, brings material truth against idealist illusion.

What is that truth? Again, a generalization from the body-gives-space thesis seems necessary: if the depicted body is not the final *object* of (pictorial) perception, because seeing it is not the consummation of pictorial viewing, or better, pictorial viewing can no longer be figured as contemplation become consummation, then the bodies viewed become the *condition of possibility* of pictorial experience, its material a priori. As each demoiselle provides her own space, so each, more generally, opens up the very possibility of there being something intelligible, meaningful to be seen. These bodies in their implacable thereness create, open, make possible a perceptual relation to the world in general: perception leans on them. Or even: instead of vision possessing these objects, these bodies possess vision—dominate, solicit, and expunge it at once. This is what I intended in claiming that the *Demoiselles* instigates or performs an axial rotation, a counter-Copernican turn, shifting from the identity thinking of the beauty system, through the negativity of ugliness, to the nonidentity of body-object with subject, the body viewed as in excess of—Picasso figuratively conceives of this as "above"—its being viewed. Only a framework having this breadth does anything like justice to Picasso's revolution.

I shall return to this claim in the next section. At this juncture, however, it might be objected that in raising Picasso's project to the realm of transcendental philosophy I am also defending myself against the *Demoiselles*, its fierceness and awfulness, as, most certainly, Steinberg himself does in celebrating the painting's sexual energy in his wildly implausible claim that "Picasso's space insinuates total initiation, like entering a disordered bed" (63). There is certainly "initiation" here, but nothing like immersion or "entering," and certainly not a disordered bed. Earlier in the essay, Steinberg takes a different approach, which is closer but still seems wrong to me, claiming that "the picture is a tidal wave of female aggression; one either experiences the *Demoiselles* as an onslaught, or shuts it off" (15). There is some kind of onslaught on the viewer, but to think of it as simply aggression loses the disorienting coolness, almost indifference, of the two central "European" figures, and reduces to a single note the masks that strike me as far more ambiguous. Following Steinberg, there has been a veritable storm of interpretations, most keying their overall interpretation to the climactic moment of the mask of the crouching figure, which is taken as the upshot of Picasso's exposure to African art. So William Rubin would see the painting as rehearsing an *agon* between Eros and Thanatos in which the different styles of painting "span the polarity from Eros to Thanatos—from the allure of the female body to "the horror" of it;"[25] Yve-Alain Bois takes that final mask as a Medusa's head, her gaze consequently castrating. For Bois, not only does the Medusa's head thesis link to a return of the repressed, but, more importantly, it is the pivot on which the painting's axial rotation turns on precise analogy with Caravaggio's employment of it in his *Medusa*: "It thematizes the spectator's petrification ... and it makes the female sex organ (the Medusa's head) the essential interrupter of narrative, the icon that challenges the (male) spectator by signifying to him that his comfortable position, outside the narrative scene, is not as secure as he might think."[26]

Each of these accounts of the vehemence of the *Demoiselles* strikes me as mastering and simplifying, as if getting the right interpretation of the painting would allow us to know what we are feeling in relation to it. This is just the relation between painting and spectator that the painting repudiates and dismantles: in the same way in which Picasso provides the conditions for pictorial experience without satisfying them, so affectively and thematically the implacable bodies and inscrutable faces freeze the viewer with their unknowableness, by which I mean not their being without affect, but the utter ambiguousness and ambivalence of their presence. It is not the agon between Eros and Thanatos that Picasso rehearses, as if the left side of the painting were all Eros and the right side all Thanatos; it is that in this setting we cannot locate where Eros ends and aggression/the death drive/castration begins. It is the female form as the power of life *and* death, of the erotic as knotted with and involving its opposite just as these figures knot sexual difference so that the very terms and conditions of the beauty system—active/masculine and passive/feminine—lose their visual purchase. It should be remembered that the head of the far left Iberian figure certainly draws on Gauguin's *The Spirit of the Dead Watching* (1892); as watcher over this scene she is both "madam" and memento mori. If the arms behind the heads of the two central European demoiselles signify their self-display, the verticality and sharpness of their elbows do not lack aggressiveness. As Steinberg comments about Cézanne's earliest use of this motif, "[T]he pose is struck as a provocation that tempers bland nakedness into a weapon."[27] Certainly the mask of the crouching figuring is frightening, but are we so sure of *what* we are frightened by here? The labels sex, death, woman, desire, or castration are just so many evasions of the irreducible difficulty of sexual encounter that Picasso means to be rehearsing. He means for us to encounter in this painting sexual encounter itself as originary, as a traumatic opening to experience rather than a moment in it. This can be so only if the paratactically presented bodies are sources—of life, death, sexual pleasure, and sexual terror; having this power is what gives these figures their authority and coolness; experiencing this power is what undoes the viewer, undoes his detachment, undoes any idea the viewer may have of being outside and master of the space viewed. Steinberg comments that "the *Demoiselles* [is] about the human condition, about that perpetual moment in which self-knowledge arises in sexual confrontation" (52). I would elaborate this claim by saying that Picasso manages to make the *Demoiselles* a moment of radical self-consciousness on the part of the viewer because the painting operates a systematic dismantling of the viewer's self-possession, hence his presumptive but unearned authority. *Les Demoiselles D'Avignon* is indeed primitive, but primitive the same way that Hobbes's state of nature is primitive, or even the way Hegel's struggle for recognition is primitive, terminating in the dialectic of master and slave. In this painting is revealed the source of the slave's power over her master; and here, for the first time perhaps in modern painting, the master shudders, quakes, even collapses. So we come to self-consciousness in the experience of an absolute otherness. Painting can thus begin again.

Stone, Bone, Geometry: The Living Body

Here perhaps is the paradox of art, a paradox that presses in harder on painting than on any other art form: how can the excess of art over conceptual meaning be located in its material sensuousness if art's materiality is, finally, nothing but dead matter—pigment on canvas? My operating hypothesis is that from 1907 on Picasso always—apart from the short span of time in which cubism reigned—had this question or the challenge implicit in it at the back of his mind (if not always at the front), that he knew in his bones that painting could only fully come to itself, authorize itself, if it could square this circle. Here are some fundamental elements that any engagement with the paradox should include. Art is connected to life itself because art, like physical beauty, operates within the ambit of a logic of whole and part, a logic that has its home in the living organism. Once it is conceded that painting operates with a logic of part and whole, its practice will come to be shadowed by the problem of organic form. Since dependence on the normative authority of organic form can look like dependence on the authority of a premodern metaphysics of life, the temptation to turn to geometric form, the logic of part plus part, can seem overwhelming. My suggestion has been that this is in fact not a real option: either geometric form is an expression of human experience, in which case the question of the "human" element has simply been hidden or deferred; or geometric form is autonomous, in which case it is unclear how it pertains to art. The embarrassment of organic form, the entwinement of art and life, cannot be avoided.

At this point, it may be argued that I am misstating the problem; after all, the fundamental question about works of art is not whether they are alive or dead, but how they mean, and meaning comes from human mindedness. From at least Lessing to the present the thought has been that matter does not mean on its own, rather mind or spirit "breathes life" into matter by giving it meaning. Among the difficulties here, the most pertinent is that this way of answering the problem generates an absolute bifurcation between the life/body system and the meaning system, a bifurcation that only makes sense in the kind of Platonic universe that no one now supposes we inhabit. Against the background of this uninviting scenario, it becomes salient to note that there is one place where the axis of dead matter versus organic life meets the axis of meaning versus dead matter, and that is paradigmatically the human body, but also necessarily, by extension, all living bodies. The human body in its *sheer material givenness*, in its matter-of-fact material self-presentation is alive and a source of meaning, meaningful in its aliveness. The human body itself means, and means beyond, before, after, and how we intentionally mean it. So the human body in its sheer being there—standing or sitting or lying, not even moving—means. And what it means first is aliveness (or deadness, which for the body is a mode of aliveness, and hence different from dead matter, material stuff). Which is to say, it is somehow the human body as itself a material presence in the world that is a source of meaning rather than consciousness or mind or spirit or language or even desire (although desire is, especially for Picasso, utterly proximate to aliveness and its absence—this is precisely the upshot of my interpretation of the *Demoiselles*). Because the body autonomously and automatically means, cannot be prevented from meaning except by being erased altogether, the body necessarily organizes visual space. Visual space is a precipitate of the bodies inhabiting it.

Or at least this becomes Picasso's theme: the body's meaning in excess of and independently of how it is meant; or, the inevitability, the ineluctable terror or passion, of its being meant (desired, wanted, seen, painted). All these themes are already there in the *Demoiselles* but require the passage through cubism and its failure to become explicit. Think of this stuttering emergence this way: Let us concede that consciousness, language, desire, and so on are sources not just of meaning but of ideality, of normative rightness. Beginning with, say, Cézanne, modern art discovered that although it was directed to the visual presence of the world, the terms of its practice were burdened with ideals from elsewhere, ideals that were extrinsic to the sheer material givenness of things as they imposed themselves on the perceptual experiences that painting was to be a record of. The most difficult and therefore most contested "thing" here must be the human body. If painting is to achieve an integrity intrinsic to its material practice, then it would have to excise all extra-bodily meaning from the body, let the body present itself, be present by itself, which in practice means either presenting it through the negation of its idealized forms or capturing it before idealization has had a chance to gain access to it: presenting it through the negation of beauty, through distortion and dismemberment, or capturing the body before beauty (which in practice may not be so different from the negative strategy).

Consider now Picasso's *Nude Standing by the Sea*.[28] I want to say that this painting recovers and deepens the *Demoiselles*' axial rotation against the beauty system by displacing cubism's own presumptive displacement of organic form. Hence, the most salient and unmistakable feature of this painting is that this monster is, for the most part, constructed, made out of geometric solids: her head is just a ball, her body a pyramid, her legs rectangles like those of a table, her breasts small sharply pointed cones, her buttocks half spheres. Moreover, the ball that is her head is without features, just a stone ball, and it is very small, tiny in proportion to the rest of her body. Not only does the smallness of her head—and I think this is general also for all the pinheaded bodies that Picasso painted at this time—drive out the possibility that her body is just an extension of her consciousness, or what self-awareness she has might be located in her head, but, for the viewer, it eliminates the possibility that in responding to her we are responding to an expressive, affect-laden irresistible human face. No eyes as windows into the soul here, no Levinas face of the other, no look or gaze or returning view. But this is also to admit that, unlike Picasso's ferocious demoiselles, this figure is open to being viewed, the way some of us used to view bodies before Picasso made it impossible (at least impossible in the old, unselfconscious way it was possible to view bodies before him). But, of course, it is not really to-be-looked-at-ness that is in question here. It is the language of cubism, the language of geometry and geometrical construction that is at issue.

In saying that Picasso flagrantly presses the fact of her geometric construction, I mean to be insisting that he is allowing in everything a painterly rationalist could want: here is a body that is nothing but pure geometrical forms. And the purity of her being nothing but a composite of geometrical forms matters not at all to her presence. In this setting her geometrical construction is not the source of her meaningful presence, but, if anything, an explicit form of testing it, resisting it: the resistance fails. The geometry of her form is sublated at every moment by those geometrical forms being those *of* a human body, human bodily form effectively sublating, overcoming, and subsuming other contestants to the throne of originating form. *We* do not breath life into the human body, we do not project meaning on to it; it exemplifies meaning and life even as geometrical construction would seek to crush it.

Further, I interpret the meaning of Picasso depicting her as something constructed and, indeed, as something that has been sculpted from stone as pressing the fact of her brute materiality, her sheer material presence as opposed to any illusory inwardness. I do not know whether we are inclined to ascribe soul or sapience to her; maybe she is more "primitive" than that, before soul or sapience the way the demoiselles may be thought of as before beauty (before the beauty system could get hold of them). And while I need to acknowledge her sapience, I do not think of it as anything "inward"; I do not know what it would mean for her to suffer. She feels, to the extent she does, precisely in proportion to the extent she is a living body, no more, no less—which is the puzzle and wonder of her. (She is emphatically turned toward the sun, "soaking" it in; but there is no heat or hotness here; her turning and facing thus occur the way a plant might turn and face the sun; the sun is her medium or element, like the blue of sea and sky.)

So the metaphorical thought Picasso is after is that her material being in the world is no different in kind from the material life afforded by her painted representation. But this presses in exactly the opposite direction to what we may have supposed: in a presentation of the human body the exchange between obdurate materiality and material meaning is immediate: she is—appears to be—alive. Because of her human form, her aliveness is necessarily given; because of her geometric construction and because of her stoniness, we are given pause: how exactly is she alive? How does or can she "feel" in her stony body? But this pause and these questions cannot fully abrogate the "sense" of her as alive, where the only possible explanation for the insistence of that sense is her human form.

Against these thematics of her brute materiality, I take her standing and uprightness, which are undeniable, to operate here as a counterpoint; that is, what her easy unselfconscious uprightness signifies is the uprising or *immanent ideality* of the human form as a sheer material presence, and hence an ideality not dependent on extrinsic ideals (like all ideals of beauty).[29] It is the combination of brute materiality and uprightness that Picasso is after, therefore, not just the utter transposability of materiality and phenomenality, of deadness and aliveness, but the increment of that joining that uprightness allows: an ideal of the human rising up in sheer being there. The painting appears to insist upon an impossible union of opposites in which the up movement from dead matter to living meaning and the down movement from ideality to inert stuff were allowed to perfectly coincide. Uprightness is not meant to provide the terms of this work's authenticity, but rather forms a further elaboration of how human bodily form possesses not just sense but even an incipient ideality in its mere givenness in ways that utterly dissolve the significance of the body's geometrical material construction.[30] I am hence urging that the nude's uprightness must be understood in relation to the general project of desublimation, and hence as a component of the attempt to close the space between matter and meaning, dead stuff and aliveness—a component of the attempt to interrogate again and again the image of the female body as where these opposites converge and coincide.

If I can put these claims in the context of my remarks on the *Demoiselles*, I would say that what is being asked of us here is *acknowledgment*, acknowledgment that what is before us is a human body with everything that means for our attitudes and comportment to it. That we can feel a curious empathic identification with the bather, wanting something from her even if we do not know what, is our acknowledgment that she is one of us, and one of us because no matter her material substance, no matter how constructed, no matter how hewn, and no matter how geometrically contrived—still, this is a human form: in the sheer having of head, body, arms, legs, breasts in approximately the right places she means, and she can only mean, the way a human form means, because there is nothing else for us to acknowledge.

Endnotes

1. Theodor W. Adorno, *Negative Dialectics*, trans. E. B. Ashton (London, 1973), p. xx.

2. Theodor W. Adorno, "On Subject and Object," in *Critical Models: Interventions and Catchwords*, trans. Henry W. Pickford (New York, 1998), p. 248.

3. The status of the *Demoiselles* is now, I suppose, secure. So Christopher Green states in his introduction to his edited volume *Picasso's "Les Demoiselles D'Avignon"* (Cambridge, 2001): "In the mythology of modernist and postmodern art history, the status of Picasso's *Demoiselles D'Avignon* as a painting that marks a dramatic break from the past and a new twentieth century beginning is now unquestioned" (p. 2).

4. In stating the stakes in the way I do I have been partially preceded by Charles Harrison, *Painting the Difference: Sex and Spectator in Modern Art* (Chicago, 2005), 172–74.

5. Rosalind Krauss, *The Picasso Papers* (Cambridge, 1999), pp. 193–94.

6. And is not what is exquisite in Robert Ryman or Agnes Martin, precisely, touch? But then why the detour through geometry and the mechanical? And what about the standing of touch?

7. Or, if not a detour, then a limb of a practice that can be described differently from the way cubism is now described. For example, in "The Polemical Part," which is an epilogue to his article "Resisting Cézanne: Picasso's *Three Women*," *Art in America* 66 and 67 (November-December 1978 and March-April 1979): pp. 114–33, 114–27, Leo Steinberg argues that cubism, as practiced by Picasso but not Braque, can be seen as one way of extending the principles of discontinuity, fragmentariness, and disunity that he pioneered in the *Demoiselles*.

8. Of course, one could argue that since geometry is one possible a priori framework for the intelligibility of space, then *logically* Picasso must be wrong in this claim. And this way of conceiving geometry and its consorts (the mechanical, etc.), would certainly make the postmodernism that emerges with minimalism look at least plausible if not downright inevitable. What is forgotten in this is that geometry is just another human practice, grounded in human needs and human bodily practices of pacing, measuring, constructing.

9. Sigmund Freud, *Three Essays on the Theory of Sexuality*, trans. James Strachey, in *On Sexuality* (New York, 1977), p. 69. Freud proposes that the curiosity underlying visual pleasure can be sublimated into art "if its interest can be shifted away from the genitals on to the shape of the body as a whole."

[10] Laura Mulvey, "Visual Pleasure and Narrative Cinema," *Screen* 16, no. 3 (Autumn 1975): p. 12.

[11] Elizabeth Cowling, *Picasso: Style and Meaning* (London, 2002), p. 179. Cowling, I should state, is almost unique in defending ugliness as a recurrent productive weapon in Picasso's painterly armory. Her tenacious defense of Picasso's plurality of styles has been exemplary for me.

[12] For the analogies see ibid. p. 168.

[13] Ibid., p. 174.

[14] Elizabeth Cowling et al., *Matisse Picasso* (London, 2002), p. 55.

[15] See Leo Steinberg, "The Algerian Women and Picasso at Large," in his *Other Criteria: Confrontations with Twentieth-Century Art* (New York, 1972), pp. 125–234, for an account of ugliness in Picasso, beginning with the *Demoiselles*, that runs from puzzlement (p. 224) to outright denial (p. 227).

[16] For a thoughtful effort at reconstructing Adorno's logic of ugliness see Peter Uwe Hohendahl, "Aesthetic Violence: The Concept of the Ugly in Adorno's *Aesthetic Theory*," *Cultural Critique* 60 (Spring 2005): pp. 170–96. For my own earlier effort see *Against Voluptuous Bodies: Late Modernism and the Meaning of Painting* (Stanford, 2006), chaps. 7 and 9.

[17] Theodor W. Adorno, *Aesthetic Theory*, trans. Robert Hullot-Kentor (Minneapolis, 1997), 45. (Hereafter *AT*; subsequent references appear parenthetically in the text.)

[18] For Adorno's attempt to find a space for primitivism, see Hohendahl, "Aesthetic Violence," pp. 173–80, which also includes a useful account of the role of Carl Einstein's Picasso-inspired account of African sculpture in the argument of Adorno's *Philosophy of Modern Music*.

[19] Theodor W. Adorno, "Parataxis: On Hölderlin's Late Poetry," in *Notes to Literature* (New York, 1992), 2: pp. 109–49.

[20] The idealization of the female form would involve standard markers of sexual desirability including body type, youth, posture, etc. And of course nakedness.

[21] All parenthetical references in the remainder of this essay are to Leo Steinberg, "The Philosophical Brothel," *October* 44 (Spring 1988): pp. 7–74, here 13; the essay was originally published in two parts in 1972 in *Art News*. This essay now, deservedly in my view, dominates the field. For a summary of responses to it see Christopher Green's introduction to *Picasso's "Les Demoiselles d'Avignon."*

[22] Cowling, *Picasso: Style and Meaning*, p. 165. Because art historians all know so well the numerous drawings that lead up to the final painting, they suppose they know the space of the painting better than they do.

23 Steinberg, "The Polemical Part," p. 124.

24 Cowling, *Picasso: Style and Meaning*, p. 178, seems to me to get all this just right.

25 William Rubin, "From Narrative to 'Iconic' in Picasso: The Buried Allegory in *Bread and Fruitdish on a Table* and the Role of *Les Demoiselles d'Avignon*," *Art Bulletin* 65, no. 4 (December 1983): p. 635. Rubin's thesis of a shift from narrative to iconic is his version of the painting's revolutionary axial rotation.

26 Yve-Alain Bois, "Painting as Trauma," in Green, *Picasso's "Les Demoiselles D'Avignon,"* p. 44.

27 Steinberg, "Resisting Cézanne," p. 120. Steinberg, I should note, persuasively interprets *Three Women* (1908) as an account of the emergence of sexual difference, just barely—out of stone.

28 Nude Standing by the Sea (1929), is in the permanent collection of the Metropolitan Museum of Art, New York, and can be viewed online at http://www.metmuseum.org/toah/works-of-art/1996.403.4. My paragraphs on this painting were originally part of a commentary to a presentation by T. J. Clark on this painting entitled "The Ordinary Optimism of Picasso" at the University of California, Berkeley, March 2, 2007. For reasons of space, I have not been able to include here either an account of Clark's interpretation of this painting or my concerns about his interpretation.

29 Her uprightness, standingness, was the key to Clark's interpretation of the painting in the presentation mentioned in the previous note.

30 I have said nothing about the woman's position. Trying the position for myself, it is not a stretch, but just a way of standing and holding oneself, which I think is the point: she may be made, constructed, but in positioning herself she is also self-constructed and, in holding herself, fully self-possessed. The depth of her self-possession converges with the density of her material being, her indissoluble independence. This is why sun, sea, sky are her elements only; Picasso removes any hint of dependence. Thanks to Gregg Horowitz for both pressing me on her pose and his suggestions about it, which I have adopted freely.

Thierry de Duve

Resisting Adorno, Revamping Kant

> *Anyone fully able to grasp why Haydn doubles the violins with a flute in* piano *might well get an intuitive glimpse into why, thousands of years ago, men gave up eating uncooked grain and began to bake bread, or why they started to smooth and polish their tools.*
> —Theodor W. Adorno[1]

THERE ARE MANY SUCH stunning remarks in Adorno: highly insightful shortcuts in time demanding commensurate short circuits in the reader's brain connections. They combine or, rather, jostle precise technical and philological knowledge of a given art form (here, music) with bold bird's-eye views of the fate of humankind, mediated by strong political consciousness of history, especially of the economic overdetermination of the period the philosopher and his readers live in. Lifted from a paragraph that starts, "As a bourgeois art music is young," the lines of my epigraph are inserted in a thorough discussion of Wagner's original talent for orchestration as a "victory of reification in instrumental practice," leading Adorno to conclude that "Wagner's oeuvre comes close to the consumer goods of the nineteenth century which knew no greater ambition than to conceal every sign of the work that went into them."[2] Lines such as these show Adorno at his best: clever, witty, fast, pugnacious, and flamboyant—and a true writer to boot. They make you want to embrace his writing wholesale, and, by the same token, they make critique of his thinking very difficult. Resisting Adorno (my title, I'm afraid, gives my intention away) does not get easier when we read on, but for reasons quite different, if not opposite:

> Works of art owe their existence to the division of labour in society, the separation of physical and mental labour. At the same time, they have their own roots in existence; their medium is not pure mind, but the mind that enters into reality and, by virtue of such movement, is able to maintain the unity of what is divided. It is this contradiction that forces works of art to make us forget that they have been made. The claim implicit in their existence and hence, too, the claim that existence has a meaning, is the more convincing, the less they contain to remind us that they have been made, and that they owe their being to something external to themselves, namely to a mental process. Art that is no longer able to perpetrate this deception with good conscience has implicitly destroyed the only element in which it can thrive.[3]

No doubt the reader who has the famous first line of the *Aesthetic Theory* in mind—"It is self-evident that nothing concerning art is self-evident anymore, not its inner life, not its relation to the world, not even its right to exist"[4]—will read this paragraph as a statement of Adorno's most intimate convictions and anxieties. The last sentence, in particular, all but betrays his profound desperation in the face of a world he sees as no longer capable of sustaining the, for him, fundamental illusion that makes works of art appear as *sui generis* entities, autonomous and as if unmade. It is no longer style and flamboyance that jump from the page, but rather ponderous gloom. The paragraph is also typically obscure. But the gloom and the obscurity, even the despair, are magnets as powerful as wit and brilliance for the committed Adorno reader.

250   Thierry de Duve

Buttressed by his immense culture and his aristocratic sense of self, they account for the unique pathos—you might call it "the pain of contradictions lived and thought through"—that tinges Adorno's writings in general. That pathos is irresistible, so much does it testify to the depth of his concerns, to the seriousness of his thoughts and, above all, to the lucidity at all costs that drives him. You are never left in doubt that art and culture matter to Adorno; moreover, that they matter because the course of the world matters, what he often names, in rather heavy terms, the totality. *"Fiat ars, pereat mundus"* is not an Adornian utterance. There is perhaps a measure of dandyish masochism in his writing, but not a trace of decadence. The pain is the price of compassion; the gloom is the mood the greatest mass murder ever perpetrated in the history of humankind—the destruction of the European Jews—commands: "The need to lend a voice to suffering is a condition of all truth. For suffering is objectivity that weighs upon the subject."[5] Because Adorno's pathos is not personal and subjective, because it is out there in the world and affects you objectively, its dark seduction is very hard to resist. If you care for the world yourself, then the pain that transpires behind Adorno's professorial authority and critical consciousness is likely to move you in a much more profound and durable manner than the pyrotechnics of a style capable of linking violins doubled by a flute in Haydn to primitive human beings baking bread for the first time.

Of course, you might quibble with the content of the paragraph even if its tone bewitches you. You might voice your surprise at such a distinguished reader of Marx invoking the *technical* "separation of physical and mental labour" in lieu of the *social* "division of labour in society." But then you would easily find a dozen quotes elsewhere in Adorno's writings that show you how aware he was that art owes its existence not to the "separation of physical and mental labour" but to the brutal fact that while one man composes music or poetry, another (wo)man has to bake his bread. My favorite one, from *Minima Moralia*, is devoid neither of the witty and insightful historical shortcuts nor of the gloom demonstrated by the paragraph on which I am commenting:

> The existence of bread factories, turning the prayer that we be given our daily bread into a mere metaphor and an avowal of desperation, argues more strongly against the possibility of Christianity than all the enlightened critiques of the life of Jesus.[6]

Granted, those lines are not directly about art and the social division of labor, but they are about bread (if this is an excuse) and the labor that industrially produced bread *conceals*. They also give a glimpse of Adorno's complicated relationship to Messianism (Jewish and Christian)—something highly relevant to the relationship to art and to history our paragraph displays. To come back to it, the twist may well be that Adorno chooses to acknowledge the division of labor in terms of the separation of body and mind only because he wants to stress the paradox of the "mental process" that gives birth to works of art as being *external* to them. But here we run into serious translation problems. The word rendered as "mental process" (and as mind in the second sentence) is actually *Geist*, a word with quite a pedigree in German philosophy. Its Hegelian origin would have been blatant had the translator rendered it as "spirit." But he seems to have systematically eclipsed the Hegelian overtones of the whole paragraph, making it perhaps not more obscure than it is, but obscure in a way that betrays its author. We will need another translation:

> Works of art owe their existence-in-the-world [*Dasein*] to the division of labor in society, the separation of physical and mental labor. By the same token, however, they themselves appear as in-the-world; their medium is not pure spirit existing for itself, but the spirit that retreats into worldly existence [*Existenz*] and, by the force of such movement, lays a claim on the unity of what is separated. This contradiction forces

works of art to make us forget that they are made: the claim their existence-in-the-world stakes, and hence the claim that existence itself is meaningful, is the more convincing, the less something in them warns us that they have been fabricated, that they owe their existence to spirit as something external to themselves. Art that is no longer able to achieve this deception with good conscience—indeed its very principle—has dissolved the only element in which it can realize itself.[7]

The gloom is still there; the anxiety as to the fate of art is still there; the fear that *Dasein* itself, not just the existence of art but existence *per se*, in other words human life, has lost its meaning, is still there. But I hope this translation makes it a bit clearer how much all that pessimism is dressed up in Hegelian garb. To read under Adorno's pen that the medium of works of art is *not* "pure spirit existing for itself" is already utterly surprising. Does Adorno need to remind us that in art spirit has material existence? Has he not accustomed us to consider the medium in its materiality and its technical specificity, first and foremost? What we witness here is Adorno presenting a Hegelian argument the better to push the anti-Hegelian counterargument according to which works of art "owe their existence to spirit as something external to themselves." For Hegel, spirit was the internal medium of art, phenomenal existence the external, and when he saw their final synthesis achieved in the wake of Romantic art, it was to the benefit of spirit. For the post-Romantic Adorno, even that ultimate stage of spirit is but a particular moment of its history. The unification of matter and spirit is *claimed* rather than achieved, and then at the cost of a regressive movement of spirit retreating, recoiling, taking refuge, as it were, in the material existence of the artworks' medium. Here Adorno concludes: "This contradiction forces works of art to make us forget that they are made." In other words, this unresolved battle of forces compels us to look at works of art as though they were not artifacts but rather products of nature. And when that battle is lost, as the last sentence dramatically announces, then art's very survival is under threat. The view that art should look like nature while we know that it is the product of spirit is so foreign to Hegel that dialectical negation of Hegel fails to account for its appearance under Adorno's pen. It is a typically Kantian view, however: "Nature was beautiful, if at the same time it looked like art; and art can only be called beautiful if we are aware that it is art and yet it looks to us like nature."[8] I wonder whether Adorno's particular brand of pathos does not result partly from his being perpetually torn between the two greatest among his predecessors in the history of German philosophy, Kant and Hegel. This is not to say that Schopenhauer and Nietzsche do not loom large in his work as well, but traveling back and forth between these two thinkers and Hegel is feasible, whereas reconciling Kant and Hegel is not—except perhaps via Schelling, but this would mean walking the Romantic route, something Adorno avoids like the plague. That Adorno's pathos results from the clash between his unrelenting longing for reconciliation and his acute awareness that reconciliation in an irreconciled world is either a lie or an impossibility is palpable everywhere in his writings. That "the pain of contradictions lived and thought through," as I called his pathos, might result, in part, from his attempt to reconcile Kant's critical with Hegel's speculative philosophies surfaces more sporadically, but where it does, it signals how impossible a task Adorno has set himself. What would such reconciliation entail?

Versöhnung is a key word in Adorno, one with complex meanings and several realms of application, and it is a dialectical word, which is to say that it necessarily implies its own negation. It resonates with the word "utopia" in the political realm and with the word "redemption" in the religious one, and carries the connotation of "promise" as ceaselessly betrayed and yet still waiting to be fulfilled. It is the word in which Adorno's hope and despair become one—no wonder it is also the most laden with pathos. For example, "Dialectics serves the end of reconciliation," and "The agony of dialectics is the world's agony raised to the level of concept."[9] To start with the easiest to grasp, one layer of meaning in Adorno's usage of "reconciliation" is the practical, social, or historical meaning of cease-fire, armistice among enemies, the taming of class and other struggles, and the state of peace obtained thereby. Such a peace is always, by necessity, provisional, never durable, and therefore not much more than a truce, yet renouncing it would mean renouncing every hope of a pacified world. A second layer of meaning has "reconciliation" refer to the more profound and in principle more durable peace that history would make with itself if it could make up for past tragedies and catastrophes, if their victims could be vindicated once and for all without calling for revenge in their turn, in short, if the process of history itself could be brought to a halt. This would be the true redemption, and no investment in progress is thinkable without positing it on the horizon, but since it calls on a teleological notion of history implying the abolition of history, it is self-contradictory and bound to fail. For example, "Utopia—the yet-to-exist—is...the imaginary reparation of the catastrophe of world history; it is freedom that, under the spell of necessity, did not and may never come to be."[10] A third layer of meaning touches on the even broader reconciliation of the sphere of human life with the global sphere encompassing all life, that is, with the order of natural phenomena, natural beings, and natural laws. This ultimate utopia must be recognized as beyond the realizable, while its promises—those made by the beauty of nature, in particular—cannot be forgotten without humanity's presence in the natural world becoming meaningless. Traversing these various layers of meaning, there runs the philosophical plane where reconciliation is defined as the dialectical uniting of opposites that resolves a contradiction; for Adorno, as for Hegel and Marx, contradictions are not just logical and formal, and they don't obey Aristotle's principle of the excluded third; they are real, concrete ordeals, embodied in worldly events, disputes, and struggles; they are the engine of history. But unlike Marx, whose materialist upturning of Hegel consists in putting the historical development of the relationships of production in lieu of the progressive unfolding of absolute spirit, Adorno articulates his critique of Hegel around a different kind of materialism: the radical refusal of synthesis, of sublation, of what Lyotard has called "result."[11] It is not only that contradictions cannot be solved; it is that they ought to remain unsolved. Their irresolvableness makes them vulnerable to further contradictions and thus keeps open the possibility of reconciliation as a potential. In the same way that Messianism requires the arrival of the Messiah to be perpetually postponed, so every momentary reconciliation requires the unity of the opposites to be in turn denied in the name of truly accomplished reconciliation. For example: "If the utopia of art were fulfilled, it would be art's temporal end."[12] Oxymoric *Wahrheitsgehalt* is, I believe, the main thrust of Adorno's highly contradictory notion of *Versöhnung* as it is applied, exemplarily, to works of art:

> The most intimate contradiction within works of art, the most threatening and fruitful, is that they are irreconcilable by way of reconciliation, while actually their constitutive irreconcilability at the same time cuts them off from reconciliation.[13]

Adorno's ambition, however, doesn't stop with the anti-Hegelian Hegelianism his project of a humanity (ir)reconciled with itself entails. For a philosopher of his background and caliber, the ultimate reconciliation must be the reconciliation of the practical and the theoretical—in Kant's terms, of ethics and nature; in Hegel's terms, of spirit and the world —all this *on* Adorno's terms, that is, as irreconcilable reconciliation. To play Hegel against himself will not suffice here. Must Kant not be played against himself too? Should a "negative" Hegel not be played against a "negative" Kant? And would that not amount to the true dialectical *Versöhnung* of Hegel with Kant? If *transcendentalism* was the solution for Kant and *dialectics* the solution for Hegel, we might have a glimpse of the enormity of the task Adorno set himself: to somehow combine *negative dialectics* with *transcendental materialism*. The latter expression is not Adorno's, but what its strategy might consist in is relatively clear: wherever Kant presupposes innate universal conditions of possibility, refer to sedimented history and ingrained social habits instead. Adorno does this systematically in the chapter of *Negative Dialectics* devoted to Kant. One superb example is the passage where he criticizes Kant for making the will the transcendental seat of freedom by saying that freedom is *freedom of the will* only insofar as men have the will to seek freedom.[14] Another is the passage in *Dialectic of Enlightenment* where he and Horkheimer pretend that Kant's transcendental *schematism*, this "hidden art in the depths of the human soul," has been mechanized by the culture industry.[15]

I doubt that Adorno ever explicitly put the ultimate reconciliation of the practical and the theoretical on his agenda, but he was highly aware that Kant's *Critique of Judgment* was an attempt at precisely such a reconciliation (though of course not on his terms): the bridging of the domains of the first and the second *Critiques* via the third, the making compatible of the laws of nature with the moral law via the reflecting judgment. He therefore knew the centrality of aesthetics for any such attempt, and thus of the realm of pleasure and pain—not just pleasure and pain theorized by a philosopher but experienced by *this* philosopher. (Indeed, "[s]uffering is objectivity that weighs upon the subject." And there is not much talk of pleasure in Adorno.) Given the central place aesthetics had for his philosophy in general, it is hard to imagine Adorno failing to reflect consciously on his own pain and not objectifying the scars left by the cultural issues that mattered to him. He never wrote on art and culture without engaging his own appreciation, and he never lost sight of the larger picture, convinced as he was that art's autonomy was precisely what allowed it *not* to be cut off from the world at large—a conviction shared by both Hegel and Kant, albeit on mutually incompatible premises.[16]

Adorno made his home in these incompatibilities. His aesthetic theory is fraught with Hegelian readings of Kantian issues (never the other way around, of course): solvable antinomies interpreted as irresolvable contradictions, ideas of reason recast as moments of spirit, ethical imperatives rewritten as historical programs, and so on. I am tempted to read the particular brand of pathos the *Aesthetic Theory* yields as the symptom of the willfully impossible reconciliation of Kant and Hegel. And I want to resist the pathos and its appeal, not only because I made my choice between Kant and Hegel long ago and don't dream of reconciling them, but also because I see no way for the skeptic to engage critically *and* respectfully with Adorno's thought other than to start by reading his pathos as the symptomatic outcome neither of his character nor of the state of the world but of his way of thinking. Indeed, negative dialectics is a way of thinking that you either embrace or reject but with which you cannot enter into discussion. If you embrace it, you cannot even settle an argument you might have with yourself. There is no arguing with someone who claims that aesthetic experience is "possibility promised by its impossibility," or that, although the utopian figure of art "is compelled toward absolute negativity, it is precisely by virtue of this negativity that it is not absolutely negative," or that "a noncontradictory theory of the history of art is not to be conceived: the essence of its history is contradictory in itself."[17] Where do you start if you don't agree? Where is *your* possibility to contradict a theory that makes of contradiction a nonfalsifiable motto? How do you wriggle out of the ensuing double bind? What do you make of the conundrum of the passage where Adorno claims that philosophy's task is to interpret art "in order to say what [art] is unable to say, whereas art is only able to say it by not saying it"?[18] Pardon? This is no longer dialectics, negative or other; it is self-contradiction run amok. Better laugh it off than whine with Adorno, I'd say.

To quote that passage out of context was a bit unfair. And to laugh Adorno's pathos away may turn out to be a symptom of its own. Consider this, one of the concluding lines of *Aesthetic Theory:* "It would be preferable that in some better times art vanish altogether than that it forget the suffering that is its expression and in which form finds its substance."[19] Would you dare laugh that off and risk passing for a philistine who wants art to paint the world rosy and pink? From Grünewald's Isenheim altarpiece to Picasso's *Guernica*; from Shakespeare's *Macbeth* to Beckett's *Endgame* (which Adorno wrote about and held in high esteem), would you deny that human suffering is the stuff great works of art are made of? You may laugh *with* Beckett, because you would be laughing at the ridiculousness of laughing, but you won't laugh *at* Beckett.[20] So you won't laugh *at* Adorno either, when he prefers to see art vanish rather than have it forget the suffering of humankind. And yet the pathos of that line! Are you willing to suffer *with* Adorno? Will you accept the sacrifice of art against the certainty of "some better times"? I, for one, shall not. I simply do not entertain, even remotely, the hope that some future day the world might be peaceful enough—harmonious, beautiful, *reconciled* enough—to allow for the vanishing of art into uselessness (which says something about what I think is the usefulness of art). I find such hope naive and futile, if not dangerous. Thus I shall refuse to share in the pathos that wants me to suffer either way, whether it is from a life without art in an otherwise happy world, or from the "damaged life" of the existing world, with art as solace.[21] Yet I can't honestly shut my ears to the intimation that makes Adorno's pathos so hard to resist: am I therefore devoid of empathy for my fellow men? Have I abandoned all hope in a better world? Have I sold out to "affirmation"? And, accessorily: have I not misunderstood Adorno? Did he not write that line as a warning because he refused the alternative it offered? Has he not consistently written against art as solace? Was he really that naive, to believe in a future perfect world? Why then does the word *Versöhnung* under his pen mean the contrary of its dictionary definition? Is the truth-value of his thinking not of practical nature? Was he not, like good old Marx, philosophizing in order to change the world rather than interpret it?

All these questions may boil down to this: what is it, signaled by Adorno's particular brand of pathos, that makes the intimation that if you don't espouse his negative dialectics you fall into affirmative ideology so strong? *Affirmation* is another key word in Adorno, and somehow a pendant to *Versöhnung*, because it is the Frankfurt School's word for false and premature reconciliation.[22] It has a practical and a theoretical side, and practice prevails, in accordance with the motto of changing the world rather than interpreting it. In theory, "affirmation" refers to every discourse, such as positivism, that silences the negative, the dark, the inassimilable, or the contradictory nature of the real. In practice, "affirmation" designates reconciliation with the world as it is, submission to so-called reality, moral resignation, political defeatism, and approval of the status quo in general. No one with progressive ideas—and I'd add, no decent intellectual—wants to be accused of endorsing such reconciliation. But precisely herein lies the catch-22 that makes Adorno's pathos irresistibly communicative: if you are a progressive in practice, you must agree with me in theory, the pathos implies; and if you disagree with me in theory, then you betray progressive politics in practice, and you are a traitor to the cause. Adorno must have had this debate with himself many times and, in my view, he succumbed to its double bind. Hence the irritating fatalism of his all-encompassing (shall I risk the word "totalitarian"?) reconciliation project. Self-contradictory as this project is, and ought to be, in order *not* to be totalitarian, it betrays a self-defeating obsession with the totality. Adorno is never satisfied with a partial or temporary or local reconciliation. Unless the totality is redeemed, redemption is illegitimate, untrue, and fraudulent. Since, however, no one but the most naive optimist will place bets on global redemption, what remains is global despair in the name of global redemption. Again, "Dialectics serves the end of reconciliation," and "The agony of dialectics is *the world's* (my emphasis) agony raised to the level of concept." For the totality should not be redeemed: "It lies in the definition of negative dialectics that it will not come to rest in itself, as if it were total. This is its form of hope."[23] If despair, then hope; if hope, then despair: opting for the fragment in the name of totality is the only move *desperate hope* (that oxymoron!) allows. The Schlegel brothers already had a glimpse of this, and Adorno is definitely their heir. How disappointing, in a sense, and yet perfectly explicable it is to realize that Adorno's "micrological" politics perhaps amount to no more than his own redemption from his obsession with the whole: "Micrology is the place where metaphysics finds a haven from totality."[24] Maybe, maybe not. Certainly, micrology was the wishful solution to Adorno's own contradictions. Adorno has, it seems to me, inherited in spite of himself the worst from Hegel: the notion that total, absolute realization of spirit in the actual world accomplishes the ineluctable process of history itself. The fact that he no longer dares to call it progress only adds to the pathos.

Philosophers who abide so rigorously by the consequences of their own thinking processes that they systematically think against themselves are undoubtedly courageous, and I know no philosopher who does that more courageously than Adorno. (Bourdieu is also in that category and in his writings, too, the pathos is palpable.)[25] When that sort of courage is combined with great intellectual powers, immense erudition, infallible intuition of the issues that count, and keen artistic judgment, it commands the greatest respect and admiration. All this I want to salute in Adorno. I also deeply sympathize with "the pain of contradictions lived and thought through" that is as endearing in the man as it is frustrating in his writings. But when all is said and done, I must confess that Adorno doesn't do much for me; he rarely helps me think. Neither does the philosophical tradition to which he belongs, starting with the Romantics: the whole string of German poets and philosophers after Kant who led his legacy astray. I said earlier that I made my choice between Kant and Hegel long ago (in favor of Kant, it goes without saying), which is roughly to say that I opted for transcendentalism against dialectics. (By "transcendentalism" I mean criticism in Kant's sense. It need not be idealistic; as Adorno surmised, transcendental materialism is perfectly conceivable.[26] Let it also be clear that my use of "transcendentalism" is as opposed as it can be to its usage by Emerson and the "American Transcendentalists."[27]) As for dialectics, whether idealist or materialist, affirmative or negative, it is, in my view, wishful thinking; it articulates theory with practice by way of a vicious circle that wants correct theory to found just practice while just practice proves the theory correct. Worse, and how paradoxically ironic: dialectical thinking wants to make the irreconcilable reconcilable (all the while acknowledging its irreconcilability, the better to prescribe its reconcilability, and so on, in circles), because it refuses to reconcile itself *with* the irreconcilable. (Notice that reconciliation with the irreconcilable, in other words, with the fact that there are irresolvable contradictions, contains no contradiction.) Hegel refused to bow before the most absolute of all irreconcilabilities, that between the finite and the infinite; in so doing, he refused to reconcile metaphysics with human finitude—precisely Kant's landmark achievement. What Kant established once and for all, and Hegel stubbornly refused, is the possibility of a philosophy radically compatible with modern science, that is, definitively godless. Dialectics is the quixotic refuge of theology, even in Adorno (to say nothing of Walter Benjamin), and, to that extent, it needs the dulcinea of a re-enchanted world to long for, and windmills such as reification to fight against. The superiority of transcendentalism over dialectics is blatant, provided it is not confused with its "affirmative" derivatives such as logical positivism, based on a very un-Kantian acceptance of the division of labor among the mental faculties. Hegel railed against the nascent positivism of his time, which he accused of ratiocination, that is, of defective thought confined in the narrow limits of the understanding. Transcendentalism in Kant's sense is not at all reducible to that sort of "affirmative" thinking. It does not forbid reason (practical as well as theoretical) to venture beyond the limits of understanding as long as reason *knows* that there is nothing to *know* beyond those limits. Kant's *Ding an sich* is and remains the most formidable antidote to the speculative temptation that seized German philosophers and poets beginning with the first reception of the *Critique of Judgment*, in the 1790s. Far from embodying this profound metaphysical essence mysteriously lodged in the heart of things it is still too often taken to be, the *thing-in-itself* is a conceit that carries the imperative: Thou shalt not pretend to know the unknowable (reconcile the irreconcilable, synthesize the unsynthesizable, present the unpresentable, and so on). Let the *thing-in-itself* rest; it is a mere heuristic supposition we finite minds need in order to think properly. Hegel is of course the most monumental of German philosophers to have maniacally refused to let the *thing-in-itself* rest and to have sought to raise it to the self-consciousness of the *thing-for-itself*, but he is far from alone. One senses the same panic before Kant's epistemological imperative in Heidegger's obsession with the ontic-ontological distinction. I wonder, sometimes, why Adorno fell under Hegel's spell, he who so cruelly and gaily (no pathos, there) dissected the pretensions of Heidegger's "jargon of authenticity."[28] Perhaps Hegel's impressive posterity, in Marx and beyond, prevented Adorno from realizing that his statement— "Philosophy which once seemed outmoded is now alive because the moment of its realization has been missed"[29]—was better applied to Kant than to Hegel.

I am aware of how bluntly I state my position. I make no apologies, except that I humbly admit lacking the intellectual equipment (not to mention the time and patience) needed to back my perhaps outrageous views on dialectics with the proper scholarly work; those views are more a matter of *Wahlverwandschaften* than of scientificity. Certainly I don't feel alone in the family of antidialectical thinkers. Minds much greater than mine—not least Michel Foucault and Gilles Deleuze—belong to it. As for my declared preference for Kant over Hegel, it goes back a long way, at least to the eighties, to my days at the *Collège de philosophie*, where I would listen to Jean-François Lyotard and Pierre-Jean Labarrière dueling over the timely relevance of both philosophers. As Kant's champion, Lyotard won the duel for me, even though "my" Kant was from the outset quite different from his. In a nutshell, Lyotard, who must be credited with having initiated a "postmodern" return to Kant—actually, to a revamped Kant that would have been unrecognizable to the neo-Kantians of yore—funnels every possible philosophical issue, from aesthetics to politics, through the *Analytic of the Sublime*.[30] My "Kant-after-Duchamp" approach to aesthetics bypasses the sublime altogether.[31] Its reading strategy addresses the *Analytic of the Beautiful,* mentally replaces every occurrence of "beauty" with "art," and assumes that the sentence "This is art" is the paradigmatic formula of a *modern* aesthetic judgment in the truest Kantian sense. I mention this here only because, to an Adornian reader, the *Analytic of the Beautiful,* and by inference my own conception of art, must appear unbearably *affirmative;* only the *Analytic of the Sublime* makes room for negativity and contradiction. To stay with Adorno, I think it needs to be stressed that he held (not surprisingly) a complex and ambiguous position vis-à-vis the Kantian sublime, which he deemed at once complicit with domination and a protest against it.[32] And he knew from experience, as I do also, that under the conditions of the culture industry, the sublime turns to kitsch. He allowed his experience and taste to shape his theory to some extent, as I think one should, in spite of the risks involved. Philippe Lacoue-Labarthe has reproached Adorno for having missed the properly *philosophical* sublimity of Schoenberg's *Moses and Aaron*.[33] Perhaps it was Adorno's *aesthetic* distaste for the sublime that made him deaf to it. Whatever the case, I would hope that my own distaste for the sublime has not made me deaf or blind to negativity and contradiction in aesthetic matters. On the contrary, my interpretation of Kant, which I admit often implies reading between the lines and sometimes against the grain, consistently stresses the particular negativity that resides in aesthetic *disagreement*. I seek to give ugliness and even disgust the voice that academic readings of the *Analytic of the Beautiful* silence. Critics of Kant who are under the impression that the said *Analytic* opens onto classical, harmonious, "affirmative" aesthetics only, never imagine Kant in the midst of an aesthetic quarrel.[34] They are, in my opinion, victims of Kant's social conformism. In aesthetics as well as in politics, Kant was reluctant to let opposition speak openly and, therefore, minimized the role dissent must have played, even against his will, in his own writings. Hence the polished, too polished, look the *Analytic of the Beautiful* projects. Beauty occupies center stage while ugliness coyly remains in the shadow, to the extent that for some readers, it is as if negative aesthetic judgments in the realm of beauty were for Kant a contradiction in terms, and thus impossible.[35] To witness the birth of an aesthetic of ugliness, some argue, we would have to wait for Karl Rosenkranz, who was seen as a Hegelian and, as such, was supposedly able to grant contradiction a nonformal, concrete role.[36] I disagree: there is room for negative aesthetic judgments in Kant, if only because it is all too obvious that without the freedom to say "This is ugly," "This is beautiful," would not be a judgment at all. But I also have more technical reasons to disagree. As Kant insisted, the pain occasioned by ugliness is not to be confused with the repulsion caused by disgust.[37] The argument that has ugliness forbid disinterestedness makes that confusion and fails to see that when something is pronounced ugly, it is so relative to the standard of beauty that the thing in question should have met. The more serious argument that has ugliness contradict the harmonious free play of the faculties suffers from another confusion, that between logical contradiction and real opposition. Isn't it ironic that Hegelians proudly think they are ahead of Kant when they promote precisely this confusion to the rank of "dialectics," whereas, in fact, even the precritical Kant had already set out to undo it?[38] In a short essay dated 1763 that has apparently no bearing on aesthetics, Kant speaks of pleasure and displeasure—the very feelings he would later see yielded by beauty and ugliness, respectively—not as concepts in logical contradiction to one another, but as opposite sensations susceptible to quantitative measurement on a continuous scale.[39] A letter contains both good and bad news; our pleasure in reading the good news is, say, rated 5; and the displeasure in reading the bad news, 3: we are left with 2 units of pleasure. We may smile at the naiveté of such protobehaviorist apprehension of feelings; it is not their measurability that matters, it is the fact that Kant proposes an articulation of the positive and the negative that results from an actual opposition of forces distinct from the logical, Aristotelian principle of contradiction. I cannot help but see in Kant's proposal an anticipated alternative to dialectics and its confusions. For it does what dialectics does: give oppositional negation an active, productive, "political" function while avoiding the confusion with linguistic negation dialectics suffers from. Psychologically speaking, pleasure is definitely a positive feeling, Kant notes. Displeasure, he then argues, can be called *negative pleasure* yet is a positive sensation, in the sense that it is positively a sensation rather than the cancellation of sensation it would be if *negative pleasure* had been a mere contradiction in terms. And he adds that, similarly, "*aversion* can be called a *negative desire*, hate a negative *love, ugliness* a *negative beauty, blame* a *negative praise*."[40] Though Kant does not adduce the argument of the "negative magnitudes" in the third *Critique*, the question of its applicability therein has great consequences for the question of whether or not the *Analytic of the Beautiful* is "affirmative." If the positiveness of *negative pleasure* is read into the *Analytic*, as I am convinced is legitimate, then to say that ugliness negates the harmony of the faculties is not enough; ugliness positively generates the *conflict* of the faculties.[41]

The notion of the harmony of the faculties is introduced in paragraph nine of the *Critique of Judgment*, perhaps the most obscure and frustrating passage in the *Analytic of the Beautiful*, inasmuch as Kant promises there "the key to the critique of taste" and then fails to deliver. Paragraph nine raises the question of "whether in the judgment of taste the feeling of pleasure precedes the judging of the object or the latter precedes the former."[42] Kant knows that the judging *must* precede the pleasure, for otherwise we would deal with mere agreeableness in sensation and not with a pure judgment about beauty; but he is unable to demonstrate it, and soon the initial question gets rephrased in terms of alleged differences between pleasures. In order not to be reducible to mere pleasure of the senses, the pleasure yielded by a pure judgment of taste must be of a different kind. Kant then fancies that this pleasure inheres in the "state of mind in the free play of the imagination and the understanding (so far as they agree with each other as is requisite for a cognition in general)."[43] Without addressing here in full the considerable difficulties of paragraph nine, let us ask ourselves how we are to conceive of this "free play." And let us formulate the issue in terms that Adorno might endorse: let us consider that rather than expressing natural, innate conditions, the suppositions about the human mind that constitute the transcendental subject transpose social and historically dated ones. Let us envisage the relationship of imagination and understanding as resulting from the division of labor—technical *and* social—among the mental faculties, even if this implies anthropomorphizing them. Imagination, one of whose tasks is to unify the raw sense data registered by sensibility into coherent gestalts or images, presents understanding with, say, a rose, and asks: "what is this?"[44] Understanding, one of whose tasks is to subsume images under concepts, answers: "a rose." Imagination bows and then asks: "what color is it?" and understanding, which possesses a conceptual definition of color (for example, wavelength) and also has as its mandate to perform logical operations on concepts, answers with the predicate "red." Imagination bows again. In all such dialogues, understanding is the master; it knows and gives answers; it is the superior faculty. Like a servant at the master's dinner table, imagination is content with presenting the dishes and begs for understanding's approval; it is the lower faculty. There is no more conflict between them than there is between the orders of society: harmony reigns when everybody stays in their assigned places. But now imagination asks understanding whether the rose is beautiful, and understanding is obliged to respond: "I don't know; beauty is not a concept, it is a matter of feeling, and I am not technically outfitted to deal with feelings." There are three possible scenarios here: in the first, the rose is neither beautiful nor ugly, and our two faculties split with a shrug of indifference. Understanding goes back to the business he knows (let's gender the faculties, in accordance with the social order of Kant's time), and imagination consults with her own servant, sensibility. The latter tells her that her sensors for inner sensations register nothing: either this particular rose leaves her totally cold (indifference) or it triggers as much pleasure as displeasure, and their opposed forces compensate and neutralize each other (equilibrium). In the second scenario, the rose is objectively beautiful,[45] and something unusual happens: imagination is not satisfied with understanding's avowal of ignorance, and she presses him to try harder. Having received sensibility's report testifying to an intense pleasure, she won't take "I don't know" for an answer, and she provokes understanding. She admits that, unlike him, she doesn't master concepts, but she relies on sensibility's gut feelings to back her claims and to empower her. Understanding is surprised and excited by such effrontery and, although the rules of the game are not his, accepts imagination's challenge to play with her. She, in turn, feels flattered by her master's dismissal of courtly etiquette, and this prompts her to more audacities: she is happy to play a game nobody can win. Though at first he resisted, understanding, too, is now happy to indulge. He challenges imagination to convince him, by the sheer energy of her own conviction, that the rose is beautiful, even though he still has no concept of the beautiful under which to subsume the rose. And so the game goes on, yielding a particularly felicitous harmony between the two partners, a harmony made of *liberté, égalité, fraternité*.

The passage in *The Conflict of the Faculties* where Kant rejoices at the enthusiasm of the spectators (not of the actors) of the French Revolution is well known.[46] Why do they, aristocrats among them, whose class interest should align them with the *Ancien Régime*, embrace the revolution? Noting the fact, Kant sees in it a sign—not more than a sign but a sign, nevertheless—that political progress and faith in the "moral disposition of the human race" are not vain words.[47] His attitude vis-à-vis the mutual excitement that imagination and understanding trigger in each other is exactly of the same order, political implications included. I would not be surprised if the (pre-Terror) events of the revolution, strictly contemporaneous with the writing of the third *Critique*, proved to have provided Kant with a *Leitfaden* for his reflections on the free play of the faculties in paragraph nine. The way the Schiller of the *Letters* shows he has read the third *Critique* no doubt encourages speculation along such lines.[48] In aesthetic experience, and only there, the social hierarchies of the *Ancien Régime* cease to rule over the faculties of the mind. Imagination and understanding are able to play with each other freely because they are on equal footing; now that they are free and equal, fraternal love reigns in their midst: such is the harmony that translates as the particular pleasure only beauty yields. Just as Kant has read the enthusiasm of the French Revolution's spectators as a sign of political progress, so he reads the harmony of the faculties in the experience of beauty as a sign, too. A sign of what? Of the universal shareability of the pleasure dispensed by beauty, which is itself a sign. A sign of what? Of the presence in all humans of the faculty of taste, which is also a sign, this time of the presence in them of the universally shared *faculty of agreeing by dint of feeling*, which Kant calls *sensus communis*. Kant's unique discovery, indeed his unsurpassable contribution to aesthetics, is to have understood that, by making positive judgments about beauty, human beings suppose their humanity to reside in their claimed common ability for having feelings in common. Call it universal empathy, if you want. The pleasure beauty yields is not the egotistic pleasure of the senses, it must be the joy one has in sharing one's pleasure with anyone and everyone. Schiller's *Ode to Joy*, put to music by Beethoven in his ninth symphony, exactly transcribes Kant's exhilarating discovery of the *sensus communis*.

Or does it? Does it not rather—much more soberly put—transcribe the Romantic, euphoric moment in the reception history of Kant's discovery, a moment that gleefully ignored Kant's prudence and skepticism (testified to by the words "suppose," "claimed," "must be," in the previous paragraph)? Adorno's reading of Kant definitely belongs to a *dysphoric* moment in that same history—a moment I don't believe we have left or will be leaving any time soon. Not that I see an even darker future than did Adorno; I simply think our historical moment has prepared us to unearth the negativity hidden in Kant's text and to bring it to the surface. Not to be inclined to confuse moments in the reception history of philosophical discoveries with dialectical moments in the (Hegelian) history of spirit is an advantage, in this respect. As I gradually realize, Kant gives me the means to accompany Adorno and to accept being led by him while addressing my resistance to his Hegelianism only. The *pathos* in "empathy" is a key, provided we use it to open doors other than Adorno's psychology or way of thinking. Empathy—in Theodor Lipp's or Wilhelm Worringer's sense—is most of the time not understood as the propensity to share in someone else's pleasure. It is the inclination or the willingness to share in someone else's pain. In light of this, Beethoven's *Ode to Joy* sounds utterly idealistic, and Kant's *sensus communis* more than a trifle too "affirmative." Not pleasure, so much, but *pain*, is the sign in aesthetic experience that Kant ought to have been attentive to. I take this to be the gist of Adorno's admonition to Kant, which his particular brand of pathos signals over and over again. Pain, not pleasure, is the only sure sign indicating that all human beings *must* be endowed with *sensus communis*. When Adorno's reading is stripped of the temptation to have Hegel fill in for Kant's shortcomings, the theoretical *must* implied by Kant's skepticism (a *müssen* for theory) comes closer and closer to a practical *ought* (a *sollen* for practice). Such transfer is in any case implied by Adorno's credo, as it assigns pain the universalizing function pleasure had for Kant. Should one stake one's hope for a reconciled humanity on aesthetic experience, that is, on art and culture, as Adorno definitely did, then one had better invest that hope in universal compassion than in universal joy. Let pathos—"a pathos that even the radically pathos-alien work is unable to slough off"—be the aesthetic bond that unites the human species.[49] Let *expression* in art "lend a voice to suffering."[50] Indeed, for Adorno, "expression is scarcely to be conceived except as the expression of suffering." He even adds that "joy has proven inimical to expression, perhaps because it has yet to exist"—which gives a measure of his historical pessimism as well as his transcendental optimism.[51] Expressionism is one art-historical name (realism is the other) of the moment when the expression of suffering was allowed to negate the idealism of classical aesthetics. And as Adorno knew, both expressionism and realism have always been associated with the controversial, yet in the end positive, assessment of ugliness. It is not certain that Kant would have understood the positiveness of that assessment, but he would have agreed that the feeling ugliness in art *stems from* is suffering, for it is the feeling ugliness *yields*. He called it pain or, more timidly, displeasure, but there is no doubt in my mind that he conceived of it not merely as a lack of pleasure (a logical negation), but as an active and *positive force of negation* making pleasure difficult or impossible. This brings us back to our rose, and to our third, not yet envisioned scenario: the rose is objectively ugly.[52]

Kant does not address the issue of ugliness explicitly in paragraph nine of the *Critique of Judgment* or anywhere else. But his problem with it is clearly the same as his problem with beauty: in order not to be reducible to mere displeasure of the senses, the pain occasioned by a negative judgment of taste must be of a different kind. There is no reason to believe that Kant went another route than with beauty, so we may surmise that the pain in question also involves imagination and understanding, but this time "so far as they" *do not* "agree with each other as is requisite for a cognition in general."[53] Cognition is antagonized. The technical and social division of labor among the mental faculties remains, but free play is out of the question. Insurrection of the lower faculties is the order of the day. When imagination presents understanding with the rose and asks him if it is ugly, "I don't know" is understanding's reply, for ugliness is no more a concept than beauty, and it is equally a matter of feeling. Here again, imagination won't take "I don't know" for an answer, but this time she is met with downright rebuttal. Not only has her effrontery not won her understanding's sympathy at all, it has succeeded in irritating him considerably. Understanding knows his own rules, and since he is the master, he is willing to abide by his rules but not by someone else's—least of all by those of a female servant *twice* ranking lower in the social order! His irritation makes him phrase his response maladroitly: instead of humbly admitting that he is not technically outfitted to deal with feelings, he barks back: "Feelings are irrelevant, as far as I (the master) am concerned." This of course infuriates imagination: the message she has received from sensibility spoke of such an intense unpleasantness that, as far as *she* is concerned, there is no doubt that feelings are relevant—and no doubt either that the rose is ugly. Her conviction grows, and so does her revolt: she is no longer asking understanding for confirmation of sensibility's gut feelings, she wants the master to acknowledge her own intuitive certainty. Understanding is impressed but doesn't budge. Though he won't admit it, he is not indifferent to such convincing display of conviction, but since the only rules he recognizes are the rules of cognition, he mistakes imagination's certainty for some mysterious feminine access to a truth that is refused to him. Now he goes after that truth. He questions imagination; he interrogates her. She is only too glad to oblige him, for she has seen in his demand her opportunity to seize power. Sensing this, and not ready to surrender his towering master's status, understanding freezes into an authoritarian posture. And so on and so forth. The game, or the conflict, goes on without ever resolving in the happiness of both parties, in a bitter stalemate at best.

Marx was certainly not as disinterested a spectator as Kant when confronted with the revolutions and counterrevolutions of his time. He was also a lot less conservative. If he had witnessed the quarrel of imagination and understanding over ugliness, he, too, might have read it as a sign and, like Kant with the French Revolution, as a sign of political progress—progress spelled "class struggle," though, not "disinterestedness." He would have given the *conflict* of the faculties a reading as positive as Kant's reading of their *harmony*, in spite of the negativity of the feelings involved. And he would have had a good reason for this: when conducted consciously under the direction of the Communist party, class struggle unfolds on behalf of classless society; the proletariat is a social class only as long as its ongoing struggle against the bourgeoisie prevents it from standing for humanity reconciled; the conflict is pursued in the name of the harmony it will eventually bring about; war is waged for the sake of its termination; negativity is legitimated by the ultimately positive, even affirmative, goal to be attained. And so on. Adorno can't afford, won't afford, Marx's optimism. He is writing his *Aesthetic Theory* with Stalin's ghost looking over his shoulder; with the crushed Budapest insurrection in memory; with the Berlin wall facing him; with the knowledge of Marx's utopia having become a totalitarian nightmare; and still more intolerable, with the awareness that there is no more redress for Auschwitz ever to be expected from the self-righteous antifascism stemming from the Eastern bloc than from the amnesia reigning in *Wirtschaftswunder* West Germany. Historical contradictions have no happy ending in negative dialectics. Yet, as desperate an answer to Marx as it may be, negative dialectics preserve an important aspect of Marx's handling of contradictions—and one, interestingly enough, that does not appear to be dialectical: its "in-the-name-of" structure. It is in the name of totality that micrology opts for the fragment; in the name of global redemption that global desperation takes over; in the name of truly accomplished reconciliation that momentary reconciliations are denounced as false and premature; in the name of beauty and harmony that ugliness and dissonance were given the leading role in virtually every significant modern art movement (not just in realism and expressionism). Adorno found precious something that the Marxist art theorists who instrumentalized art (Lukács is Adorno's favorite foil) were only too eager to sacrifice: the intuition that the autonomy of truly ambitious art, its radicalism, its abstraction, its so-called formalism, its active deskilling, have a lot to do with this "in-the-name-of" handling of contradictions. The failure of art for art's sake was not that the artists in that movement were making art in the name of art; it was that they failed to understand that they had to make *anti-art* in the name of art. (Gautier not *getting* Manet would be to the point.) The art for art's sake artists conceived of art's autonomy as a closed territory fearfully cleansed of all inner conflict and fenced off from the "totality." They did not see, as Adorno did, and how exemplarily, that only the art that willfully lets the dirt and the violence of the "totality" contaminate its autonomy truly establishes that autonomy. When Adorno writes, "For the sake of reconciliation, authentic works must blot out every trace of reconciliation in memory," he is close to Marx.[54] He is also closer to Kant than he might think. To resolve contradictions by coping with them instead, in the name of their resolution, is not exclusive to Adorno's negative dialectics, or to Marx's dialectical materialism. It is also what dialectics in Kant's sense—that is, the resolution of antinomies—does. In paragraph fifty-seven of the third *Critique*, located in the section entitled *The Dialectic of the Aesthetic Power of Judgment*, the antinomy of taste gets resolved when the concept on which our aesthetic judgments ought to be based, and which is missing, is shown to be nothing but the regulative idea *in the name of which* each one of our aesthetic judgments speaks: the idea of a supersensible substratum of humanity, where we are "to seek the unifying point of all our faculties."[55]

To anthropomorphize the faculties of the mind when reading Kant, as I did, is not the most orthodox interpretive strategy. Yet it has the useful effect of historicizing and socializing the transcendental subject. Instead of the solipsistic, sovereign entity it is often taken to be, the transcendental subject is better described as a society of faculties analogous to a society of human beings, with its historical existence and its unresolved conflicts.[56] (I think Hegel saw this in Kant and used it against him.) The cognitive faculties are the product of the technical and social division of labor; they are gendered; they entertain relationships of production with each other; they can play freely or enter into conflicts with one another; they ought to be living in peace and harmony, and they don't. They don't empirically—there is enough evidence of *that*—and they don't transcendentally either. The supersensible substratum where we are "to seek the unifying point of all our faculties" is an idea, a *mere* idea. Orthodox, classical, or otherwise "affirmative" readings of the third *Critique*—possibly including Kant's own, inasmuch as he hoped to give the third *Critique* the level of apodicticity he thought he had given the first—tend to take the unity and the harmony of the subject's faculties for granted. (They do this with a vengeance if they are incorporated in a critique meant to dismiss Kant's transcendental subject.) By the same token, they take *sensus communis*—the intersubjective extension of the subject's faculties—to be a factual reality: humans *are* naturally endowed with the mutual empathy that makes them recognize their common humanity in all others. Such orthodox and "affirmative" readings also focus on beauty and leave the negativity of ugliness aside, or simply expel it from Kant's aesthetics. When their biases are corrected, when the issue of ugliness is raised from within the third *Critique* and allowed to occupy center stage, when suffering, the negative feeling ugliness yields, is assessed positively, when the conflict of the faculties, of which the feeling of ugliness is the sign, is granted a place in aesthetic theory, then the violence reigning among humans comes to the fore and casts doubt on the factual reality of *sensus communis*; then the harmony of the subject's faculties can no more be taken for granted than harmony among humans. The faculties' unity is not given; it may or may not, some day, be the outcome of their reconciliation, but there is no guarantee whatsoever that history is moving that way. Human history is no more teleologically oriented than natural evolution—a salutary antidote to the false hopes of progress as historical determinism, be they Hegelian or Marxist in inspiration. Just as the Enlightenment's ideal of emancipation, seen through Kantian eyes, was not a project but rather a maxim,[57] so peace among the faculties of the mind is not a goal humanity will achieve when it has grown wiser; it must forever be conceived as nothing more and nothing less than a *hic et nunc* requirement of reason: a *müssen* for theory and a *sollen* for practice. Between Kant's time and ours, Adorno implicitly warns us, the cursor has moved a long way in the direction of the *sollen*, because in the meantime we have been forced to think that *sensus communis* is definitely *not* a natural endowment of humankind and therefore *must* be an idea, a mere regulative idea: we have had to come to terms with the "fact" that we humans are *not* graced with the faculty of spontaneously empathizing with the human in us all—not an easy thing to swallow.

What demonstrates this lack of empathy to be a "fact" has a

name, and that name is Auschwitz. Kant had left the question of *sensus communis* open. Rightly or wrongly, Adorno understood that Auschwitz definitively closed it with a negative answer: *sensus communis* is a chimera; the sad truth is that humans *are* wolves to one another. In one of the rare passages in the third *Critique* where Kant allows himself to muse on the future, he asks himself "whether there is in fact such a common sense,... or whether a yet higher principle of reason only makes it into a regulative principle for us first to produce a common sense in ourselves for higher ends, thus whether taste is an original and natural faculty, or only the idea of one that is yet to be acquired," and he leaves the answer pending.[58] My understanding of Adorno's famous statement that writing poetry after Auschwitz is barbaric is that he takes it to be a fact that *sensus communis* is not a fact. He "reads" the Nazis philosophically, as having experimentally demonstrated that humanity does not and cannot form a community of feelings. The Nazis made one exception to the unity of the human race when they decided to physically eliminate the Jewish People, and in so doing they proved that they, not the Jews, were the true exception. They exempted themselves from having to share in the common definition of what makes humans human, thereby proving that empathy does not extend to the whole of humanity; such is the *fact* the name Auschwitz stands for. Of course, Adorno doesn't speak in terms of *sensus communis*. He once again takes the Hegelian road rather than the Kantian and falls prey to its historical determinism. He sees in Auschwitz the intolerable ultimate step in the progress of reification, reached when people are exterminated "administratively," not as individuals but as specimens. Auschwitz spells for him "the final stage of the dialectic of culture and barbarism." The extent to which he is aware that Auschwitz also spells the final stage of his negative dialectics, the stage where he can no longer escape its philosophical impasse, is hard to tell. But he knows himself to be engulfed in a Hegelian nightmare where the absolute realization of spirit has turned into its absolute reification. The passage in "Kulturkritik und Gesellschaft" (1951) where the ban on poetry after Auschwitz is pronounced is also where this Hegelian nightmare appears. It is worth quoting in full:

> The more total society is, the more reified is spirit and the more paradoxical its effort to escape reification on its own. Even the most extreme consciousness of doom threatens to degenerate into idle chatter. Cultural criticism finds itself faced with the final stage of the dialectic of culture and barbarism: to write a poem after Auschwitz is barbaric, and this corrodes even the recognition of why it has become impossible to write poetry today. As long as it remains by itself in self-satisfied contemplation, critical spirit has not yet risen to [the challenge of] absolute reification, which presupposed the progress of spirit as one of its elements and is now preparing to absorb it entirely.[59]

The last sentence is telling. I had to add the word "challenge" to convey what Adorno meant, at the cost of suppressing the stunning and no doubt deliberate stylistic effect that produced an unbearable proximity between the evil of absolute reification and the elevated task critical spirit must accomplish so as to be on the level: *"Der absoluten Verdinglichung...ist der kritische Geist nicht gewachsen."*[60] Such proximity leaves no room for the kind of "negation-of-negation-that-denies-its-inevitable-inversion-into-positivity" that negative dialectics typically requires. As Lyotard has argued, when Adorno makes of the name Auschwitz a "model" for negative dialectics (1966) and thus suggests that it puts an end to the affirmative kind only, he creates for himself the philosophical aporia I called a Hegelian nightmare, and which Lyotard pinpointed as "the wound of nihilism, not an accidental wound but an absolutely philosophical one."[61] Adorno's pathos here verges on the sublime: "Thought honors itself by defending what is damned as nihilism," he pompously writes at the end of a splendid paragraph where he salutes Beckett for being the only writer to have, in his literary work (*Dichtung:* poetry in the widest sense), reacted adequately to the situation of the concentration camps.[62] I don't know what I admire most in this passage: whether it is the Beckettian somersault—if sublime, then ridiculous; if ridiculous, then sublime—with which Adorno extricates himself from the double bind Lyotard called the "rule of immanent derivation that defines negative dialectics: if p, then *non-p*; if *non-p*, then p";[63] or whether it is his offhand recognition that poetry after Auschwitz is possible, after all. He has admitted a few pages before and, not by chance, a paragraph or so after having mentioned Beckett's *Endgame* for the first time, that "it may have been wrong to say that after Auschwitz you could no longer write poems."[64] But he has retracted a few pages down the road: "Auschwitz demonstrated irrefutably that culture had failed." And, a little further: "All post-Auschwitz culture, including its urgent critique, is garbage."[65] Obviously, he is utterly reluctant to amend his outrageous claim of fifteen years earlier, even as he is resting his case on the work of the one great writer who he admits has proved him wrong. His embarrassment is enough of an indication, I think, that what is at stake is not whether poetry, the other arts, and culture at large have become barbaric after the unnamable. Adorno knows that it's the other way round: Auschwitz is one name of the unnamable because it names that *in the name of which* it is impossible, without being barbaric, to write poetry, to make art, or otherwise to speak publicly.[66] Yet he doesn't reach for the "in-the-name-of" argument. He focuses on the ultimate dialectical reversal that makes it a duty for poetry, or for art, or for "critical spirit," to rise to the level of obscenity of the unnamable—witness, in *Endgame*, the abjection of Hamm's parents having to live in garbage cans[67]—and he leaves unattended the nondialectical reversal that justifies the obscenity in question: that poetry be written, or art be made, in the name of "Auschwitz never again." What this "never again" formulates is not dialectical: a negation it is, but a negation that doesn't pair up with what it negates. Even *negative* dialectical fusion of the contraries (whatever that means) is here impossible: the abominable event happened; the command "never again" forbids, but is impotent to prevent, its happening again. And it is a positive command, in spite of its negative content, which is why it affirms Auschwitz in a transhistorical, essentially philosophical way. As an imperative, it makes of Auschwitz a *fact*—in Kant's Latinized German, *Faktum*—the *fact* that *sensus communis* is not a fact. There is more than a play on words, here. I think that Adorno has had a keen intuition of this *fact* (italicized) but that he failed to theorize adequately its difference from a fact (roman), in the empirical sense. Should we succeed in theorizing that difference, we might find the transcendentalist's way out of the dialectician's Hegelian nightmare. Or, to borrow Lyotard's words: we might avoid the "wound of nihilism," possibly the deepest and most hidden source of Adorno's pathos. It's worth trying.

 Kant's resorting to Latin is often indicative of some paradoxical play with usual terms. Just as *sensus communis* doesn't refer to common sense in the commonsensical sense—indeed, it means common sentiment, not common understanding—so Kant's usage of *Faktum* instead of *Fakt* or *Tatsache* indicates that he intends it to mean something different from fact, in the factual, demonstrable sense. The word *Faktum* appears in the *Critique of Practical Reason,* where it refers to moral conscience and to nothing else.[68] It is a *fact,* an undeniable, immediately intuitive though indemonstrable *fact,* that moral law is given to us, from no one knows where, and this *fact* is enough to call us to our supersensible destiny, which is to realize the highest good in the sensible world. Is this task within our reach, given that there are few illusions to be entertained regarding humankind's morality? Is implementation of morally good deeds in the sensible world even possible, given that free moral action, as such, produces no tangible proof of its efficiency? Ever the pessimist, Kant writes: "We are fortunate, if only we can be sufficiently assured that there is no proof of its impossibility."[69] Still, is there something that mediates between the arid sphere of morality, where only the categorical imperative rules, and the earthly sphere where we finite beings made of flesh and blood—as much as we yearn and may strive for the highest good—are prone to letting the penchants of our fallible human nature dictate our behavior? In less dramatic and more philosophical terms: is there a mediating ground between ethical conduct (the domain of the second *Critique*) and the world ruled by the laws of natural sciences (the domain of the first) to give us hope that the realization of the highest good in the sensible world is at least not impossible? Even though no feelings are admitted as the ground of moral conduct except respect, feelings such as pleasure and happiness definitely partake in the highest good and are morally compatible with it. Given that feelings can on the other hand be accounted for by psychology, physiology, and the natural sciences in general, couldn't the sphere of feelings, if not directly then at least analogically, provide this mediating ground? This becomes the great question of the *Critique of Judgment*, with the realm of aesthetic experience standing as the paradigm for the sphere of feelings at large. Kant reads the call on universal agreement issued by every judgment of taste as the sign that we presuppose in others the same faculty of agreeing by dint of feeling that we sense in ourselves. The issue now is whether that faculty—call it in Kant's Latin *sensus communis* or, in plain English, universally shared empathy for our fellow men—is our natural endowment, or not; whether or not it exists, in fact (roman). The *Critique of Judgment* leaves the issue open. To quote Kant again: "Whether there is in fact such a common sense...or whether [it is] only [an] idea...that is yet to be acquired..., this we would not and cannot yet investigate here."[70] It is possible to read the whole "Critique of the Teleological Judgment" as the investigation Kant postponed in the just quoted paragraph twenty-two, but the issue doesn't get settled there either. *Sensus communis* is definitely an idea, but whether it is also a natural propensity with which we come equipped—something like an instinct—Kant doesn't know.

We ought to know, I understand Adorno to reply: Auschwitz reveals the fact (roman) that we are not so equipped. It is my contention that *fact*, here, should have been italicized, in accordance with Kant's *Faktum*.

Why the cold shower—of our not being equipped with *sensus communis*—had to take the ultraviolent form of Auschwitz is the incomprehensible scandal that I think drove Adorno (and Horkheimer) to conceive the extreme, and in my view fundamentally flawed, theory that totalitarianism, and "German fascism" in particular, was the logical outcome of Kant's rationalism. In the chapter of *Dialectic of Enlightenment* entitled "Juliette or Enlightenment and Morality," the caricaturing of Kant as obsessively systematic and prototypically bourgeois, and the reduction of science to the most mindless positivism, are so gross that they don't even deserve comment. On the other hand, the pairing of Kant with the marquis de Sade in that same chapter, although improperly theorized,[71] is the most insightful acknowledgment I know of that Auschwitz names the *fact*—in Kant's sense of *Faktum*—that *sensus communis* is not a fact in the empirical, verifiable sense. Unfortunately, Horkheimer and Adorno misrepresent Kant's *Faktum* and, therefore, mistake *fact* for fact:

> Kant, to be sure, had so purified the moral law within the self of any heteronymous belief that respect, despite his assurances, could be no more than a psychological fact of nature, as the starry sky above the self was a physical one. "A fact of reason," he called it.[72]

The authors' conflation of a *fact* of reason with a fact of nature—a heresy for Kant, as it should be for anyone—is crucial to the poetry-after-Auschwitz issue and beyond, to the question of whether a Kantian, more particularly, the "Kant-after-Duchamp," approach to aesthetics, is able to respond to a negativity of the magnitude of Auschwitz without simply putting a ban on all art practice. Does Auschwitz name a *fact* of reason or a fact of nature?

What is intuitively right in Horkheimer's and Adorno's take on the issue is that the answer is both. What is wrong is that this is no license to conflate and confound the two, not even dialectically. The fact of nature (in Kant's sense of nature) is that Auschwitz happened; the gas chambers were real. The *fact* of reason is that Auschwitz ought never have happened. The moral law, Kant's *Faktum*, should never have allowed it to happen, which is why the moral law now reads: "Auschwitz never again." No new law is thereby uttered: "Auschwitz never again" is the law, Kant's one and only categorical imperative, historicized under its new, post-Shoah name. By conflating Auschwitz as a fact of nature (that is, of history) and Auschwitz as negatively naming the moral law, Horkheimer and Adorno feign to understand Kant as upholding the theory that the moral law is deducible from the laws of nature. (I can't imagine this to be feasible without a measure of disingenuousness.)[73] They might have been better (or more honestly) inspired to keep in mind the "as if"–reasoning with which Kant articulated the relation between the moral law and the laws of nature, for example, in the second formulation of the categorical imperative:

> Ask yourself whether, if the action you propose were to take place by a law of nature, of which you were yourself a part, you could indeed regard it as possible for your will.[74]

This formulation gives us the exact understanding of the relation Kant's *Faktum* has vis-à-vis the notion of fact in the empirical sense. Kant proposes to the hesitant ethical subject a simple test: if the action you project to accomplish were to be the outcome of a natural law (such as Newton's law of universal gravity, always on Kant's mind when he thinks of nature), rather than the result of your free will, would you still approve of it? If the answer is no, then your action is immoral. Transposed to the issue of whether *sensus communis* is a fact of nature, the test yields a theoretical lesson. If the relationships you have with other human beings were to obey your natural instincts and nothing else, could you still call them ethical? The answer would be yes if you were sure that *all* your instincts are charitable, good, and respectful of others—quite an improbable event. And it would definitely be no if you were sure that *all* your sentiments vis-à-vis others are like those of the wolf for the lamb, also an unlikely event if, like the rest of us, you have affectionate feelings at least for the ones close to you. The practical maxim Kant would draw from this test is: don't trust your feelings in ethical matters; they are sometimes good and sometimes bad, but they offer no a priori certainty because they are not universalizable; let the cold and impartial inner voice of the categorical imperative dictate your conduct. Never mind if we don't have a superego that weighs every single ethical action against the inevitability of the laws of nature; we don't need to espouse Kant's moral rigor to grasp the implications the test's theoretical lesson has in store for the *Critique of Judgment:* if it were an established fact of nature that all of us humans are endowed with *sensus communis*, then our good feelings—I mean, the feelings that make us feel good, those we revel in when we are happy, those signaled to us by the free play of our faculties in aesthetic pleasure, and perhaps those we spontaneously share with our loved ones—would be universalizable, in fact. This in turn means that we would realize the highest good in the sensible world simply by following our natural inclinations. And if by any chance it were an established fact of nature that we humans are *not* equipped with *sensus communis*, then none of our good, pleasurable feelings would be universalizable. Egotism, *jouissance*, and self-interest—Horkheimer and Adorno speak of self-preservation—would be ruling *all* human relations. The chances are that the only universalizable feelings would be negative feelings: fear and distrust of others, anger and aggressiveness, a sense of generalized competition that sees in anyone a potential enemy, a paranoid defense of one's identity, all sorts of ideologically motivated hatreds and hate-fueled ideologies. The aesthetic culture produced by a humanity really (that is, in fact) driven by such feelings would be a Babel of stolen pleasures and a sea of grievances among competing rackets, for whom destroying the art and culture of "the other" is more vital than producing an art and culture of one's own—a fairly good definition of barbarism.

Notwithstanding Adorno's constant insistence that *Dialectic of Enlightenment* was "the joint work of Horkheimer and myself, to the extent that every sentence belongs to us both," this was hardly the case.[75] Evidence from the posthumous papers of both co-authors, as well as the testimonies of Gretel Adorno, Jürgen Habermas, and Rolf Tiedemann indicate that Horkheimer wrote most, if not all, of the chapter I am discussing here, "the Sade chapter," as Habermas calls it.[76] If this is true, then it was Horkheimer's insight to bring in Sade, and Adorno must have applauded; he might even have pardoned Horkheimer for crassly oversimplifying and distorting Kant in exchange for a peek into the *Philosophy in the Bedroom* that gave him an anticipated glimpse into his own future negative dialectics. As is shown by the record of their discussions in the immediate postwar years, when they were finalizing the manuscript and projecting a second volume on dialectics, Adorno already had a much darker vision of enlightened rationalism than did Horkheimer. "Reason is its own sickness," he replied to his colleague, when the latter called on what remained of "healthy reason" in his effort to "rescue the Enlightenment."[77] The barbarism of all post-Auschwitz culture was already on Adorno's mind, and it was the barbarism of the kind of humanity driven by mutual hate I described earlier, the barbarism of a world where we would be certain, apodictically certain, that humanity is not endowed with *sensus communis*. It is definitely to Horkheimer's credit to have intuited that the world of Sade, or of the sadist, is, or rather *ought to be*, such a world. But Horkheimer made the mistake of confusing *is* with *ought* (fact with *fact*, again), and so he congratulated Sade—whom he saluted as the most intransigent critic of Kant, while casting the latter as the epitome of the bourgeois thinker—for having unveiled self-preservation and material interest as the real founding ground of "the respect without which civilization cannot exist."[78] And he missed the true import of Sade's *Philosophy in the Bedroom* totally. For a philosophy it is: not an empirical rebuttal of Kant's morals or a genealogy à la Nietzsche, but a thought experiment in inverted Kantianism, perversely but rigorously faithful to the original. How much more to the point than Horkheimer's pitting of Sade against Kant is Lacan's pairing of Kant with Sade:

> *Philosophy in the Bedroom* came eight years after the *Critique of Practical Reason*. If, after showing that the former is consistent with the latter, I can demonstrate that the former completes the latter, I shall be able to claim that it yields the truth of the *Critique*.[79]

Alas, the sadist complains, the world where only egotism and *jouissance* rule is not a fact. It is our *moral* task to bring it to existence: "Yet another effort, Frenchmen." Still too much benevolence, compassion, and weakness of heart render ethical relations impure. Let us sweep all that sentimentality away, espouse Kant's rigor, and clear the air for the cold and impartial inner voice. And to make sure that this task, unlike the achievement of the highest good in the sensible world, is not impossible, let us invert Kant's categorical imperative. Instead of calling it a duty for everyone never to make use of anyone else as a means to an end, let us call it a right for everyone always to use and abuse anyone else as a means to one's own ends, no matter how wicked.[80] Let us create a world where "delight in evil" is the highest good. Lacan writes:

> If one eliminates from morality every element of sentiment, if one removes or invalidates all guidance to be found in sentiment, then in the final analysis the Sadian world is conceivable—even if it is its inversion, its caricature—as one of

the possible forms of the world governed by a radical ethics, by the Kantian ethics as elaborated in 1788.[81]

Kant's test has shown that whether *sensus communis* exists or not is undecidable, and Sade apparently agrees. He also seems to have seen through the lines of the not yet written third *Critique* something Kant himself was reluctant to see: that, if it was a theoretical necessity to postulate that *sensus communis* exists, it was also a quasi-moral obligation to make that postulate; and that the less plausible the postulate's factual reality was, the more the cursor of the quasi-moral obligation had to move in the direction of the moral *tout court*. Sade's thought experiment in inverted Kantianism pushes the cursor all the way in the direction of the moral—of the morally evil, that is. The sadist calls it a moral obligation to make the theoretical postulate that *sensus communis* does *not* exist, and follows through with the corresponding practical maxim: one ought to make sure that it does not exist; one ought to suppress all love, compassion, and sympathy—all shareable feelings—from one's conduct. It is left to us, readers of Sade, to redress the inverted Kantianism where it must be redressed: only in the practical maxim. The theoretical postulate remains the Sadian one: that *sensus communis* does *not* exist. This is how I read Horkheimer's insight in the "Sade chapter" of *Dialectic of Enlightenment*. It is as much an insight into the deepest historical sources of Adorno's pathos as it is into the meaning of the *Philosophy in the Bedroom*. Horkheimer—and Adorno with him, for, after all, he cosigned the text—are wrong when they see in Sade a dialectical critic of Kant: the inversion Sade imprints on Kant is not dialectical. But they are right on target when they virtually suggest that Sade has written "poetry after Auschwitz" long before Auschwitz. Through the *divin marquis*, literature has risen to the level of obscenity of the unnamable. Perhaps Sade did worse, too, and, unlike Beckett, could afford to speak *in the name of the unnamable* without being barbaric because, even in those days of Terror, the unnamable was still unthinkable. It was left to Pier Paolo Pasolini's film *Salò, or the 120 Days of Sodom* to unpack the full sadistic barbarism of the unthinkable having become a fact and to redress the "in-the-name-of" procedure.

What kind of aesthetic theory the post-Auschwitz world requires will of course not be settled today. Adorno raised the question for everyone working in the field, and though he has not made our task easier, we are in his debt. The work that remains to be done is enormous. I hope to have convinced at least a fraction of my readers that looking toward Kant for help is far from absurd or obsolete, and less aporetic than turning to Hegel. To bring this essay to a close, I want to return to the quotation with which I began:

> Works of art ... appear as in-the-world; their medium is not pure spirit existing for itself, but the spirit that retreats into worldly existence and, by the force of such movement, lays a claim on the unity of what is separated. This contradiction forces works of art to make us forget that they are made: the claim their existence-in-the-world stakes, and hence the claim that existence itself is meaningful, is the more convincing, the less something in them warns us that they have been fabricated, that they owe their existence to spirit as something external to themselves. Art that is no longer able to achieve this deception with good conscience—indeed its very principle—has dissolved the only element in which it can realize itself.[82]

What to do with the ominous last sentence that threatens art in its very existence? Should there be room in a post-Auschwitz aesthetic theory for "art that is no longer able to achieve this deception with good conscience"? Should the theory then accommodate art that has lost "its very principle"—art that is only nominally art but lacks the conviction? Or is art worthy of the name still obliged to "achieve this deception," albeit with *bad* conscience? If the former, why hold on to the word "art"? If the latter, how to escape the pathos of repressed guilt? In reading that passage when I embarked on the writing of this paper, I wondered why Adorno had inserted the typically Kantian view that art should look like nature while we know that it is art in an otherwise typically Hegelian argument, and I saw in this a symptom of his struggle with both philosophers. Now I realize that in selecting that passage, I must have had an inkling of a more profound question: Why was Adorno essentially right when he made the view that art should appear as-if-unmade the touchstone of the judgment that decides whether something deserves to be called art or not? The long answer would involve making deep excursions into *transcendental materialism* as the result of the modern disenchantment of the world and explaining why the Romantic path that led from Kant to Hegel via Schelling missed it. The place to start would be Kant's theory of genius and its non-Romantic update.[83] The short answer is this: Kant's God died at Auschwitz for the third time. The God of the first *Critique* died right there, in the fourth antinomy. Modern biology, Darwinism, cybernetics, killed the God of the third *Critique*. The God who gets annihilated at Auschwitz is the God of the second *Critique*, God as postulate of practical reason. As I said earlier: not an easy thing to swallow, even a century after Nietzsche. At stake is an issue as old or, I should say, as young as modernity (what, indeed, are two hundred years compared with the one hundred thousand that separate us from the first tombs containing traces of red ochre, possibly the most ancient manifestation of aesthetic *and* religious behavior?): Is a truly secular art possible? Will art survive the demise of religion? Adorno never tackled the question head-on because he shared with his friend Benjamin the modernist conviction that politics have displaced religion once and for all—not their best insight in view of the overwhelming confusion of politics and religion that has recently threatened us from all sides. Today's *doxa* notwithstanding, I think that art's autonomy from religion—and whether it is thinkable, whether it is viable at all—

was Adorno's unacknowledged concern when he doubted the right of art to exist.[84] If I may say so, my "Kant-after-Duchamp" approach to the aesthetic theory of art is an attempt to construct that autonomy intellectually. It rests on the conviction that the unsurpassable lesson Kant had learned from his philosophical investigation of the beautiful in nature has been transferred to the domain of art. "This artifact is art" replacing "This fruit of nature is beautiful" as the canonical utterance of a *pure* aesthetic judgment expresses this transfer.[85] Until recently, I was content with attributing the need of that transfer to the death of the God of the first and third *Critique*s. In an essay published a few years ago, paraphrasing Kant's double reflexive loop—"Nature was beautiful, if at the same time it looked like art; and art can only be called beautiful if we are aware that it is art and yet it looks to us like nature"[86]—I wrote:

> In simple words: beauty in nature arises when we look at nature as if it were God-made, and beauty in art arises when we look at artifacts as if nobody had made them. No matter what creationists and religious fundamentalists believe, it is no longer possible to look at nature as if it were God-made. The question is whether we can still look at man-made things as though nobody had made them. The answer is not: yes, we can; it is: yes, we must. A strange "must" on the verge of "ought," as if poised between *müssen* and *sollen*. A quasi-ethical obligation to endow all humans with the faculty of agreeing, that overshadows the theoretical necessity to endow all humans with the faculty of taste.[87]

Barack Obama was to me an unknown name then. I find my "yes we can/yes we must" quip pleasantly uncanny in view of his election and its economic context, but that's an aside. I was thinking ahead of myself, then, not fully realizing, as I do better today, that the reason serious art is invested with unprecedented ethical gravity goes far beyond the intellectual solitude the modern disenchantment of the world has thrown us into. It has everything to do with the monsters the dreadful twentieth century has engendered and the moral abandonment that has ensued. May the transcendentalist live and think through the contradictions of our time with less pain than the dialectician and face the future with more energetic optimism. But forget that the cursor has definitely moved all the way into the direction of the *sollen* he may not.

Endnotes

[1] Theodor W. Adorno, *In Search of Wagner*, trans. Rodney Livingstone (London, 1991), p. 83.

[2] Ibid., pp. 82 and 83.

[3] Ibid.

[4] Theodor W. Adorno, *Aesthetic Theory*, trans. Robert Hullot-Kentor (Minneapolis, 1997), p. 1.

[5] Theodor W. Adorno, *Negative Dialectics*, trans. E. B. Ashton (New York, 1997), pp. 17–18.

[6] Theodor W. Adorno, *Minima Moralia: Reflections from Damaged Life*, trans. E. F. N. Jephcott (London, 1974), p. 110.

[7] Here is the German original: "Die Kunstwerke verdanken ihr Dasein der gesellschaftlichen Arbeitsteilung, der Trennung geistiger und körperlicher Arbeit. Dabei jedoch treten sie selbst als Dasein auf; ihr Medium ist nicht der reine, für sich seiende Geist, sondern der, welcher in die Existenz sich zurückbegibt und kraft solcher Bewegung das Getrennte als vereint behauptet. Dieser Widerspruch zwingt die Kunstwerke dazu, vergessen zu lassen, daß sie gemacht sind: der Anspruch ihres Dasein, und damit der von Dasein selber als eines Sinnvollen, gerät um so überzeugender, je weniger mehr in ihnen daran mahnt, daß sie hervorgebracht wurden, daß sie dem Geist als einem ihnen selber Äußerlichen sich verdanken. Kunst, welche nicht mehr das gute Gewissen hat zu solchem Trug, ihrem eigenen Prinzip, hat bereits das Element aufgelöst, in dem einzig sie sich realisieren kann"; Theodor W. Adorno, *Versuch über Wagner* (Berlin, 1952), p. 104. I am grateful to Christian Katti for his help with the translation of this and other quotations, as well as for his precious advice with regard to Adorno and the Adorno literature. Whether or not to leave the word *Dasein* untranslated was a question, because it is unclear from the context whether Adorno borrowed it from Heidegger or from Hegel. *Versuch über Wagner* precedes *Jargon der Eigentlichkeit* by twelve years, so we cannot expect Adorno to have yet articulated the virulent critique of Heidegger the later book contains. Precisely for this reason, I preferred to forge the not-quite-Heideggerian expression "existence-in-the-world" to translate *Dasein* in this paragraph because I think that this is literally what Adorno meant. (Unless otherwise noted, all translations are my own.)

[8] Immanuel Kant, *Critique of the Power of Judgment*, trans. Paul Guyer and Eric Matthews (Cambridge, 2000), p.185.

[9] Adorno, *Negative Dialectics*, p. 6 (translation modified).

[10] Adorno, *Aesthetic Theory*, p. 135 (translation modified).

[11] Commenting on Adorno's "models" in the last part of *Negative Dialectics*, Lyotard writes: "The idea of the model corresponds to this reversal in the destiny of dialectics: the model is the name for a kind of para-experience, where dialectics would encounter a non-negatable negative, and would abide in the impossibility of redoubling that negative into a 'result'"; Jean-François Lyotard, *The Differend*, trans. Georges Van Den Abbeele (Minneapolis, 1989), p. 88.

[12] Adorno, *Aesthetic Theory*, p. 32.

[13] Ibid., p. 190 (translation modified).

[14] Adorno, *Negative Dialectics*, pp. 261–65.

[15] Max Horkheimer and Theodor W. Adorno, *Dialectic of Enlightenment*, trans. Edmund Jephcott (Stanford, CA, 2002), p. 98. Kant's description of schematism is to be found in the *Critique of Pure Reason*, trans. Paul Guyer and Allen W. Wood (Cambridge, 1998), p. 273.

[16] "Natural beauty" replaces "art" in Kant's case, but Adorno most often ignores the substitution, one sign among many that he has a Hegelian reading of Kant.

[17] Adorno, *Aesthetic Theory*, pp. 135–36, 233, 210.

[18] Ibid., p. 72.

[19] Ibid., p. 260 (translation modified).

[20] See Theodor W. Adorno, "Ist die Kunst heiter?" in *Versuch das "Endspiel" zu verstehen* (Frankfurt, 1972), p. 14.

[21] I borrow the expression "damaged life" (beschädigtes Leben) from the subtitle of *Minima Moralia: Reflections from Damaged Life*.

[22] Within the Frankfurt School, the German word *Affirmation*, much rarer than the customary *Bejahung*, is used mostly by Adorno and Herbert Marcuse. The latter has added psychosexual connotations (false happiness through "repressive desublimation") to the mainly political ones the word conveyed for Adorno.

[23] Adorno, *Negative Dialectics*, p. 406.

[24] Ibid., p. 407.

[25] The pathos is especially palpable in *Homo Academicus* (Paris, 1984), where Pierre Bourdieu closely observed the social group in which he intimately took part, and went so far as to assume—not without pain or courage—the personal consequences of the demystification of the consensus apparently projected by academics as a class.

[26] See my essay, "Some Philosophical Implications of Eric Cameron's 'Routine Extremism,'" forthcoming.

27 Although Emerson claimed Kantian filiation for his brand of transcendentalism, it is as if he picked the wrong Immanuel. His definition of transcendentalism as "the Saturnalia or excess of Faith," his opinion that the Transcendentalist believes in miracles and in ecstasy, and his claim that "Nature is transcendental" owe more to Swedenborg than to Kant. See Ralph Waldo Emerson, "The Transcendentalist" (1842), in *Essays and Lectures* (New York, 1983), pp. 196 and 198.

28 Theodor W. Adorno, *The Jargon of Authenticity*, trans. Knut Tarnowski and Frederic Will (London, 1973).

29 Quoted without reference by Trent Schroyer in his foreword to ibid., p. vii.

30 See, among other texts, Jean-François Lyotard, *Lessons on the Analytic of the Sublime*, trans. Elizabeth Rottenberg (Stanford, CA, 1994).

31 See my book, *Kant after Duchamp* (Cambridge, MA, 1996).

32 Adorno, *Aesthetic Theory*, pp. 196–99.

33 Philippe Lacoue-Labarthe, *Musica ficta (Figures de Wagner)* (Paris, 1991), pp. 238–42.

34 When I teach aesthetics, I regularly present Kant as witnessing an aesthetic quarrel (*A* pretending that "this rose" is beautiful, *B* that it is ugly; or *A* pretending that "this object" is art, *B* that it is not) into which he is dragged by virtue of the fact that, seeing the rose or the object, he inevitably forms a judgment himself. I did this once in writing, too. See my essay, "Do Artists Speak on Behalf of All of Us?" in Diarmuid Costello and Dominic Willsdon, eds., *The Life and Death of Images: Ethics and Aesthetics* (London, 2008), pp. 139–56.

35 See, for example, Paul Guyer, "Kant on the Purity of the Ugly," in *Values of Beauty: Historical Essays in Aesthetics* (Cambridge, 2005), pp. 141–62; Reinhard Brandt, "Zur Logik des ästhetischen Urteils," in Herman Parret, ed., *Kants Ästhetik/Kant's Aesthetics/L'esthétique de Kant* (Berlin, 1998), pp. 229–45; Daniel Dumouchel, "La laideur introuvable—Les multiples visages du déplaisir," in Christophe Bouton, Fabienne Brugère, and Claudie Lavaud, eds., *L'année 1790—Kant—Critique de la faculté de juger—Beauté, vie, liberté* (Paris, 2008), pp. 13–27; Herman Parret, "The Ugly as the Beyond of the Sublime," in Christian Madelein, Jan Pieters, and Bart Vandenabeele, eds., *Histories of the Sublime* (Brussels, 2005), pp. 59–68. For an interesting defense of the possibility of an aesthetics of ugliness in Kant, see: Christian Strub, "Das Hässliche und die 'Kritik der Ästhetischen Urteilskraft'. Überlegungen zu einer systematischen Lücke," *Kantstudien* 80 (1989): pp. 416–46.

36 Karl Rosenkranz, *Aesthetik des Häßlichen* (1853), ed. Walther Gose and Walter Sachs (Stuttgart-Bad Cannstatt, 1968). As a Hegelian, however, Rosenkranz is utterly unconvincing. His book is not much more than a

typology of the different sorts of ugliness.

37 "Only one kind of ugliness cannot be represented in a way adequate to nature without destroying all aesthetic satisfaction, hence beauty in art, namely, that which arouses loathing"; Kant, *Critique of the Power of Judgment*, p. 190. Let it be said in passing that the "Kant-after-Duchamp" approach amends Kant so as to admit loathing or disgust into the list of legitimate aesthetic feelings. Nothing essential in Kant's contribution to aesthetics is thereby put into question, even though disinterestedness gets problematized and receives a new reading.

38 Hegel showed the way by assimilating actual opposition (light vs. darkness, for example) to reflective determination (light containing its negation as part of its truth). See the three "Remarks on Contradiction" in G. W. F. Hegel, *Science of Logic*, trans. A. V. Miller (Amherst, NY, 1969), pp. 435-43.

39 Immanuel Kant, "Attempt to Introduce the Concept of Negative Magnitudes into Philosophy" (1763), in *Theoretical Philosophy, 1755–1770*, trans. David Walford in collaboration with Ralph Meerbote (Cambridge, 1992), pp. 205–41. See p. 219 in particular.

40 Ibid., p. 221.

41 The pun is not irrelevant. Of course, when Kant wrote *The Conflict of the Faculties* (*Der Streit der Fakultäten*, 1798), the conflict in question involved the faculties in the sense of the schools composing the Prussian University, not in the sense of the faculties of the mind (*Vermögen*). Yet the idea that the conflict among the former might be the institutional transposition of a conflict among the latter (both are *facultates*, in Latin) must have occurred to Kant and amused him.

42 Kant, *Critique of the Power of Judgment*, p. 102.

43 Ibid., p. 103.

44 Imagination, in Kant's sense, has both the productive function our present-day usage of the word carries and the receptive function we would assign to perception. Sensibility takes care of what we would call sensations, i.e., raw sense data not yet organized into percepts.

45 Of course, the rose is not *objectively* beautiful the way it is *objectively* red. The question of the "objectivity" of aesthetic judgment is too complex to be dealt with here. Let me simply state that, on this point, I *almost* completely adhere to what Adorno has to say: "The strongest buttress of subjective aesthetics, the concept of aesthetic feeling, derives from objectivity, not the reverse. Aesthetic feeling says that something is thus; Kant would have attributed such aesthetic feeling, as 'taste,' exclusively to one who was capable of discriminating in the object"; *Aesthetic Theory*, p. 164 (translation slightly modified). I disagree only with the last

sentence: to discriminate among discriminating and nondiscriminating people in matters of taste was not Kant's business as a philosopher. Whether he thought he could do this "in real life" depends on how much confidence he had in his own taste. Needless to say, the matter is speculative.

46 Immanuel Kant, *The Conflict of the Faculties* (1798), trans. Mary J. Gregor and Robert Anchor, in *Religion and Rational Theology*, ed. Allen W. Wood and George Di Giovanni (Cambridge, 1996), pp. 301–3. See Jean-François Lyotard, "Le Différend et le signe de l'histoire," *Change International* 1 (Fall 1983): pp. 114–19.

47 Kant, *The Conflict of the Faculties*, p. 302.

48 See Friedrich Schiller, *On the Aesthetic Education of Man, in a Series of Letters* (1794), trans. Reginald Snell (New Haven, 1954).

49 Adorno, *Aesthetic Theory*, p. 101.

50 Adorno, *Negative Dialectics*, p. 17.

51 Adorno, *Aesthetic Theory*, p. 110. Note Adorno's strange turn of words in the already quoted sentence: "It would be preferable that in some better times art vanish altogether than that it forget the suffering that is its expression and in which form finds its substance" (p. 260, translation modified). He does not speak of suffering as a content that art *expresses* but rather of the suffering that *is* art's expression; neither does he speak of suffering finding its form in works of art, but of form finding its substance in the suffering. In the next sentence, he adds: "This suffering is the humane content [*der humane Gehalt*, not *Inhalt*] that unfreedom counterfeits as positivity" (ibid.).

52 Of course, the rose is no more *objectively* ugly than it is *objectively* beautiful. (See note 45.)

53 Kant, *Critique of the Power of Judgment*, p. 103. (See note 43.)

54 Adorno, *Aesthetic Theory*, p. 234.

55 Kant, *Critique of the Power of Judgment*, p. 217.

56 A similar, less anthropomorphic and perhaps less naive description—one that imparts a linguistic turn to Kant's notoriously language-blind philosophy—can be found in Lyotard's notion of the "archipelago of phrase regimens." See *The Differend*, passim.

57 See the last chapter of my book, *Kant after Duchamp*: "Archaeology of Practical Modernism."

58 Kant, *Critique of the Power of Judgment*, p. 124.

59 Theodor W. Adorno, "Cultural Criticism and Society," in *Prisms*, trans. Samuel and Shierry Weber (London, 1967), p. 34. I modified the

translation on some crucial points where Adorno's Hegelian turn of mind was lost. Compare with the German: "Je totaler die Gesellschaft, um so verdinglichter auch der Geist und um so paradoxer sein Beginnen, der Verdinglichung aus eigenem sich zu entwinden. Noch das äußerste Bewußtsein vom Verhängnis droht zum Geschwätz zu entarten. Kulturkritik findet sich der letzten Stufe der Dialektik von Kultur und Barbarei gegenüber: nach Auschwitz ein Gedicht zu schreiben, ist barbarisch, und das frißt auch die Erkenntnis an, die ausspricht, warum es unmöglich ward, heute Gedichte zu schreiben. Der absoluten Verdinglichung, die den Fortschritt des Geistes als eines ihrer Elemente voraussetzte und die ihn heute gänzlich aufzusaugen sich anschickt, ist der kritische Geist nicht gewachsen, so lange er bei sich bleibt in selbstgenügsamer Kontemplation"; Theodor W. Adorno, "Kulturkritik und Gesellschaft," in Rolf Tiedemann, ed., *Prismen, Gesammelte Schriften* (Frankfurt, 1977), 10.1: p. 30.

60 Literally: "To absolute reification, critical spirit has not grown." The translators of *Prisms*, Sam and Shierry Weber, have had recourse to the same expedient as I: they slipped in the word "challenge." In addition, they split Adorno's long sentence in two: "Absolute reification, which presupposed intellectual progress as one of its elements, is now preparing to absorb the mind entirely. Critical intelligence cannot be equal to this challenge as long as it confines itself to self-satisfied contemplation"; *Prisms*, p. 34.

61 Jean-François Lyotard, "Discussions, ou: phraser 'après Auschwitz,'" in Philippe Lacoue-Labarthe and Jean-Luc Nancy, eds., *Les fins de l'homme, À partir du travail de Jacques Derrida* (Paris, 1981), pp. 289 and 290.

62 Adorno, *Negative Dialectics*, p. 381.

63 Lyotard, "Discussions, ou: phraser 'après Auschwitz,'" p. 291.

64 Adorno, *Negative Dialectics*, p. 362.

65 Ibid., pp. 366 and 367.

66 Auschwitz is not the only name of the unnamable: Treblinka or Sobibor stand for the same *fact*.

67 The just-quoted "All post-Auschwitz culture, including its urgent critique, is garbage" is dialectically echoed in the following, from Adorno's essay on *Endgame*: "Beckett's garbage cans are emblems of the culture that was reconstructed after Auschwitz"; *Versuch das 'Endspiel' zu verstehen*, p. 201.

68 Immanuel Kant, *Critique of Practical Reason*, in *Practical Philosophy*, trans. Mary J. Gregor (Cambridge, 1996), pp. 173–77. The Cambridge edition does not underline the Latin subtext in *Faktum*, which it translates as "fact," but J. Gibelin's French translation does. On its first occurrence, in the first sentence of the "Deduction of the Principles of Pure Practical

Reason," the translator uses the French "fait" followed by the Latin *"factum"* in parentheses; *Critique de la raison pratique* (Paris, 1974), p. 55.

69 Kant, *Critique of Practical Reason*, p. 215.

70 Kant, *Critique of the Power of Judgment*, p. 124. I allowed myself to compress the sentence somewhat because it is clear that here, as elsewhere (but not everywhere), Kant considers taste and *sensus communis* as one and the same faculty. Kant's German for "in fact" is *"in der Tat"* (no trace of *Faktum*, here).

71 The authors see Sade the way they see Nietzsche (in *On the Genealogy of Morals*): as having uttered the most intransigent critique of Kant's *Critique of Practical Reason*, as having unearthed the natural principle (self-conservation) behind Kant's lofty moralism, and as having revealed the true nature of the bourgeois subject emancipated by the Enlightenment. I shall seek another pairing of Kant with Sade a little further on, one that I think is much more to the point.

72 Horkheimer and Adorno, *Dialectic of Enlightenment*, p. 74. The authors paraphrase here the often cited first line of Kant's conclusion of the *Critique of Practical Reason* (p. 269): "Two things fill the mind with ever new and increasing admiration and reverence ... : the starry heavens above me and the moral law within me." Kant speaks of the moral law as "a fact of pure reason," p. 177 of the *Critique of Practical Reason*.

73 If the moral law were so deducible, its relation to natural laws would be *schematic*—precisely what Kant, in the second *Critique*, took such great care to refute, to the point of even coining a new word to mediate that relation: moral law, he said, finds its *type* (not its *scheme*) in natural law, which means that what both have in common is no more than the *form* of universal legislation; *Critique of Practical Reason*, pp. 194–98.

74 Ibid., p. 196 (translation slightly modified). The first formulation of the categorical imperative was the following: "Act in such a way that the maxim of your will could always hold at the same time as a principle in a universal legislation" (p. 164; translation modified).

75 Adorno (quoting himself in a letter to Karl Thieme), letter to Horkheimer, 2 June 1949, cited by Gunzelin Schmid Noerr, "Editor's Afterword," in Horkheimer and Adorno, *Dialectic of Enlightenment*, p. 220.

76 Ibid., p. 224.

77 Horkheimer and Adorno, "Rettung der Aufklärung. Diskussion über eine geplante Schrift zur Dialektik" (October 14, 1946), in Max Horkheimer, *Gesammelte Schriften* (Frankfurt, 1985), 12: p. 602.

78 Horkheimer and Adorno, *Dialectic of Enlightenment*, p. 67. Later in the chapter, and not surprisingly, Horkheimer congratulates Nietzsche for having unveiled the same "truth" in *On the Genealogy of Morals*: always a

matter of reducing the moral law to the laws of nature.

79 Jacques Lacan, "Kant with Sade," in *Ecrits*, trans. Bruce Fink (New York, 2006), p. 646.

80 "'I have the right to enjoy your body,' anyone can say to me, 'and I will exercise this right without any limit to the capriciousness of the exactions I may wish to satiate with your body'"; Marquis de Sade, *Philosophy in the Bedroom*, quoted by Lacan, "Kant with Sade," p. 648. Compare with Kant's third formula for the categorical imperative: "So act that you use humanity, whether in your own person or in the person of any other, always at the same time as an end, never merely as a means"; Immanuel Kant, *Groundwork of the Metaphysics of Morals*, in *Practical Philosophy*, p. 80.

81 Jacques Lacan, *The Ethics of Psychoanalysis, 1959–60*, trans. Dennis Porter (New York, 1992), p. 79.

82 Adorno, *Versuch über Wagner*, p. 104. (See note 7.)

83 I have modestly started this inquiry in two as yet unpublished essays, the already cited "Some Philosophical Implications of Eric Cameron's 'Routine Extremism,'" and "Joseph Beuys and the German Past, Tentatively," both forthcoming.

84 Witness, again, the famous first line of Adorno's *Aesthetic Theory*: "It is self-evident that nothing concerning art is self-evident anymore, not its inner life, not its relation to the world, not even its right to exist" (p. 1).

85 Yes, *pure*. The gist of the "Kant-after-Duchamp" approach to aesthetics and art theory is the following: apply to art what Kant said about beauty in nature and forget everything he had to say about art. The latter is obviously dated and could not survive the demise of the Fine Arts (actually: Beautiful Arts, *Schöne Künste, Beaux-Arts*) system enforced in his time. This is where Duchamp intervenes: he was the messenger who brought us the (good or bad) news that we have moved from the Fine Arts system to the "Art-in-General" system, where (1) the representation of beauty no longer mediates between nature and art; (2) the boundaries between the individual arts have been challenged and, in some cases, dissolved; (3) anything can a priori be art; (4) the decision whether or not something deserves to be called art ultimately rests on the individual aesthetic judgment.

86 Kant, *Critique of the Power of Judgment*, p.185.

87 de Duve, "Do Artists Speak on Behalf of All of Us?" p. 154.

Contributors

ANTHONY J. CASCARDI is Sidney and Margaret Ancker Professor of Comparative Literature, Rhetoric, and Spanish at the University of California, Berkeley.

FRED RUSH is Associate Professor of Philosophy at the University of Notre Dame.

CLAUDIA BRODSKY is Professor of Comparative Literature at Princeton University.

ROBERT KAUFMAN is Assistant Professor of Comparative Literature the University of California, Berkeley.

ALEŠ ERJAVEC is Research Professor at the Institute of Philosophy, Ljubljana, Slovenia.

J. M. BERNSTEIN is University Distinguished Professor of Philosophy at the New School for Social Research.

THIERRY DE DUVE is Professor of Aesthetics and Art History at Université Charles-de-Gaulle Lille 3 in Villeneuve d'Ascq, France.

www.ingramcontent.com/pod-product-compliance
Lightning Source LLC
Chambersburg PA
CBHW031235290426
44109CB00012B/305